3230091455

D0102289

†15-95

Nobody ever told us school mattered

Raising the educational attainments of children in public care

Acknowledgements

I would like to thank first the many children and young people who have shared with me their experiences, sometimes painful ones, of school and education. I never came away from one of those encounters without mixed feelings of sadness and anger at the unrealised hopes and wasted potential that our conversations so often revealed. They gave me the energy to keep insisting on the crucial importance of education for children in care when this still seemed invisible to most social workers.

The editor of an anthology is indebted to many people: Thanks to Dr Lindsey St.Claire and Dr Marilyn Osborn for permission to reprint an abridged version of the paper first published in *Early Childhood Development*; to the *Oxford Review of Education* for permission to reprint papers by Mike Stein and by Roger Bullock, Michael Little and Spencer Millham from the special issue on the Education of Children in Need; to the *British Journal of Social Work* for permission to reprint the paper by Anthony Heath, Matthew Colton and Jane Aldgate; to the *Times Educational Supplement* for permission to reprint the article by Peter McParlin and Eric Graham; and of course to all the authors.

Friends at the Who Cares? Trust, especially Susanna Cheal, and at Children in Wales have made many helpful suggestions and I owe as much of my knowledge of the care system to my association with them as from formal research. I am also grateful for suggestions to my colleagues at the University of Wales Swansea Centre for Applied Social Studies: Nigel Thomas, Bob Sanders and Matthew Colton.

I would like to thank Shaila Shah of BAAF for commissioning me to edit this book, which has been a most interesting though not always an easy task, and for her helpful advice and patience. Thanks finally to my husband, Derek Greenwood for his invaluable support, innumerable cups of tea and coffee, and his tolerance of my long periods wedded to the computer.

Nobody ever told us school mattered
Raising the educational attainments of children in public care

Edited by
Sonia Jackson

NF 039942

060207

British
Agencies
for **A**doption
and **F**ostering

Published by
British Agencies for Adoption & Fostering
(BAAF)
Skyline House
200 Union Street
London SE1 0LX

Charity registration 275689

© Sonia Jackson 2001

**British Library Cataloguing in Publication
Data**
A catalogue record for this book is available
from the British Library

ISBN 1 873868 98 7

Project management by Shaila Shah, Head of
Communications, BAAF
Photographs on cover by John Birdsall
Photography www.JohnBirdsall.co.uk
Designed by Andrew Haig & Associates
Typeset by Avon Dataset Ltd, Bidford on Avon
Printed by Russell Press Ltd. (TU),
Nottingham

NF 039942
060202
(370.941)
N6b

All rights reserved. Except as permitted under
the Copyright, Designs and Patents Act 1988,
this publication may not be reproduced, stored
in a retrieval system, or transmitted in any
form or by any means, without the prior
written permission of the publishers.

Contents

Introduction

Sonia Jackson

There has never been a better moment for those who care about improving educational opportunities for looked after children. Frank Dobson, when Secretary of State for Social Services, made education the central plank of the Quality Protects programme (in 1998) and described educational achievement as 'the single most significant measure of the effectiveness of local authority parenting'. Since then, following extensive consultation, the Department for Education and Employment and the Department of Health have, for the first time ever, issued joint Guidance, *The Education of Children and Young People in Public Care*, some elements of which have statutory force (DfEE/DH, 2000).

The idea for this book was first suggested to me by Donal Giltinan, then Director of BAAF's Scottish Centre, following a discussion at BAAF's Publications Advisory Group. He pointed out that much of the previous literature on the subject had been published in places not likely to be easily accessible to practitioners or students. Would it not be interesting to chart the way the education of children in care has moved over a period of 20 years from total obscurity to becoming recognised as a crucial aspect of good parenting and a key indicator of quality? What were the most important texts that had contributed to this shift in attitudes? So the book was originally conceived entirely as an anthology of published work. Later, when Shaila Shah took over the editorial role, it was decided to commission a number of new chapters identifying key issues and current developments in the education of looked after children.

The first part of the book consists of an abridged version of a position paper, *The Education of Children in Care* (Jackson, 1983), originally commissioned by the Social Science Research Council (later the Economic and Social Research Council (ESRC)) in 1983. It was used as the basis for a call for proposals on the subject, to which Anthony Heath and his colleagues at Oxford University and Felicity Fletcher-Campbell of the National Foundation for Educational Research were successful applicants, but otherwise it languished unseen in some ESRC office.

1

Eventually it was published by the University of Bristol School of Applied Social Studies as the first in its series of occasional papers. Since the School no longer exists the paper is virtually unobtainable in its original form but is still very frequently cited. Has anyone actually read it, I sometimes wonder?

I had not looked at it for many years. Returning to it after so long was a curious experience. Although so much has changed in caring for children away from home, the neglect of their education remains one of the worst failings of the system, which we are only just beginning to address in any serious way. The problems are much the same and many of the suggestions for improvement in this modest pamphlet seem as valid today as when they were written. I have resisted the temptation to rewrite it with hindsight and have simply cut the sections which are less relevant, usually because they refer to forms of provision that no longer exist. For space reasons I have also omitted the Appendix which reproduced my evidence to the House of Commons Social Services Committee Inquiry into Children in Care. Thanks to the late Barbara Kahan, who was expert advisor to that Committee, this did not go without notice in the Committee Report (House of Commons, 1984) and may have had some influence on subsequent policy.

When the paper was published in 1987, along with five others on various topics, it attracted a great deal of media attention, mostly around the theme of "Children in care only fit for the dole". This was very unpopular with some of my colleagues but, alas, Mike Stein's paper reprinted in this volume shows that it was no more than the truth and to some extent still is. Of course that is not a criticism of young people who are looked after but of the system that has failed them.

The second part of the book reprints several papers mainly based on research carried out in the 1980s which confirmed previous evidence of the low attainment and school problems of looked after children. The first of these, by Lindsey St.Claire and the sadly missed "Oz" Osborn, comes from the Bristol child cohort study which began in 1970 and analyses the data relating to children who spent any time in care or were separated from their mothers for more than a month. The findings of this report are closely in line with the earlier data from the National Child Development Study (the longitudinal study of all children born in one week in 1958) discussed in the ESRC report. Reading the paper (which has had to be much reduced in length) one is struck by the way the discussion is framed by the theoretical preoccupations of the time – for instance the debate on maternal deprivation or separation and its effects. The main research question, having shown that the performance and behaviour of children who have been in care are significantly worse than that of others, is to establish by statistical procedures if this is due to the care experience or to the pre-care environment. This same question preoccupied the Oxford group of researchers led by Anthony Heath. There seemed almost a desire at that time to exonerate the care system from any responsibility for the children's poor performance.

St.Claire and Osborn conclude that the family background of children in care accounts for most of the variance. Their findings on family background correspond closely with those of Bebbington and Miles (1989). Most children who enter care are not only socially disadvantaged in many obvious ways, such as having a single parent, substandard housing, low income, many siblings, and poor health, but also suffer from complex family problems.

The authors note that being in residential care was associated with particularly poor attainment and behaviour but did not seem to consider the possibility that a better quality of care might bring about improvements.

This rather despondent view of care was echoed in the early publications of the Oxford researchers. The 50 children in care in their study scored lower on standardised tests than a comparison group of children from socially disadvantaged homes, even though the study children were in stable long-term foster homes described as "middle-class". The conclusions of this part of the study were similar to those of St.Claire and Osborn (Heath, Aldgate and Colton, 1989).

The next publication to emerge from the ESRC initiative was very different. Felicity Fletcher-Campbell and Christopher Hall concluded from their study of children in the care of 43 local authorities that the main obstacles to educational achievement lay in the system and not in the children (Fletcher-Campbell and Hall, 1990). This very important book did not attract the attention it deserved from social workers and social services managers, possibly because it was published by the

National Foundation for Educational Research (NFER) and was seen as belonging in the education sector rather than social care.

After this the issue seemed to fall off the agenda again. In an attempt to restore it to its rightful place Matthew Colton and I, with support from NCH, organised a London conference in 1992, which was very well attended, and included a moving contribution from a group of young people who came with Tory Laughland, the founder of the Who Cares? Trust. The main papers were published two years later as a special issue of the *Oxford Review of Education* (Heath, Colton and Jackson, 1994).

The second reprinted paper in Part II is another publication from the Oxford research. It is interesting to note the difference in tone from the earlier paper. Although the findings are no more encouraging, in that the in-care group failed to catch up with their peers, the conclusion is different: not that children in care are doomed to failure but that exceptional inputs are needed to compensate for the disadvantages that the children bring with them into care. Ordinary, good quality foster care is not enough.

Two papers from the *Oxford Review* special issue follow. Although research based, they are both grounded in practice. Roger Bullock and his colleagues consider the experiences of children going back into school after a period away in care and conclude that far more needs to be done by social workers, carers and schools to ease the transition and ensure continuity. Of course, the same is true for children changing schools as a result of a placement move and this continues to be a major problem for looked after children (see Jackson and Thomas, 1999). The other paper, by Mike Stein, is about how educational failure affects the future employment and life chances of careleavers. It reports on three studies carried out over a period of several years and paints a bleak picture of life after care for the 80 per cent of young people who leave with no qualifications. Once again, this is an issue which is regrettably still very much alive.

The two remaining chapters in Part II are different. Peter McParlin, an educational psychologist, writes partly from his own experience of care. He escaped from catering college to achieve his ambition of going to Cambridge, but without any assistance from the care system. We owe a great debt to those few people – another is Fred Fever – who, succeeding from care, have the courage to share their experiences (see Fever, 1990).

Tory Laughland did more than anyone to raise the profile of children in care and draw attention to the weaknesses of the care system. The lecture which I gave in her memory has not previously been published though I am often asked for copies. It seems to retain its relevance today and concludes this section.

Part III of the book is made up of newly commissioned chapters which show how far we have travelled, but also how far we have yet to go before looked after children and young people can truly enjoy "equal chances" with those who live with their own families. Felicity Fletcher-Campbell reviews the implications for looked after children of the government's numerous new initiatives. Barbara Fletcher and Howard Firth show what can be achieved when a local authority really does act as a corporate parent in relation to education. Tricia Skuse and Ray Evans suggest that the Looking After Children materials, if properly used, can make an effective contribution to improving the educational care of looked after children.

With Kate Cairns' chapter we move into quite different territory. Although we know that over half of looked after children come into care as a result of neglect or abuse, rather little has been written about the effects of traumatic experiences on their behaviour, even though problem behaviour is strongly associated with school exclusion and placement breakdown. This chapter links the literature on post-traumatic stress disorder (PTSD) with the practical experience of fostering and shows how the symptoms of PTSD affect learning, attachment and behaviour.

Nevertheless, as both the next two chapters argue, we should not look at problems of school attendance and behaviour as arising mainly from the characteristics of the child. Eric Blyth exposes the contradictions in government policy that primarily account for the high rate of exclusions suffered by looked after children, and suggests some remedies. Tim Walker opens up a subject curiously little discussed in the British child care literature – the role of independent agencies and the contribution they can make to improvements in attainment and keeping looked after children in mainstream education.

The next two chapters are both by American authors, though Randy Lee Comfort writes partly from her experience of running a community project to support foster and adoptive families in an ethnically mixed area of Bristol. Jack Richman and Lawrence Rosenfeld describe an approach which has been extensively used in the USA to identify the social support needs of educationally "at-risk" children. They argue that providing targeted social support may be more effective than any direct educational input in improving morale and attainment, and provide evidence that children in public care typically lack many forms of support that young people at home can take for granted. The School Success Profile offers a means of identifying such needs in consultation with the young people themselves, and in a way that avoids stigmatising them.

Finally, Joy Rees describes the experience of a three-year project to improve the educational environment in residential children's homes. Many of the previous chapters identify residential care as the least likely setting to promote school success, so the insights and achievements of this project have enormous practical relevance.

There are still many gaps in our knowledge and understanding of the education of looked after children. Very little, for example, is known about disabled children in care, though valuable new evidence has emerged from a re-analysis of the OPCS Disability Survey (Gordon *et al*, 2000). This shows that children with disabilities are much more likely to be in local authority care (5.7 per cent compared with 0.55 per cent for the whole child population). Among children with disabilities living in some form of residential establishment, 83 per cent are in care, most of them under compulsory orders. Among disabled children living in foster homes, 40 per cent had severe and multiple disabilities.

Some of the detailed findings of this study may have been superseded but the main patterns are likely to hold good. For example, children in care were much less likely to attend ordinary schools if they had physical or sensory disabilities or any degree of learning difficulty compared with children in their own families, where only those with multiple disabilities did not go to ordinary schools. Although the nature of disabilities among children in care was far less severe than among children who were not in care, they were less likely to be attending a special or ordinary day school. The authors comment that this raises the question of the extent to which their learning difficulties arose from, or were exacerbated by the experience of being in care. Clearly this is an issue that needs urgent investigation.

The reprinted papers in Parts I and II of the book are reproduced essentially in the form in which they first appeared, apart from Chapters 1 and 2, both originally substantial papers from which some sections have been cut, as indicated. In addition to problems of length, there were also questions of terminology. Language does not stand still; usage changes and some terms which were acceptable at the time of writing would now be considered inappropriate or even offensive. I have left them unchanged in the interests of historical accuracy but enclosed them in quotation marks. Similarly, the term "foster parent" is used by some authors of earlier papers instead of the now more usual "foster carer". Where the author wrote "foster parent" in Parts I and II of the book it has been allowed to stand, but in the newly commissioned parts (Part III) "foster carer" has been substituted.

An anthology does not have to be comprehensive, and this one makes no claim to be. What it tries to do is to remind readers how long it has taken us to recognise the importance of educational success for children in public care and to urge them to take maximum advantage of this promising moment.

References

Bebbington, A, and Miles, J (1989) 'The background of children who enter local authority care', *British Journal of Social Work*, 19:5, pp 349–68.

DfEE/DH (2000) *Guidance on the Education of Children and Young People in Public Care*, LAC (2000) 13, London: Department of Health.

Fever, F (1990) *Who Cares? Memories of a childhood in Barnardo's*, London: Warner.

Fletcher-Campbell, F, and Hall, C (1990) *Changing Schools? Changing People? The education of children in care*, Slough: NFER.

Gordon, D, Parker, R, Loughran, F, with Heslop, P (2000) *Disabled Children in Britain: A re-analysis of the OPCS Disability Survey*, London: The Stationery Office.

Heath, A, Colton, M, and Aldgate, J (1989) 'The educational progress of children in and out of care', *British Journal of Social Work*, 19:6, pp 447–60.

Heath, A, Colton M and Jackson, S (eds) (1994) *Oxford Review of Education*, 20:3, *Special issue: The Education of Children in Need.*

House of Commons (1984) *Second Report of the House of Commons Social Services Committee 1983–4*, London: HMSO.

Jackson, S (1983) *The Education of Children in Care*, Report to the Social Sciences Research Council, unpublished.

Jackson, S, and Thomas, N (1999) *On the Move Again? What works in creating stability for looked after children*, Ilford: Barnardo's.

Part I

Raising the issue

1 The education of children in care

Sonia Jackson

This is an abridged version of a report to the Economic and Social Research Council, 1983, later published as 'Bristol Papers in Applied Social Studies No. 1' (1987), University of Bristol.

Introduction

School is a central experience of all our childhoods. It has enormous power to make us happy or miserable and to shape our view of ourselves. Whatever else is happening in our lives we are expected to attend five days a week, 40 weeks a year, at least from the age of five to 16. For this, if for no other reason, the education of children in care is a matter of great importance. But what happens to us during those 13,000 hours has consequences which usually shape the rest of our lives.

It is at school that most people learn what is considered appropriate behaviour outside the family, how to cope with conflict and authority, how to acquire and apply knowledge. They form an opinion about their ability in relation to others in their age group, and they are given continual feedback, positive and negative, about their performance. The climax of this process for some is the inexorable verdict of public examinations which determine what further educational and job opportunities open out, or alternatively are closed, at least in the short term. And for others, school days just peter out, a sentence served.

This paper is therefore concerned with, firstly, the adjustment and happiness at school of children in the care of local authorities. Then with the repercussions that maladjustment and unhappiness may have on other aspects of their lives. And thirdly, with their educational attainment which, it is argued, is intimately bound up with their self-esteem and has far-reaching consequences for their future occupations, life-style and relationships.

School children in care

In March 1984 there were nearly 79,000 children in the care of local authorities in England and Wales. The number of under-fives admitted to care has gradually dropped but there has been a corresponding rise in the admission of older children as a result of court orders. About half the children in voluntary care, under what is now section 2 of the Child Care Act 1980, only stay for a short period though this figure may disguise some repeat admissions. The finding that those who stay for more than six months are likely to remain for a very long time, normally throughout their childhood (Rowe and Lambert, 1973), remains broadly true. Two-thirds of children in care (62 per cent in 1984) are of compulsory school age. However, as care orders normally remain in force until children reach 18, the number who have legitimately left school is substantial (27 per cent) and their educational needs are as worthy of discussion.

Of those at school, 13,400 (17 per cent) are under ten and 35,500 (45 per cent) aged 10–15; 2,200 are placed in maintained and voluntary special boarding schools and 2,800 in Community Homes with Education (CHEs).[1] The number receiving special education in day schools is not known. Many more, for whom precise figures are not available, may be placed in independent boarding schools.

Children attending neighbourhood schools either from residential homes or foster homes make up the equivalent of 45 average-sized primary schools and 24 large comprehensives.

How many of these children come into care with already well-established educational problems? This is hard to estimate since statistics usually only quote the "main reason" for reception into care. It is very probable that, especially with older children, school difficulties and in particular disruptive behaviour, are a major contributing factor.

---

[1] The number of children and young people looked after in March 1999 was 55,000. Community Homes with Education no longer exist. However, this section has been retained to establish the context in which the paper was written.

The educational experience of children in care: some questions

What are the responsibilities of the local authority in relation to those who spend all or part of their childhood in care? There is no doubt that it is responsible, as are parents, to ensure that these children receive efficient full-time education – in other words, that they attend school. How far this extends beyond seeing the child is on the premises is more open to interpretation. Perhaps one end of the spectrum would be best expressed in the famous words of the Hadow Report (Board of Education, 1931):

What a wise and good parent would desire for his own
children, that a nation must desire for all children. (p xxix)

At the other end is the principle of less eligibility, usually now unspoken but clearly implicit in much financial decision-making and summed up in the words of one senior official: 'It is no part of our job to try to provide for a child better than its own parents could have done'.

To express it in another way, should it be the aim of the social services department to provide a standard of care and education superior in quality but similar in kind to what the child might have expected to experience in an adequately functioning family of the same social class as his or her family of origin? Or should the department attempt to compensate for the social class disadvantages as well as the particular inadequacies or problems which caused this child to be taken into care? Should it aspire for this child to a degree of educational success which is rarely achieved by those of similar family backgrounds and therefore become an agent of social mobility?

Until quite recently such a question could not have been asked – most people over 40 will, after all, remember singing in assembly:

The rich man in his castle,
The poor man at the gate,
He made them high and lowly,
And ordered their estate.

Domestic service, farmwork or the armed forces were assumed to be the destination of children brought up in care, and anything but the most rudimentary education and training would have been viewed as a waste of public funds (Middleton, 1979). In these more generous times the formal objective of social service departments would no doubt be that children in care should attend school regularly and do as well as their abilities allow. This paper draws together evidence on the educational experience and attainment of those who have spent part of their childhood in care and suggests some implications for child care practice. Some of the questions to which it attempts to offer preliminary answers are:

- How is the duty to further children's education reflected in practice?
- Are some forms of care more effective than others in promoting educational adjustment and success?
- How do children in care perceive their own experience of school and education?
- Are there schemes or projects which lay special emphasis on the educational role of social workers and/or direct caregivers?
- In what areas do we need more knowledge?

Sources of information

This paper draws on information from a number of different sources:
1. Books and articles, with special emphasis on those published since 1970;
2. Unpublished material from research in progress;
3. Interviews with researchers, administrators and with young people who have been in care; and
4. Local authority guidelines, manuals and job descriptions.

In the first category, the aim was to identify any book or article in the English language dealing directly with the topic, and also to find out how much attention was given to it in publications concerned with children in care in general. A computer search was undertaken using a number of different databases. In addition, the education, social work, sociology and psychology journals were scanned for relevant articles.

A systematic programme of interviewing was not possible in the time available. However, a large number of informal conversations and a few longer interviews with people who have thought about the issues involved, both as providers and receivers of care, yielded much useful information. Finally, documents such as manuals and guidelines for field workers and job specifications for residential workers were collected from a number of social services departments.

The dichotomy between care and education

The early stages of the literature search provoked feelings of increasing frustration, until it became clear that the absence of published material was in itself important evidence. So far as it is possible to discover, there is not one single book published in the UK or the USA concerned with the education and welfare of children in public care who attend neighbourhood schools. There are of course books about the education of "handicapped", "maladjusted" and educationally subnormal children, some of whom may be in care.[2] And the Schools Inspectorate did produce a discussion paper on Community Homes with Education (DES, 1980) which Malcolm Dean described in *The Guardian* as 'the most damning education report of the decade', but that is outside the scope of this paper.

The computer research revealed an enormous number of publications on children in care, over 8,000 on foster care alone, and a much larger number on educational disadvantage. Of these, only a tiny handful focus on the education of children in foster and residential care. They are discussed in more detail below. This finding is in line with Hilary Prosser's review of the literature on residential care since 1966, which includes only one title concerned with schools or education out of 142 books and articles abstracted (Prosser, 1976). The companion volume on foster care (Prosser, 1978) has only four relevant items out of 243 abstracted.

The conclusion is inescapable: researchers and practitioners do not see education as a particularly interesting or important aspect of care for

---

[2] Despite rereading these words with a sense of acute discomfort I decided it would be more honest to let them stand. I hope the change in current terminology also reflects a change in thinking.

separated children. Conversely, for educationists and teachers, children in care are not perceived as a discrete category, even though it would be generally agreed that they are among the most disadvantaged groups of children in the population.

It might be argued that because education is only one aspect of a child's life it would be unreasonable to expect whole books to be devoted to it. How then is education treated in the wide literature on child care? Most frequently the answer is not at all. Rarely is the subject even listed in the index. For example, two books by Paul Brearley and his colleagues, *Admission to Residential Care* (1980) and *Leaving Residential Care* (1982) never mention schools, although both entering and leaving residential establishments carry a high risk of educational disruption.

The DHSS *Guide to Fostering Practice* (1976) does not mention education. Interestingly, the earlier *Guide to Adoption Practice* (Home Office, 1970) does include a brief paragraph on the subject in relation to the assessment of applicants. It advises that information should be obtained not only about the facts of the prospective adoptive parents' education, training and present occupation, but also about their feelings and attitudes to their own education and that of any child they might bring up.

> *Agencies should try to select adoptive parents who will not put undue pressure on their children to achieve educational or work standards beyond their real ability, or develop interests in line with the adopters' personalities rather than their own.*

This was written at a time when adoption was still confined to babies and very young children. Nevertheless, there is surely an implication that the children's "real" ability is more likely to correspond with that of their probably working-class natural parents than that of their middle-class adopters. And not only their intelligence but their interests, too, are likely to be inherited. "A" levels and Mozart are not for the lower orders. There is no suggestion that adopting parents might be specially selected to give educationally stimulating care, nor that there might be problems if they fail to do so. That the consequences can be quite as serious is illustrated by Felicity Seighart's saddening case studies of gifted children adopted by couples of limited intelligence (Seighart, 1979).

On the other hand, a number of studies by the National Children's Bureau have shown adopted children to be conspicuously successful in education (Seglow, Pringle and Wedge, 1972). More recently, Owen Gill and Barbara Jackson (1983) looked at a potentially problematic group of black adolescents growing up in white, mostly suburban middle-class homes. The children in all the 36 families studied were doing well at school, most being described as average or above in ability and in the effort they put into their work. The girls especially compared favourably with their peers in their ability to channel their energies into school work. In 19 cases out of 22, the adoptive parents were very happy with their progress.

Barbara Tizard's finding, in a study of children adopted from institutions after infancy, were similar. Perhaps influenced by the same anxieties as the Home Office official quoted above, she looked particularly for evidence of adoptive parents putting pressure on children to achieve educational success, but found none (Tizard, 1977). The negative emphasis of the *Guide to Adoption Practice* (Home Office, 1970) is only an extreme example of the low expectations of the performance of children in care which pervade the literature. Almost all the meagre references to education and schools in the child care practice literature relate to problems of attendance or classroom behaviour. Nowhere is there a sense of school as a central part of a child's life, or education as the key to their future.

Social workers are not noted for basing their decisions on books, so it could be that the slight importance given to education in the child care literature bears little relation to practice. It would be comforting to believe this, but there is a telling piece of evidence to the contrary.

Melotte (1979) studied placement decisions over a two-month period in one local authority. Fifty-six children, aged three months to 16 years were admitted to care during that time. All the social workers involved (including seniors and area officers) were asked: 'What factors influenced you when you decided to place this child?' Twenty factors were mentioned by at least one social worker. None included school or education.

Although, as was pointed out at the beginning of this paper, the number of children in the education system who are in local authority care is by no means insignificant, some schools will have none, and most only one or two. This may explain why there is no reference to them in the huge literature on educational disadvantage. It is more surprising to find that the education of children in care is not discussed in books which are specifically designed to bridge the education/social work divide – those dealing with social work in schools.

Failure in communication between the social worker and the teacher is a central theme of Katrin Fitzherbert's *Child Care Services and the Teacher* (1977). She writes:

> *The different facets of a child's growth and development are so inter-dependent that they make nonsense of the division of our helping professions into separate and often antagonistic camps.* (p 185)

She is very critical of the low value placed by social workers on school attendance and their failure to consult or work closely with teachers to identify children at risk and take preventive action. Margaret Robinson's *Schools and Social Work* (1978), which is written more from a social work point of view and aims to be informative rather than polemical, gives the basic facts about care orders, but is otherwise exclusively concerned with the problems of children living in their own families.

So education and discussion of the educational experience of children in care is thin on the ground. What there is comes from very few sources.

Mia Kellmer Pringle had a unique ability to keep a foot in both education and social work camps. She saw the importance of education to children in care and early recognised them as a specially disadvantaged group (Pringle, 1965). These perceptions were built into her National Child Development Study, which later provided important evidence on many aspects of the lives of children in care. She first saw the significance of what the children themselves might have to say and initiated the "Who Cares?" scheme, which led to the formation of the National Association for Young People in Care (NAYPIC).

Another name which recurs is that of Barbara Kahan who, as Children's Officer of Oxfordshire, always gave a high priority to the educational needs of children in care, and whose book *Growing Up in Care*

(1979) most unusually includes a whole chapter on "Education and Teachers".

School attainments of children in care

No information is formally collected about the educational performance of the 79,000 children in care.[3]

No returns are made either to the DES (Department of Educational Sciences) or DHSS (Department of Health and Social Security) of examinations passed or other qualifications obtained by children in care, nor have I been able to trace any other official statistics on the matter, for example, from answers to Parliamentary Questions.

Social services departments do not normally have this kind of information. Case papers may or may not include school reports; social workers may mention that a child is working for a public examination, but often omit to record the result. Fact sheets do not include a space for educational achievements, and even when a child leaves care at 18, it is usually a matter for the individual social worker whether or not any facts about the young person's educational level are recorded.

Turning to the literature, there is general agreement, when the subject is mentioned at all, that children in care are likely to have difficulties at school and probably perform below their potential, but there is a lack of hard data.

Essen, Lambert and Head (1976), reviewing the available information, found that far more attention had been paid to the social and emotional progress of children in care than to their cognitive development. Two previous studies (Ferguson, 1966; Pringle and Bossio, 1965) had found well below average scores on IQ and attainment tests among children in care, especially those who had first been admitted to care under the age of five. Ferguson also followed up the children after discharge from care and looked at the implications of their low school attainment for employment and social adaptation.

---

[3] This remained true until the issue of government *Guidance on the Education of Children and Young People in Public Care* (DfEE/DH, 2000).

Table 1

Average scores at 11 years – National Child Development Study

	Mean reading score	*Mean maths score*
Early in care	9.2	9.5
Later in care	10.1	10.3
Never in care	11.1	11.1

Source: Essen *et al*, 1976.

Juliet Essen *et al*'s (1976) study remains the only published British research on the school attainment of children who are or have been in care which is based on a large sample – 414 children, 3.4 per cent of the total National Child Development Study 1958 cohort. Her report is based on findings from the 7- and 11-year-old follow-up, that is, on data collected nearly 20 years ago. Although this has to be taken into account, and one would hope that some improvements in child care practice might have taken place since then, it is unlikely that the picture has altered radically.

Over 80 per cent of the children who had been in care at some time were no longer in care by the time of the 11-year follow-up, having either returned to live with a parent or been adopted, and the study does not distinguish between those who might have been in care for a short period around the time of their seventh birthday and those who were continuously in care from early childhood. Of children first in care before the age of six months, 6.4 per cent were later adopted, which would usually imply a dramatic change in their social circumstances, and this is a confusing factor. Otherwise, children who had been in care at any age generally came from an extremely disadvantaged group, and were likely at 11 to be living in large families with low incomes, poor overcrowded housing, and either with only one parent or with a father in semi- or unskilled manual work.

All these factors make interpretation of the results difficult. Quite clearly the school performance of the group as a whole was poor whether or not they were in care at the time of testing, as the above table shows.

Analyses of variance were used to exclude social class, family size, region, receipt of free school meals, overcrowding, birth weight and maternal age (all factors correlating with educational problems). Even allowing for these, children who first came into care after the age of seven were, on average, six months behind on reading and seven months behind in mathematics. Those first in care before seven were 14 months behind in reading and 12 months behind in mathematics in comparison with children from the same social background who had never been in care.

The authors are unable to reach any conclusion whether the experience of being in care actually leads to or contributes to low attainment. For the "later in care" group, the results provide no clear answer. Their scores were already below average at seven, before they came into care, and did not change relatively to those not in care during the period when they were in care. Their attainment was low even allowing for "standard" social disadvantage, but Essen *et al* (1976) suggest that admission into care may be a symptom of problems which could be more important in terms of child development than the actual experience of being in care. Additional negative factors could be marital conflict, illness, lack of attention, lack of interest in schooling, and low teacher expectation.

This fails to explain why the "early in care" group scored consistently lower than those coming into care later both at seven and 11, and why their performance deteriorated relatively to those never in care. It could be that very early admission to care reflects greater incapacity in the family and that delays in learning in early childhood disproportionately affect later development. The implications which the authors draw from the study are that it is not being in care which is educationally damaging so much as the conditions which make it necessary, and that preventive action which only aims to keep children out of care will not do anything to avert school failure.

One could, however, look at it another way. Local authority care, on this evidence, is at best neutral. It clearly does nothing to improve the educational attainment of this most severely disadvantaged group.

Looking at behaviour, rather than attainment, the same three authors (Essen, Lambert and Head, 1977) found that children who had been in care at any time before the age of 11 were thought by their teachers to be less well adjusted to school than children with similar backgrounds who had not been in care. They tended to be anti-social rather than withdrawn, and hostile towards adults and other children.

As with attainment it was found that children admitted to care later already had more behavioural problems at seven than those of similar socio-economic background who never came into care, but the behaviour of the whole "in care" group deteriorated between seven and 11 relative to children never in care. Even those out of care by the age of 11 continued to behave poorly. In this case, the authors have less hesitation in ascribing the problem at least partly to the experience of being taken into care rather than the antecedent family conditions. They conclude: 'The possible consequences of deterioration of behaviour in school in children who have been in care should not be underestimated' (Essen *et al*, 1976).

Akhurst (1975) used Rutter's 'Children's Behaviour Questionnaire' to assess the level of behaviour disorders reported by houseparents and teachers in a group of 182 children in long-term residential care. All children had been in their current homes for more than six months and had no formally recognised "handicap". Akhurst found a much higher prevalence of severe behaviour disorder than in the general population, particularly among boys in the local authority homes. They were described by their teachers as anti-social, restless, disobedient and destructive.

Looking back

What do people who are, or have been, in care think of their educational experience? Certainly they do not think it unimportant – school is a dominant theme in autobiographies and reminiscences of those brought up in care and in reports of group discussions. The prevailing tone is one of regret for missed opportunities, talents undeveloped, avenues blocked off. Most blame themselves, a few express fierce resentment (see Hitchman, 1960; Timms, 1973).

This is selective evidence. Most children do not write autobiographies or join pressure groups, and among those who do, one would expect to find a high proportion of above average ability who are dissatisfied with some aspect of their life in care. But perhaps they are in the best position to tell us why the school attainment of children in care is so disappointing.

A number of themes emerge from many different sources. It does not seem to matter if the year is 1930 or 1975, if the child is black or white, boy or girl, lives in Bradford or Wandsworth – the experience is essentially the same. Children in care are educationally "handicapped" by both external and internal factors.

Among the external factors the most damaging is undoubtedly disruption. A change of school is disturbing even for a well-adjusted child living with his or her family. New faces, new demands, new rules, new customs have to be learnt before the child is in a state to absorb any formal instruction – and this can take a long time. Almost always for a child in care, a change in placement involves a change of school, and this is rarely given much significance in the placement decision. Frequent moves are a common feature of life in care; ten or twelve over five years are not unknown.

Changes of placement made for behavioural reasons often have educational implications which are overlooked or ignored. There is never any sense of a long-term educational plan such as most middle-class parents make for their children, explicitly or implicitly. Despite the apparatus of assessment, the convenience of adults rather than the needs or abilities of the child is what decides his or her educational opportunities.

This is best illustrated by Graham Gaskin's account of his childhood (MacVeigh, 1982). Constantly on the move, he was often placed in settings where no educational provision was made at all. At one stage he was labelled educationally subnormal and sent to a school for backward children. He remarks bitterly, 'This was because I hadn't managed to scrounge myself a teacher, books and a class during all the periods they kept me away from school' (p 39).

Attitudes of professionals – social workers and teachers – are another important external factor. Both are criticised for expecting too little of children in care. Living conditions, especially in family group residential homes, are often mentioned as a problem in connection with homework. The internal factors which appear over and over again are low self-esteem and lack of motivation. Looking back, many people could see that their attitude to school was strongly coloured by how much the adults caring for them were concerned about their educational progress – and most were not.

Barbara Kahan (1979) reports on a series of discussion meetings held with a group of ten adults who had spent time in care from 1942 to 1969. School, she found, was 'a largely unsatisfactory experience for them'. Some had deep feelings of regret about the educational opportunities they had missed or not used as fully as they might have done. Grown up, they could see the connection between achievement at school and subsequent employment prospects, but at the time no one, they felt, had explained it with enough force. 'They didn't really impress upon you how important your education was until your last year in school' – and by that time it was too late. 'I looked upon it as a routine, just a chore to go through every day' (p 157).

Small kindnesses and sympathetic responses from teachers were remembered with gratitude many years later. And yet they did not want to be treated differently from other children. They resented discrimination even when it was well meant. 'I felt that I wanted somebody to expect a lot more and demand a lot more'. Some members of this group were old enough to be parents and two of them described how they gave their own children the kind of close personal atten-tion and encouragement which they felt they had lacked themselves: quite simple things like attending school open days, helping with homework – 'Spurring them on to do the thing that's just a bit too difficult at first'.

Placement decisions, the group thought, were made with very little detailed knowledge, and the child's voice never listened to. Andrew Demetri (1982) tells how he was sent to a special school at the age of nine. He was never told why, but thinks it was probably because he was found in bed with a girl.

No one should be able to label a child maladjusted. I have borne that mark like a stigma on my body since I was nine. Perhaps that above everything else has made me feel different. I bitterly resent the fact that I am largely uneducated. I am intelligent enough to have profited from a normal education but because of the label I was sent to a school where there were so many disturbed boys that it was quite impossible to give those of us who were at all interested a reasonable education.

All the same, he tried hard at first. He liked the teachers who taught

English and RE; perhaps he might have learnt something worthwhile even from that school. But he could not resist indefinitely the unrelenting attack on his self-esteem:

I never liked being told I was worthless, and I was told this many times. They said I would never get anywhere in life. I believed them. Maybe it was at this point that I began to give up. I just regressed. At the end of my stay at school I was doing no work at all.

Leon Parker, later a full-time worker for the National Association for Young People in Care (NAYPIC), wrote an education autobiography (unpublished but from which I was given permission to quote) in which the themes of disruption leading to retardation, attention-seeking, labelling, low self-esteem, lack of support and poor motivation can all be clearly seen.

I think my education received its first setback in 1964; in that one year I went from home to foster home about six times. It must have had some effect on me because in 1965 my mental age was six months behind my actual age.

He managed to learn something from one or two of the ten different schools he attended over the next few years, but a constant thread running through his account is the fragility of his self-concept and how easily it could be undermined by an insensitive teacher.

My first English Language teacher was Taffy Thomas, who was the deputy head. His method of trying to improve your English was that he would give us essays to do, then we would hand them in to him. He would call out our names in order and tell us our mark in front of the whole class. If you had a low mark like I always had, he would shout at you and say what a load of rubbish it was, in front of all your classmates. His theory was to humiliate you in front of everyone. Because he made me feel inferior to other students and that I could not do as well as them, I lost my confidence in my ability to write English essays.

For Leon Parker the way out of this familiar downward spiral came through Further Education College and the understanding of one English teacher who was able to tolerate his initially disruptive behaviour and recognise his ability.

After all those years of let downs and failures I have now improved so much that I am getting As for my essays. At school I dreamed of getting As, now the dream has become reality in one subject at least.

The many changes of placement recorded in this account, most of them having significant educational consequences, must have resulted from social work decisions, but Leon makes no reference at all to social workers. As so often, the changes appeared to the child arbitrary and purposeless – 'You can be moved at the drop of a hat'. Certainly there is no indication of any plan being discussed with him. One may hope that this will change as children in care increasingly make themselves heard.

Different types of care

Up to this point children in care have been discussed as if they were a homogeneous group. In a sense this is true, in that they are drawn predominantly from what Hilary Prosser (1978) describes as 'chronically deprived lower class families facing crises', and typically children who spend long periods in care pass through many different types of provision. For example, 75 per cent of children in care have undergone at least one residential experience (Millham *et al*, 1980). But it may be useful to look at some of these different settings from an educational viewpoint. What can we say about children in foster care of the traditional kind, in "professional" foster homes, in children's homes?

Foster care

Some evidence here comes from the chapter on 'The study child at school' from the Columbia University longitudinal investigation into children in foster care (Fanshel and Shinn, 1978). The authors start from the proposition that although foster children are vulnerable, coming as they do from the most disadvantaged groups in the population, it is conceivable that foster care:

. . . offers some children respite from the anxieties of troubled and unpredictable environments, with concomitant improvement in school

performance. A secure foster home or stable institutional placement might free the child's cognitive resources as a result of cessation of anxiety. (p 227)

They suggest that, overall, school adjustment is a barometer indicating the child's general well-being. In this they found themselves to be treading new ground: 'Our review of the literature showed very little data on the school performance of foster children, which was somewhat surprising since the foster care system is given the task of attending to the child's educational needs' – a remark equally applicable to the British literature on fostering.

The investigation looked at level of performance on entering foster care, trends over time and comparison between long-term and short-term care. It was more comprehensive than the National Children's Bureau study (Essen *et al*, 1976), covering the assessment of performance on 11 school subjects, attitudes to school, and relationships with teacher and classmates. Another major difference is that three-quarters of the subjects in the North American study were black or Puerto Rican. The findings, however, are not dissimilar to those reported by Essen and her colleagues. On each assessment occasion the majority of these children performed at a level below normal for their age (Essen *et al*, 1976). A third of the group were almost two years behind in reading ability. But then 70 per cent of the subjects were already substantially behind in reading at the time of entering foster care, and looking at the children over the whole five-year period some modest improvement seemed to occur. So do the data support the hope with which the study began that foster care might have a positive influence on school performance? The authors feel this would be going too far:

Minimally we can state that these data do not support any notion that remaining in foster care (as opposed to returning to disadvantaged homes) is a markedly depriving experience for children.

Nor could it be said that foster care in general is an effective form of compensation for educational disadvantage. On entry 59 per cent of the children were performing below their age levels; after five years this had reduced only slightly to 53 per cent. Fanshel and Shinn (1978) conclude:

We would emphasise the need for a concentrated effort to enhance the school performance of foster children since this obviously has serious implications for their future ability to be well-employed, self-sustaining adults. Investment in this area should have high priority. (p 256)

This perception is no better recognised in the North American practice literature than in our own. Social and emotional adjustment are given overriding importance.

There is little direct evidence from British research on the relationship between long-term foster care and educational attainment. It would seem reasonable to assume, though, that where fostering is of the "exclusive" quasi-adoptive type, the influence of the foster carers would be similar to that of birth parents. A large number of studies have shown that children's school achievement is intimately bound up with their parents' education, attitudes, aspirations and expectations, and that these tend to follow a social class gradient (see Newson and Newson, 1977).

Two studies which have examined the characteristics of foster carers are those of Victor George (1970) and Gilvray Adamson (1973) and their findings were very similar. George's work, based on analysis of case papers and interviews with social workers, also throws some light on selection of foster carers and what factors were considered relevant at the time.

Gilvray Adamson (1973) studied 92 foster families. She found that most belonged to social classes III and IV. The largest group of foster fathers were unskilled manual workers (52 per cent) and another quarter had routine clerical or skilled manual work. Their weekly income was rather below the national average, and their style was lower-middle or "respectable" working class (Adamson's terms), characterised by orderliness and regularity.

The foster mothers' education was limited. Only 14 out of 92 stayed at school beyond minimum school-leaving age (well below the average for that time); 76 per cent had no further training; 17 per cent had learnt typing and a few others had nursing or technical training. The most common job before marriage was domestic.

All the foster mothers are described as very "home-centred". Few had any outside interests or intellectual pursuits; 57 per cent of the mothers and 79 per cent of the fathers belonged to no clubs or organisations.

Victor George (1970) found foster parents concentrated among the skilled working class. Other writers have attributed this to the low rates of boarding out payments balanced against the minimum physical standards acceptable to child care workers. George suggests that historical factors are more important – the upper classes were excluded because it was thought essential for boarding out supervisors to be of a higher social class than foster parents.

Hilary Prosser (1978), summarising the evidence on characteristics of foster parents, described them as predominantly working class (up to 85 per cent in some studies), aged 40 or over, representing a fairly settled population, neither socially nor geographically mobile, with few outside activities or cultural pursuits.

In so far as the evidence is drawn from case papers it cannot be very reliable. George (1970), comparing records in three contrasting areas, found that, even when information about foster parents' educational background was recorded, there was no discussion of what this meant to the foster parent or how it was likely to affect the care offered. In only one report did a social worker suggest that the foster parents 'could provide very good stimulation for a child of potentially high intelligence'. Several reports expressed concern about excessively high expectations, but no report described the foster parents' expectations of children as excessively low. Leisure activities of foster parents were even less often recorded – like education this was not considered a factor of much significance for foster care.

The main focus of George's book (1970) is on fostering breakdown and how to reduce its high incidence. He recommends a move towards a higher paid foster care service with much more rigorous selection and training. This idea was taken up, and the first special foster care scheme is described by Nancy Hazel in her book *A Bridge to Independence* (Hazel, 1981). It is interesting to note that she gives far more attention to education than any previous writer on foster care, and that the results of a specific focus on school adjustment and performance were rather encouraging. The "professional" foster parents were drawn from a very different social group from those interviewed by Adamson. It was common for both partners to have been successful in the education system. Many had higher education or relevant qualifications.

Community homes

It may be informative to take a parallel look at the characteristics of residential careworkers. According to Barbara Kahan (1979), 80 per cent of staff in residential establishments for children have no relevant training – that is the drive behind the Gatsby Project training scheme (Clode, 1983). But the Dartington Research Unit's study of care staff on Certificate in the Residential Care of Children and Young People courses (Millham, Bullock and Hosie, 1980) suggests that even trained staff may have attitudes towards school and education which could be unhelpful to the children in their care.

Only 32 per cent of the care staff studied had enjoyed their own school days. Sixty-two per cent of those who had taken the 11 plus failed. Fifty-nine per cent had left school by the age of 16. Their attainments had been "mediocre", usually a few CSE or O level passes. Millham *et al* sum up the findings as follows:

> *We have identified that those residential social workers who seek training tend not to have been particularly successful at school and that the majority seem to have left full time education with alacrity.*
> (p 109)

The research team found marked differences between the attitudes of these students and those of Certificate of Qualification in Social Work students who had followed a more conventional educational path.

This might be thought slight evidence on which to base any theory about residential workers' attitudes to education, and these students are not necessarily typical of the wider group of untrained workers, though they will tend to be concentrated in key positions. But we might expect that they would be inclined to undervalue conventional school achievement. In addition, they would tend to view education in instrumental terms, not as something which pervades all aspects of life. So they might make sure that children attend school regularly but give little thought to providing an environment or leisure activities designed to stimulate cognitive and intellectual development.

Relations with schools and teachers may also be complicated by residential workers' sense of professional marginality, on which Millham and his colleagues (1980) place great emphasis, and by their own unhappy school experiences. One might hypothesise that they would be likely to reduce anxiety by avoiding contact with teachers, preferring telephone to face-to-face encounters, and visiting schools only when it becomes unavoidable. As no one seems to have looked specifically at this aspect of residential carers' work these speculations are untestable. There are some clues though.

Brown and Solomon (1974) report on a study by Manchester University students of 37 children aged 11–16 who had all been in care for at least six months, ten of them for over four years. No significant differences appeared between the 16 different homes in which the children were living. The students commented on the absence of creative activities. Individual interests, such as collecting things, painting or craft work, were 'most exceptional'. They found that children spent most of their time watching television or listening to pop records. No attempt was made to introduce them to a wider range of music or to television programmes other than comedies and thrillers. Comics and teenage magazines were read but books were for school only. Hardly any used the public library. Weekend activities consisted of 'watching telly' or 'messing about'. Unsurprisingly, most children said they were frequently bored or fed up.

The task of residential workers was made more difficult by the failure of field social workers to supply any information about the leisure activities or interests of children coming into care, or to give the residential staff any encouragement. The authors recognise too that the children's narrow range of interests and tastes partly reflect their social class origins and the effects of external influences. But on this evidence they suggest that residential care workers do much less than they could to redress the balance. They urge social services departments to:

> look beyond the essential feeding and clothing needs of the children in their care and direct their attention immediately to the quality of life in their caring institutions.

More recent research by David Berridge (1985) indicates modest progress in this direction, but many of the homes he studied were exactly like those described by Brown and Solomon.

Berridge's (1985) findings, based on a small sample of 20 homes, confirm the hypothesis that both the concern for education and the quality of life in a home are related to the educational experiences of the care staff themselves. He found enormous variation between homes even in the same authority. There was rarely any policy or direction from above: the crucial factor was the head of the home, his or her social class origins and educational level. In some London boroughs there has been a dramatic change over recent years, many residential workers having degrees and social work qualifications. Their attitude to education is markedly different. They see it as an important dimension of a child's life. This has brought about a big improvement in liaison between children's homes and schools. In three-quarters of the homes studied, care staff attended school functions and teachers were invited to case conferences or reviews, and if unable to attend submitted written reports. On the school side, teachers were showing more sensitivity to the special needs of children from homes and, again mostly in London, making arrangements to accommodate them. Berridge visited some schools where one teacher took special responsibility for children in care. All of these mentioned underachievement, low levels of attainment, lack of confidence and emotional problems as characteristics of children from homes.

Taking a wider view of education, the picture is similar. A minority of homes had plenty of books and staff made a point of playing educational games with children, and encouraged them to take up individual hobbies or to join local clubs. Few had a policy of using the public library. Classical music was never listened to. One girl in a local authority home played the oboe, but she had started before coming into care and was a very untypical child from a middle-class family.

Establishments more in charge of their own resources were likely to lay more stress on education, on choosing the appropriate school for a particular child, and on developing individual talents. These were more likely to be homes in the private sector (Berridge, 1985).

Clearly the attempts made by residential homes to combat the massive educational disadvantage of children in care are still very half-hearted.

For example, although 60 per cent of the children were in secondary school, only three homes out of the 20 studied recognised their need for suitable conditions for homework. Still less did they take an interest in the work, check that it was done, give help if necessary or ask to see the teacher's comments afterwards. Many failed even to leave a time slot when the work could be done – even if the child wanted to do it despite little encouragement.

First it's teatime, then it's clearing up time, then it's bathtime, then it's bedtime. You get detention in school for not doing homework, but when?

It would be unfair to put all the blame on residential workers for this state of affairs; much of the responsibility rests on management. I was able to examine job specifications for officers in charge and care staff from several social services departments. Some spelt out in great detail the duties attached to the post, particularly in relation to physical care, but also in less practical areas such as providing emotional support to disturbed children and relating to parents. None suggested that it was any part of a residential child care worker's job to help children achieve success in school.

The path to educational failure

The educational "handicaps" suffered by almost all children in care are interrelated and mutually reinforcing, but it is possible from the evidence reviewed above to identify five distinct elements which play a key part.

Pre-care experiences

The majority of children in long-term care come from severely disadvantaged families, most of whose energies have gone into simply keeping afloat and who have ultimately failed. Eva Holmes (1977), discussing the educational needs of children in care, suggests that they will already have learned, before they get anywhere near a school, that

. . . finding out is discouraged, that adults will rarely listen or answer questions, that adult behaviour is often quite inconsistent and

unhelpful, that no one notices or cares about trying something new or difficult, that toys invariably get lost or broken.

The only defence is a kind of pseudo-self-reliance. It is safer not to admit any need or ask for help. At school, the teacher sees a child who cannot concentrate, does not listen, is restless and will only work under constant supervision. A high proportion of these children, in the words of Wedge and Prosser (1973) are 'born to fail', and coming into care only gives them a push on the way.

Low self-esteem

Coming into care, at whatever age, confirms what disadvantaged children have often already learned: that adults are unreliable, parents do not care, no one is really interested in them or their feelings or their achievements. Attempts to succeed, even to please, are almost certain to fail. The only defence is not to try, or to seek attention by disruptive behaviour.

Failure at school is not only an important component in the children's poor self-image. It also reinforces their early assumptions about the irrelevance and hopelessness of learning, of trying to make sense of the world, understanding something new or achieving anything – feelings which often manifest themselves as boredom, restlessness and passivity (Holmes, 1977). There are many indications that such children will underestimate their own potential, will not expect to do well at school, and will aim for low-level occupations, if any.

Broken schooling

There is evidence that this in itself, as common sense would suggest, is a potent cause of educational underachievement. Studies of service families, whose children undergo frequent moves, show that even with strong parental concern and backup, each move causes an interruption of educational progress which may be cumulative. This is of course addressed by sending officers' and diplomats' children to fee-paying boarding schools at public expense. Changes of placement for children in care can be just as frequent as army postings and are often made, as has been shown, with little regard for their educational side effects.

Lack of continuity

Many children and young people who have been in care express the feeling that nobody cares about them. At any one time they might be quite wrong. Social workers and residential staff do care, often intensely, about the children for whom they are responsible. But what the children are expressing is the lack of personal investment in them as individuals, extending over a lifetime, which is the normal experience of people brought up in their own families. The very rapid turnover of field workers and care staff occurring during the 1970s has now slowed down (Berridge, 1983), but most children in care, with the exception of the minority in successful long-term foster placements, will have no consistent figure in the background throughout their schooling, and most will experience multiple changes of social worker and caregiver.

Even the most untroubled school days include patches of boredom, loss of direction, conflict with teachers, through which successful children are steered by their parents. Not only do most children in care lack that kind of support, but as Eva Holmes (1977) says:

It is unrealistic to expect them to care about their own progress unless they know that someone else whom they have learned to trust also cares.

Low expectations

The assumption that children in care will move into unskilled manual jobs, or at least working-class occupations, persists strongly. The influence of historical tradition has been shown in many aspects of child care – for instance, in the wide differences in boarding out rates in different parts of the country – and this one goes back beyond Dickens. It is not surprising then that educational success is not seen as a priority by social workers or substitute carers. Indeed it will normally be perceived as a success if a child in care attends regularly up to official leaving age, acquires the minimum skills of literacy and numeracy required for survival in an industrial society, and displays no serious behaviour problems.

For their part, teachers do not expect that a child known to be in care will be industrious or academically gifted, and are more likely, sometimes unhelpfully, to make allowances than to provide extra help. The depressing effect on achievement of low teacher expectation has of course been demonstrated in relation to other disadvantaged groups (Pidgeon, 1970; Pilling and Pringle, 1978).

Glimmers of hope

Not all children who grow up in care are unsuccessful at school. Some who are unable to come to terms with the school system find alternative routes to satisfying jobs and lives. They can often trace their success to the influence of one person who took a special interest in them at a crucial time. Some countries and agencies give higher priority to co-ordinating care and education and, where special efforts have been made to do this, the results look very promising. The following section reviews very briefly approaches in some other countries and describes a number of projects which include enhancing the school performance of children in care among their aims.

Ideas from abroad

A number of other countries emphasise the educational side of substitute care for children more than is usual in Britain or the USA. Payne and White (1979) point to Israel and Canada as making positive use of residential institutions: 18 per cent of Israeli young people between the ages of 13 and 17 are educated in residential settings, as compared with 1.9 per cent in England and Wales. Children with widely differing social backgrounds, abilities and achievements are placed together as a matter of conscious policy in the belief that middle-class children can serve as models both cognitively and affectively.

Kashti and Arieli (1979) found favourable effects for disadvantaged pupils on several measures – social skills, attitude to school, attitude to education, self-concept as pupils and scholastic achievement. They suggest that residential schools in Israel offer such pupils entry into the class and culture which determine the criteria for success in society as a whole. They do this through the peer group, recognised to be the most significant factor in influencing the child's motivation and attitudes, and by trying to give each child a sense of achievement. Because residential schools in Israel were traditionally associated with pioneering ideologies – many started as agricultural training centres – occupational values tend to be recognised and rewarded as much as success in studies. According to Feuerstein and Krassilovsky (1971), the effect of experiencing approval, often for the first time, is to alter young people's perception of study and of people who spend their time following scholastic pursuits, to reduce anxiety and permit them to make renewed attempts at study themselves.

Perhaps the most interesting thing about this is the enviable certainty of the writers' views. They are not plagued by the self-doubt that would blur the issue for most American and English commentators: Have we any right to impose our values and interests on children from other cultures, thereby possibly cutting them off from their own community and family of origin? No, Kashti and Arieli (1979) are quite confident that education is an absolute good, and the way to success lies in learning to study, working towards future goals, adopting middle-class values, attitudes and interests.

In Poland, foster care is the responsibility of the Ministry of Education, and this is reflected in the regulations which emphasise the foster parents' duty to provide good conditions for the child's education and preparation for adult life. Two-thirds of Polish foster parents have completed secondary and higher education. At least one foster parent is a teacher in half of foster homes. Ziemska (1979), in what one suspects may be a rather rose-coloured account of a typical foster family, mentions that the older children do homework from 3pm, after their main meal of the day, until 6pm. 'They need quite a lot of time because they must do some additional reading exercises. Their home work is checked by the mother. Father (a doctor) comes home for dinner at 4pm and organises physical and sporting activities'.

The French word for a residential child care worker is *educateur*, and this is a reflection of the more integrated approach to care and education for delinquent and disturbed children developed originally in Quebec (Gauthier, 1980) and known as "psychoeducation". According to Cozens (1981), the approach draws from several different sources: the Rudolf Steiner theory of necessary stages which must not be unduly hastened; milieu therapy – recognising the need to plan for 24 hours a day; and some aspects of the treatment model with a phased plan, individual counselling and a key worker for each child or adolescent. Unlike residential workers in this country, *psycho-educateurs* are highly trained, preparing for their specific professional role by a four-year, full-time course leading to a Masters degree.

Educational support for children in care

Among those who have thought about the subject at all there is unanimous agreement on the educational disadvantages suffered by children in care. There must be many social workers in area teams and residential homes who recognise the problems and work hard to overcome them. But very few planned schemes have found their way into print.

Support schemes in the USA

There are a few accounts in American journals of special programmes designed to enhance the educational prospects of foster children.

The Detroit Foster Homes Project is described (Ambinder and Falik, 1966) as 'focusing attention on the adjustment of the foster child to school as a major aspect of adjustment to life'. The strategy was to develop much closer, more regular contact with schools at all levels, from discussion with the principal to direct help for classroom teachers. Foster parents were fully involved and built up a close working relationship with case workers to help the child with school problems. Sometimes an outsider was brought in as an academic tutor to work with child, foster parents and school in a supportive and consultative role. Ambinder stresses the importance of sharing relevant information with the school, as an ongoing process, not as a "once and for all" experience at the time of the placement.

Apart from reducing the number of school problems experienced by foster children, two main benefits resulted from the scheme. Making contacts with higher level administrative staff in the school system opened channels of communication which meant that, when special arrangements for the child were necessary, the agency was likely to get co-operation. Secondly, where this kind of work was done to help the child adjust and succeed in school, the foster family placement proved much more stable.

Taylor (1973) describes a more ambitious remedial education programme developed by the Association for Jewish Children in New York. Most of the children came from families characterised by 'low income, marital conflict, mental illness'. Teachers were asked to involve foster children in extra-curricular activities, to watch for manifestations of interest or talent, and to encourage or enable participation where possible (art, drama, music, sports, science, photography are some examples given). Schools undertook to maintain complete records on the child so that they could contribute to case reviews and placement decisions. Foster parents were helped to become much more directly involved in the child's school experience. The way in which this last objective was achieved is of most interest. Partly it was through conventional participation in the PTA, attendance at school events and field-trips, volunteer activities and club sponsorship and partly through a structured programme to reinforce learning activities at home.

Each evening a specific period was set aside (usually from 20 to 45 minutes) for a one-to-one focus on school happenings: 'Abandoning a sterile tutoring format, they utilise child-centred games, songs, colourful materials and informal discussions'.

Foster parents taking part in the scheme attend training meetings presenting a variety of techniques and approaches. The aim is to strengthen enjoyment of learning experiences and demonstrate to the child that the foster parents place high value on education, rather than to teach skills and information. The results are not quantified but are said to be encouraging. Children seem much happier at school and the role of the foster parents has been significantly broadened.

One further North American article worth noting is Elaine Walizer's (1980) discussion of the neglected question of how to resettle into school a child who has been in a residential placement. There is a welcome note of realism about this article, which makes no attempt to gloss over things that can go wrong. A key problem, which many social workers will recognise, is how to develop a co-operative, non-antagonistic relationship with the school, even though acting as an advocate for the young person. Deciding what information to share is also hard – enough to engage the sympathies of the teacher without implying that allowances should be made. Social workers should give 'minimal background information' and 'the meeting should not be a gossip session' (a view that would certainly get a lot of support from young people in care).

Support schemes in Britain

In this country there have been very few planned attempts to enhance the educational prospects of children in care. Where an effort has been made, it is often due to the dedication of a few individuals.

The Kent family placement project

The importance of good relationships at the administrative level, emphasised by Taylor (1973), also emerges clearly from Nancy Hazel's study of the Kent Family Placement Project (Hazel, 1981). The adolescents in this scheme often had a long history of truancy and school difficulties, so it was seen as important to develop a partnership with the school system. The Chief Education Officer, involved at an early stage, sent a circular to heads of all the secondary schools in Kent, explaining the project and pointing out that the foster parents were paid workers who, it was anticipated, would play a very active role in promoting the education of adolescents.

School placements were made in consultation with the foster parents, birth parents, project worker, divisional education officer, head of former and proposed schools and sometimes the educational psychologist. Face-to-face collaboration between foster parents and teachers was extremely good. Teachers showed imagination and flexibility in helping the young people to catch up and co-operated closely with the foster parents to prevent truancy. The foster parents' relatively high level of education and confidence proved very useful in enabling them to negotiate with the schools and sometimes to intercede for the young people in their charge.

The educational progress of adolescents in the scheme was monitored by means of a questionnaire sent to the school every six months. The results are described only as being 'as good as could be expected given the fact that most adolescents are restless and unsettled during their last year at school'. This seems rather too modest a claim considering the high risk group from which these young people were drawn. Most of them were in the lower streams at school and tended to perform relatively poorly even there. But their behaviour was normal (when it had been extremely disruptive) their ability to mix with their peers had improved greatly and, in general, the changes reported by schools since placement were very favourable. One boy went to university and, despite their poor educational background, a substantial number went on to technical colleges or successfully completed vocational courses.

Reading and literacy

John Bald, tutor in charge of Essex Education Department's Reading and Language Centre at Clacton, set up an experiment in one community home with 12 children – two teenagers, seven primary school children and two pre-schoolers (Bald, 1982). His idea was to improve 'constructive communication' between teachers and social workers by providing a clear and mutually accepted point of focus – in this case the provision of consistent adult support for reading.[4]

As a starting point, each child was allowed to choose £10 worth of books from a local shop, and each staff member took responsibility for listening to particular children read. The basic commitment was to listen to each child regularly for ten minutes, several days a week, in conditions of peace and quiet, and to discuss the books or stories read.

The scheme had emotional as well as educational benefits. Hearing children read proved an excellent way of getting to know them better. It encouraged closeness and affectionate relationships. It provided an opportunity to enlarge the child's understanding and ability to reflect on his or her own experience. It also ensured that for a very short time most days the child had an adult's undivided attention.

But significantly, it turned out to be extremely difficult to get the scheme off the ground, despite the goodwill of all concerned. It was so foreign to residential workers to give planned time to individual children, or to make reading a high priority in their work. Not until a capable volunteer undertook to organise the community home end of the scheme did the staff begin to provide the consistent, regular support that was essential.

---

[4] This work bore fruit many years later in the Who Cares? Trust project, *A Book of My Own* (Bald, Bean and Meegan, 1995).

The Clacton scheme is a variant of the experiments involving parents more closely in teaching children to read which have been tried with success in Rochdale, Hackney and Haringey (Tizard, Schofield and Hewison, 1982). Hewison and Tizard (1980) set up a scheme for collaboration between teachers and parents in teaching children to read. Even though some of the parents were non-English speaking or even illiterate, parent-coached children of all ability levels showed significant improvement, whereas those who received extra teaching at school made only limited gains, and low-achieving children almost none.

Bald (1982) suggests that residential child care workers and foster parents can successfully take on the role of parents in the Tizard experiment, and indeed that it is vital for them to do so. Children in care are educationally vulnerable and special efforts have to be made to ensure that they become fluent readers. This needs careful organisation and planning, and above all, higher priority. Children's books and reading should be important topics in social work and foster parent training and in-service training for child care workers. Children should be encouraged to form their own collections of books and care staff should create comfortable conditions for reading and make time to talk about books to children.

Models of good practice

In residential care, as David Berridge (1985) found, the attitude of the head of home is of overriding importance. The key elements here seem to be continuity, an intense personal interest in the education of each child, practical measures to encourage learning and study, and willingness to take on the advocate role.

All these points are illustrated by the work of Maureen Coppard, officer in charge of a community home in a London borough. When she took over the home in 1972, she made a commitment to herself to stay until the 12 children then resident left care. Right from the start she took a great interest in schooling and spent a lot of time talking to the children about it. Staff from the home always go to open evenings at school and ask advice from the teachers: 'What can we do to help?' On average she visits a school once or twice a week.

Over the years she has built up a detailed knowledge of schools in the area and chooses schools which are sympathetic to children in care. This counts for a lot because 'sometimes it's a real fight to keep kids in school'. She may have to stick out for her point of view against a fieldwork decision made for reasons of convenience.

Everything is done to make study easy and attractive to the children. They are encouraged to buy books and join libraries. They can do homework wherever they like but everyone has a table, bookshelf and desk light in their bedroom. Staff always ask what homework the children have been set and check if they say none. If children have difficulties with particular subjects they try to help or find someone else who can, often husbands or friends from outside.

Problems are always liable to arise, often due to events in the child's life outside school:

Last year one girl who had just started 'A' levels was suspended from the English Literature class. She was devastated. I asked for a meeting and really pleaded with the head of department and the English teacher. It was really hard work, but they accepted her back and she's doing fine now.

Career guidance is taken seriously, in contrast to the defeatist attitude to be found in many children's homes: 'We make sure they go to school sessions, write to everywhere for information, talk about it a lot, go to interviews with them and encourage them to use resources.' Recently, much more effort has gone into encouragement of leisure activities. Children from the home belong to the sports centre and learn ice-skating, ballet, musical instruments and singing. One boy irritated everyone by tapping all the time, so she organised drum lessons with a Covent Garden musician. Another, interested in photography, was able to buy a camera with a grant from a charity, and has now made it his career.

Of the original 12 children, one is aiming for university, several have taken 'O' or 'A' levels, and all are now employed or in education. There have been failures. And the negative attitudes of junior care staff have often created problems. But on the whole this is a success story, which shows what can be done by one person with a firm conviction of the importance of education and good support from management

Does education matter?

Although we have remarkably little evidence on the education of children in care, it is entirely consistent and all points one way. It is not too hard to think of simple, low-cost measures to improve the situation quite significantly.

But in discussing initial findings with colleagues and social workers, and attempting to summarise them as evidence for the House of Commons Social Services Committee's Inquiry into Children in Care (1984), other points of view emerged. The argument is strongly made that children with severe emotional difficulties cannot be expected to give their attention to academic learning. Social workers are right to focus their attention on the child's relationships and leave education to those who know about it. A concern for academic achievement, it is argued, would simply lay another burden on children who are intolerably overburdened already.

The suggestion that local authorities should be required to publish figures on the educational attainments of children leaving their care was greeted with horror. Wouldn't that suggest that exam passes were the only thing that mattered? And wouldn't it encourage league tables and invidious comparisons between social service departments which might face very different problems and have different resources to cope with them?

A more fundamental challenge is to the value of the formal education system for these vulnerable children. What use is book learning to them – what they need are social and survival skills, not irrelevant exam passes. And do we really want to pressure them all to join the rat-race and become driven middle-class professionals like ourselves?

Young people in care, or their spokespersons, seem profoundly disillusioned about school-based education. So much of what is taught seems pointless and boring to them, and they see little prospect of a job at the end, whether they pass examinations and collect qualifications or not. Further education, which at least treats them more like adults, might have more to offer, but then there are all the money problems and the fact that the welfare system seems anxious to make it as hard to study as possible. What counts in the end is not education but enterprise.

All these are arguments seriously put forward, but I must confess to finding them hard to engage with. They seem to have so little connection with the hopeless situation of the young person leaving care at 16 with one CSE if he is lucky, few social skills, no support and the prospect of life on the dole. The idea that educational qualifications are no help in finding a job is simply wrong. When jobs are scarce employers can demand higher qualifications for the same job. Studies by the Inner London Education Authority and by the TUC in Bristol have shown that the incidence of unemployment is closely related to formal qualifications at every level.

That is not to say that collecting examination passes is the only aim of education. There are many things that children in care need to learn, like all children, as well as academic subjects. But the indications are that those settings which fail to provide education and support for young people also fail to provide training in social skills and independence, or to offer a wide range of leisure and cultural interests.

I would also take a pessimistic view of social workers' ability to compensate children in care for the terrible emotional burden of knowing that no one in their family cared enough about them to provide them with a home. Perhaps we should concentrate on things we can do something about. I would share Roy Parker's (1980) view that:

> *Placements away from the family do not always meet the most basic emotional needs of a child, but alternative care under "public" supervision does offer opportunities for repairing gaps in a child's physical and intellectual development by identifying those problems which can be rectified with reasonable certainty (such as being unable to read) and which will strengthen the social skills and confidence of deprived children.* (p 112)

The argument favoured by some social workers that intellectual development and academic achievement must wait on emotional stability rests on shaky ground. Payne and White (1979) say in their introduction to *Caring for Deprived Children*:

> *The effectiveness of the British public school system is rarely*

*questioned, it self-evidently works. The task facing those who admin-
ister or work in residential environments for the deprived members of
society is to make them as successful.* (p 12)

Yet it would be hard to claim that the British "public" school provides
the ideal environment for emotional development. One could point
to a great deal of evidence from literature as well as from the
Dartington Social Research team's earlier research (Lambert and
Millham, 1968; Lambert, Millham and Bullock, 1975) to indicate the
reverse. The "success" to which Payne and White refer lies in producing
reasonably conforming members of society who pass through the
right hoops and mostly get good jobs in the end. So the suggestions
which follow are made from the position that those who have responsibility for children separated from their families should do everything
possible to equip them with skills for living a satisfying life, which
includes the qualifications for getting an interesting and preferably
well-paid job. If success in education creates divisions between them
and the families and communities into which they were born, that is a
different problem, and one which many young people not in care also
experience.

Summary and conclusions

Evidence on the education of children in care is thin because in general
the questions have not been asked. But everything points to the conclusion that a child who comes into care, at any age, for whatever reason,
and (though here the ground is less certain) for whatever length of time,
is at high risk of educational failure. The probability that he or she will
have difficulties at school and fall behind academically is greater than
for children, even those of similar social background, who do not come
into care.

Five main contributing factors are identified: pre-care experience;
disrupted schooling; low expectations; low self-esteem; lack of continuity. All of these are compounded by the low priority given to
education by social workers who bear the main responsibility for the
welfare and progress of children in care, and by lingering traces of the

notion of less eligibility. Apart from special projects and scattered individual initiatives, there is as yet little sign of change either at face-to-face or management level.

There are large tracts of uncharted territory here, as in other aspects of the lives of children who move in and out of care. Proposals for research are made in the next section. But to say that we need to know more before we can take action would be an evasion of our responsibility to those children who are currently in the care system and whose chances are even now slipping away.

Proposals for research and action

Research is needed at several different levels. First, to map out the dimensions of the problem and fill the gaps in basic data. Secondly, to explore less tangible factors from the view point of policy-makers, decision-takers and consumers. And thirdly to monitor and evaluate innovations in practice. The suggestions below fall into these three categories.

Baseline data

We do not at present know, except in very general terms what schools children in care attend, how many are in remedial streams, how many are entered for public examinations and what proportion succeed, which local authorities use their powers to provide educational assistance beyond 18 and how many young people take advantage of them.

Longitudinal data

What is the process by which children coming into care fall increasingly behind in education? The Dartington Research Unit's concept of a "care career" could usefully be focused on an education career in care. Are there critical points at which children should be screened and intensive remedial action taken if necessary? These might be, for example:

Pre-school: role of foster carers, language development, nursery or play group experience, choice of infant school.

Six to seven years: mastery of basic skills in reading, writing and number-work; attitude of care-takers to reading and books; relations

47

between caregivers and school; beginnings of development of individual interests.

12–13 years: school relationships, homework, choice of fourth year options, examination courses, early career discussion.

School-leaving age: staying on, transferring to further education, career planning

Children's views

What do young people in care now think about education and school? As was pointed out earlier, the evidence we have on this, besides possibly being out of date, is derived from an atypical group of unusually articulate and sometimes very angry young people. The experience of more ordinary children and adolescents could help pinpoint areas where change is most needed.

Management practice

It would be useful to undertake a more systematic survey of manuals, guidelines, job specifications and in-service training programmes to see how they could be used to give greater weight to educational issues. Attempts could also be made to identify innovative practice which might stem from a policy lead from higher management or from the initiative of individual social workers, team leaders or officers in charge of residential establishments.

Collaborative research

Perhaps the best hope for change lies in planning, evaluating and disseminating schemes which recognise the educational needs of children in care and make a systematic attempt to meet them. Both academic and practice components are essential if these objectives are to be achieved.

Some ideas which could be incorporated in such a scheme are set out in my evidence to the House of Commons Social Services Committee.

I would like to add one thought not included there which might help to meet the absolutely fundamental problem of how to provide continuity for children whose families cannot do so. Building on Leonard Davis's notion of the 'reliable, caring adult' (Davis *et al*, 1982), could we not find people who would be prepared to undertake a long-term commitment to oversee the educational progress of children in care, wherever they happened to be placed at any particular moment? Something beyond the now rather discredited social aunt and uncle, more like a conscientious godparent without the religious function. There might be people like this in the community who would hesitate to offer full-time care, and might be unsuited by age, personality or situation to do so, but who would gladly make a more limited commitment which would have the potential to grow into a valuable and long-lasting relationship.

References

Adamson, G (1973) *The Caretakers*, London: Bookstall Publications.

Akhurst, B A (1975) 'The prevalence of behaviour problems among children in care', *Education Research*, pp 137–42.

Ambinder, W J and Falik, L H (1966) 'Keeping emotionally disturbed foster children in school', *Children*, p 13.

Bald, J (1982) 'Children in care need books', *Concern*, 44, pp 18–21.

Bald, J, Bean, J and Meegan, F (1995) *A Book of My Own*, London: Who Cares? Trust.

Berridge, D (1983) 'Staff movement in community homes: some grounds for optimism', *Social Work Today*, 14:35, pp 7–10.

Berridge, D (1985) *Children's Homes*, Oxford: Blackwell.

Board of Education (1931) *Report of the Consultative Committee on the Primary School* (Hadow Report), London: HMSO.

Brearley, P, Hall, F, Gutridge, P, Jones, G and Roberts, G (1980) *Admission to Residential Care*, London: Tavistock.

Brearley, P, Hall, F, Gutridge, P, Jones, G and Roberts, G (1982) *Leaving Residential Care*, London: Tavistock.

Brown, J and Solomon, D (1974) 'Leisure time interests of children in residential homes', *Residential Social Work*, 14:8, pp 246–49.

Clode, D (1983) 'Testing time for Gatsby', *Social Work Today*, 14:22, pp 6–7.

Cozens, A (1981) *The Canadian Psycho-Education Model in the Context of Residential Social Work Theory*, MSc Dissertation in Applied Social Studies, (unpublished), Oxford University.

Davis, L, James, G, Kelleher, C and Ford, J (1982) *The Reliable Caring Adult*, Voice for the Child in Care Papers, No. 5, London: VCC.

Demetri, A (1982) *The Demetri Papers*, Voice for the Child in Care Papers, No. 2, London: VCC.

Department of Education and Sciences (1980) *Community Homes with Education*, HMI Series: Matters for Discussion 10, London: HMSO.

Department of Health and Social Security (1976) *Guide to Fostering Practice*, Report of a DHSS working party on fostering practice, London: HMSO.

Essen, J, Lambert, L and Head, J (1976) 'School attainment of children who have been in care', *Child Care, Health and Development*, 2, pp 339–51.

Essen, J, Lambert, L and Head, J (1977) 'Variations in behaviour ratings of children who have been in care', *Journal of Child Psychology & Psychiatry*, 18, pp 335–46.

Fanshel, D and Shinn, E B (1978) *Children in Foster Care: A longitudinal investigation*, New York: Columbia University Press.

Ferguson, T (1966) *Children in Care – and After*, London: Oxford University Press.

Feurstein, R and Krassilovsky, D (1971) 'The treatment group technique', in Wolins, M and Gottesman, M (eds) *Group Care: An Israeli Approach*, New York: Gordon & Breach.

Fitzherbert, K (1977) *Child Care Services and the Teacher*, London: Temple Smith.

Gauthier, P (1980) 'Psycho-education as a re-education model: theoretical foundations and practical implications,' in Jansen, E (ed), *The Therapeutic Community*, London: Croom Helm.

George, V (1970) *Foster Care: Theory and practice,* London: Routledge and Kegan Paul.

Gill, O and Jackson, B (1983) *Adoption and Race: Black, Asian and mixed race children in white families*, London: Batsford.

Hazel, N (1981) *A Bridge to Independence*, Oxford: Blackwell.

Hewison, J and Tizard, J (1980) 'Parental involvement and reading attainment', *British Journal of Educational Psychology*, 50, pp 209–15.

Hitchman, J (1960) *The King of the Barbareens*, Harmondsworth: Penguin.

Holmes, E (1977) 'The education needs of children in care', *Concern*, 26, pp 22–25.

Home Office/Social Work Services Group, Scotland (1970) *A Guide to Adoption Practice*, London: HMSO.

House of Commons (1984) *Second Report from the Social Services Committee. Children in Care*, Session 1983–4 HC360 I, II & III.

Kahan, B (1979) *Growing Up in Care*, Oxford: Blackwell.

Kashti, Y and Arieli, M (1979) 'Israel: Residential Education', in Payne, C and White, K (eds) *Caring for Deprived Children*, London: Croom Helm.

Lambert, L, Essen, J and Head, J (1977) 'Variations in behaviour ratings of children who have been in care', *Journal of Child Psychology & Psychiatry*, 18, pp 335–46.

Lambert, R and Millham, S (1968) *The Hothouse Society*, London: Weidenfeld & Nicholson.

Lambert, R, Millham, S and Bullock, R (1975) *The Chance of a Lifetime?* London: Weidenfeld & Nicholson.

MacVeigh, J (1982) *Gaskin*, London: Jonathan Cape.

Melotte, C J (1979) 'The placement decision', *Adoption & Fostering*, 95:1, pp 56–62 and 72.

Middleton, N (1979) *When Family Failed*, London: Victor Gollancz.

Millham, S, Bullock, R and Hosie, K (1980) *Learning to Care: The training of staff for residential social work with young people*, Farnborough: Gower.

Newson, J and Newson, E with Barnes, P (1977) *Perspectives on School at Seven Years Old*, London: George Allen & Unwin.

Parker, R A (ed) (1980) *Caring for Separated Children: Plans, procedures and priorities*, Report of a National Children's Bureau working party, London: Macmillan.

Payne, C J and White, K J (eds) (1979) *Caring for Deprived Children*, London: Macmillan.

Pidgeon, D A (1970) *Expectation and Pupil Performance*, Windsor: NFER.

Pilling, D and Pringle, M L K (1978) *Controversial Issues in Child Development*, London: Paul Elek.

Pringle, M L K (ed) (1965) *Investment in Children: A symposium on positive childcare and constructive education*, London: Longmans.

Pringle, M L K and Bossio, V (1965) 'Intellectual, emotional and social development of deprived children', in Pringle, M L K, *Deprivation and Education*, London: Longmans.

Prosser, H (1976) *Perspectives on Residential Care*, Windsor: NFER.

Prosser, H (1978) *Perspectives on Foster Care*, Windsor: NFER.

Robinson, M (1978) *Schools and Social Work*, London: Routledge & Kegan Paul.

Rowe, J and Lambert, L (1973) *Children who Wait*, London: Association of British Adoption Agencies.

Seglow, J, Pringle, M L K and Wedge, P (1972) *Growing Up Adopted*, Windsor: NFER.

Seighart, F (1979) 'Gifted children', *Adoption & Fostering*, 96, pp 26–9 and p 37.

Taylor, J L (1973) 'Remedial education of children in foster care', *Child Welfare*, 52:2.

Timms, N (ed) (1973) *The Receiving End: Consumer accounts of social help for children*, London: Routledge & Kegan Paul.

Tizard, B (1977) *Adoption: A second chance*, London: Routledge & Kegan Paul.

Tizard, J, Schofield, W N and Hewison, J (1982) 'Collaboration between teachers and parents in assisting children's reading', *British Journal of Educational Psychology*, 52, pp 1–15.

Walizer, E (1980) 'Achieving success in post treatment education placements', *Child Welfare*, 59:5.

Wedge, P and Prosser, H (1973) *Born to Fail*, London: Arrow Books for the National Children's Bureau.

Ziemska, M (1979) 'Poland: foster family homes', in Payne, C and White, K (eds) *Caring for Deprived Children*, London: Croom Helm.

Proving the point

2 The ability and behaviour of children who have been "in care" or separated from their parents

Lindsey St.Claire and Albert F. Osborn

This chapter is extracted from a report of the Child Health and Education Study (CHES) prepared for the Economic and Social Science Research Council. It was originally published in 'Early Child Development and Care', 1987, Vol. 28, pp 187–354.

The purpose of this study was to determine the extent to which the poorer cognitive development and increased risk of behavioural deviance typically shown by children in care (Essen, Lambert and Head, 1976; Lambert, Essen and Head, 1977) could be attributed to the in-care experience itself as compared with the alternative hypothesis that these developmental problems are the result of background circumstances or contextual factors associated with being taken into care.

Main findings

Children are statutorily taken into the care of the local authority only as a last resort when the family situation is considered to be so bad that to leave them with their own parents would entail a greater risk than the act of removing them and (usually) placing them with strangers. Implicit in this process is the belief that separation of children from their parents and familiar home circumstances is likely to be detrimental to their emotional and psychological well-being, although this belief need not imply a commitment to the concept that maternal deprivation (i.e. loss of the natural or biological mother) is responsible for the ill-effects (Rutter, 1981).

In contrast to statutory care is voluntary care, when parents, for one reason or another, are unable to care for their child themselves. In this case the parents retain the right to reclaim their child but, since children are often removed from their familiar home surroundings to be looked after by strangers, this too is likely to be a traumatic experience.

The legal distinction carries no implications for type of placement or children's actual experience of care. For this reason, instead of classifying the sample in terms of whether or not children had experienced a period in care and their legal status, the present research concentrated on type of placement. Residential or foster care and adoption provide the bases of a clear classification which is independent of the (unknown) infinity of day-to-day living arrangements and which accords with a common sense approach to children in care as those who have been temporarily or permanently separated from natural parents who were unwilling or unable to bear the responsibility of looking after them. It excludes children placed at home with their parents but includes children in residential or foster or adoptive homes who have never been taken into care in the formal legal sense.

Numbers of children in care

About eight per 1,000 children under the age of 18 in Britain are in care at any one time. Because of the turnover of children entering and leaving care, however, the proportion of children who experience a period in care before the age of 18 is much greater than the proportion in care at any one time. Boys outnumber girls in care by a ratio of about three to two, although this varies according to children's age and reason for being in care. Considering the substantial numbers involved, it is perhaps surprising that so little is known about the long-term behavioural and developmental consequences for children who have been in care.

Source of information

Based on the National Child Development Study (NCDS), a longitudinal survey of children born in one week of 1958, Mapstone (1969) and Essen *et al* (1976) reported that children who had experienced a period of care between birth and 11 years yielded poorer educational scores than those who had not. Similarly, and using the same data, Lambert *et al* (1977) found that the behaviour of these children was rated significantly worse than that of controls.

Clearly these findings are deeply disturbing: they suggest that almost 100,000 children in care at any one time and the still greater number who have experienced it at some stage during their childhood, are in danger of failing at school or developing behaviour problems. Still more disturbing, they raise the suspicion that the in-care experience itself might mar their cognitive and behavioural development. Essen *et al* (1976) however, warned against implicating the in-care experience *per se*. They pointed out that adverse social factors, emotional problems, family illness, or lack of attention and interest were often associated with such experiences and might account for poorer educational and behavioural outcomes.

The primary purpose of the present study was to shed light on this issue using data collected under the aegis of the Child Health and Education Study (CHES). Like the NCDS this was a longitudinal survey of British children born during one week (5–11 April, 1970). In addition to updating the work of Essen and Lambert, the intention was also to extend and clarify it, by using a classification based on type of placement rather than the in-care/not in-care dichotomy.

Of over 16,000 children in England, Scotland and Wales who took part in the CHES birth survey (Chamberlain *et al*, 1975), 13,135 were followed up at the age of five (Osborn, Butler and Morris, 1984) and 14,906 at ten (Butler *et al*, 1982). The five- and ten-year surveys collected a wide range of data covering the social background of the children, their health, use of services, educational experience and a number of developmental and educational tests and behavioural assessments.

Both five- and ten-year surveys included a question which identified children who had been in the care of their local authority. Another question inquired about mother–child separations of a month or more duration in the period between birth and five. The responses to these questions formed the basis of the "in-care" classification used in this study.

The "in-care" study groups

Of the total 13,135 children in the five-year follow-up, 127 (1.0 per cent) had been with foster parents, 48 (0.4 per cent) in residential care, and 18 (0.1 per cent) had been fostered and in residential care at some time during the first five years of life. In addition, 515 (3.9 per cent) had been separated from their mothers for at least a month between birth and five years but had not been formally taken into care. Adopted children formed a separate category and totalled 96 (0.7 per cent) out of the five-year sample. Finally, reference to the ten-year follow-up showed that 55 (0.4 per cent) children who had not experienced care before the age of five had subsequently been taken into care between five and ten. This group was defined at five as being "destined" for care. The balance of 12,276 (93.5 per cent) children surveyed at five who were in none of these categories, formed a control group.

The reasons why children were taken into care varied considerably, but the most frequently mentioned were temporary maternal illness or pregnancy. More serious reasons, such as abandonment of the child, family violence or marital breakdown, whilst occurring less frequently, tended to be associated with longer periods in care.

Social background of children in care

The five-year study groups were compared in terms of a wide range of social and personal factors describing the family socio-economic circumstances (e.g. social class, accommodation, parental employment and income), family configuration (e.g. number and ages of siblings, age of parents and the relationship of the parents to the child), characteristics of the mother (e.g. her attitudes to child rearing practices and other issues, and a scale of maternal depression), and characteristics of the child (e.g. gender, ethnic origin, physical or mental handicap, measures of behaviour, self-concept and sociability).

The findings consistently showed the groups who had been in foster or residential care to be disadvantaged in many ways when compared with the controls who had never been in care or separated. They were more likely than controls to come from low social class backgrounds, to live in substandard and crowded accommodation, to have many siblings, to be physically or mentally "handicapped", and to have parents with an authoritarian approach to child rearing and little interest in their education. Given this social background, it was not surprising to find that the social and cognitive development of the in-care groups fell considerably behind that of the controls.

In contrast, adopted children showed just the opposite pattern since they tended to be in socially advantaged, child-centred families and to have above average scores on the behavioural and cognitive measures. The former was not surprising considering the rigorous selection procedures that are undertaken before a child is placed with adoptive parents, but the latter was of considerable theoretical interest because it suggested that the effects of a disadvantaged start in life (for example, with poor circumstances, rejection by the natural mother, and being placed in care while awaiting adoption) were more than compensated for by a dramatically improved family and social situation following adoption.

Children who had been separated from their mother but without the formality of being taken into care, formed an interesting comparison group with those who had been in care. Examination of the social and family background of these children revealed that, although they were marginally disadvantaged compared with controls in some respects they were not so disadvantaged as the in-care groups. These differences were also reflected in the cognitive and behavioural outcomes at five and ten which showed that the "separated" children were doing less well than the controls but not so badly as the in-care groups. Again, this suggested that at least part of the reason for the poor cognitive and behavioural development associated with having been in care can be attributed to the poor social background of the children.

Further support for this hypothesis was suggested by the finding that the cognitive and behavioural development and home background at the age of five, of children "destined" to go into care between five and ten was very similar to that of children who had already been in care, and therefore the maternal separation and "in-care" effects were likely to be small in comparison with these contextual factors. In addition, because behavioural deviance in the "destined" group was at about the same level as in the in-care groups, behaviour problems may have been a contributory factor in the decision to take a child into care, rather than the in-care experience itself resulting in behavioural deviance.

These findings indicate the need to take account of differences in family background when assessing the effects of various separation and in-care experiences on children's cognitive development and behavioural adjustment.

[One factor known to be relevant to children's attainment is the educational level achieved by their mothers.] Among the control group, 55 per cent of the mothers had no educational qualifications compared with 59 per cent of the "separated" and 45 per cent of the adopted groups. However, up to 86 per cent of mothers whose children had been or would be formally placed in care were unqualified. [Most of the other findings on social and family characteristics of the four groups followed a similar pattern.]

Parental interest in children's education

The ten-year data base offered an opportunity to examine parental interest in children's education, which has been identified as one of the most potent influences on cognitive outcomes (Jackson, 1983). Happily the proportion of mothers rated "uninterested" by children's class teachers was only three per cent for control and "separated" groups, compared with one per cent for adoptees. On the other hand (excluding those in care at the time of testing), teachers thought that seven per cent of mothers whose children had been taken into care were uninterested and at approximately 15 per cent the proportion showing "very little interest" was three times that of controls.

At the other extreme, nearly half (48 per cent) of control mothers were rated "very interested" compared with 41 per cent and 63 per cent of those whose children were in separated and adopted groups, respectively, while proportions for the in-care groups were considerably lower: only 33 per cent and 22 per cent for mothers of children taken into care before and after five.

Cross-tabulations based on type of placement suggest the least interest was shown by mothers whose children had experienced residential care (10 per cent) which was almost double the rate for children who had been fostered.

Parents were asked when their children would probably leave school and 40 per cent of control and "separated" groups said 16, with almost exactly the same proportion expected to leave at 18. For adopted children, however, scales began to tilt, 34 per cent being expected to leave school at 16 compared with 47 per cent at 18, and they were steeply tilted in the opposite direction for children who had an in-care episode, 60 per cent of whom were expected to leave school at 16, with only 28 per cent of those whose first episode occurred before five and 27 per cent of the "after five" group expected to stay on till 18.

Similarly, 41 per cent of control parents expected their children to continue training after school, while the proportion was slightly higher for the separated children and adoptees. At 29 per cent, figures for children who had had an in-care experience were much lower, and as before, expectations were lowest for those who had been in residential care.

The analysis of social variables excluded children who were actually in care at the time of testing since it was not possible to determine whether their data referred to their families of origin or the substitute families with whom they were living. Interestingly, inclusion of children currently in care left the figures for educational qualifications virtually unaltered, which suggests that substitute mothers of children in foster or residential care were as likely as their natural mothers to be unqualified, consistent with Adamson's finding ten years earlier (1973).

Cognitive and behavioural outcomes for children experiencing different types of placement

Three ability measures were administered in the five-year survey. These were the English Picture Vocabulary Test (EPVT), Human Figure Drawing and Copying Designs Tests (described in detail in Osborn, Butler and Morris, 1984). In the ten-year follow-up, four tests of cognitive ability were administered. These included a shortened form of the British Ability Scales, a Picture Language Comprehension Test, a CHES Mathematics Test and a Shorthand Edinburgh Reading Test. [These tests, together with details of scoring and standardisation procedures are described in Appendix 2.3 to the original report.]

Figures 1 and 2 show the deviations from mean standardised scores for each five-year study group. Analysis of variance (ANOVA) confirmed that differences between groups were significant on each test at the

Figure 1

Cognitive outcomes at 5 years

Standardised English Picture Vocabulary Test (EPVT) Scores

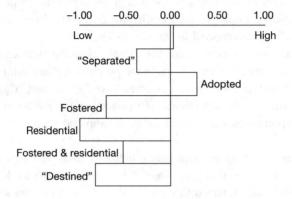

Figure 2

Behaviour outcomes at 5 years

Standardised Behaviour Scores – Antisocial Behaviour

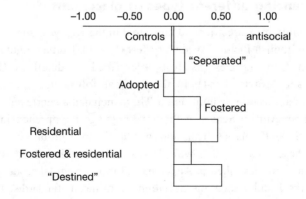

p<.0001 level or better, that is that they could not have arisen by chance.

The EPVT differentiated most dramatically between study groups, but profiles across all three tests were similar. Compared with controls: adopted children stood out as the best performers; children who had at some time been separated from their mothers but not taken into care showed a small yet consistent deficit, while those in fostered and, more especially, residential groups showed consistent, substantial deficits. Most interesting, however, was that the "destined" group showed consistent deficits which were as large – or larger – than children who had already been in care. Scores on cognitive tests at ten and behavioural scores showed the same pattern (Figures 3, 4 and 5). Children who came into care for the first time after five years already showed deficits in cognitive and behaviour scores at five for which, by definition, the in-care experience could not have been responsible. Indeed to take a transactional view, it seems just as likely that the children's behaviour contributed to their placement away from home. [The authors comment: 'it seems shocking that children who were to have in-care episodes some time after their fifth birthdays, were so clearly distinguishable from controls beforehand and Wedge and Prosser's (1973) phrase "born to fail" springs to mind'.]

The findings from the CHES study are essentially in agreement with those of the NCDS 12 years earlier, which found that children who had been in care were by 11 between one and two years behind in mathematics and reading compared with those who had never been in care.

The ten-year follow-up asked teachers whether children attended remedial classes. The answer was yes for 16 per cent of children who were taken into care before five years, a rate roughly three times that of the controls. More important, 25 per cent of children who had been in foster care were identified as not getting remedial help from which their teachers believed they would benefit. Among those who had been in residential care, the figure rose to 40 per cent needing help and not getting it.

Figure 3

Cognitive outcomes at 10 years and type of placement

Figure 3a: Standardised Picture Language Scores – deviations from the mean

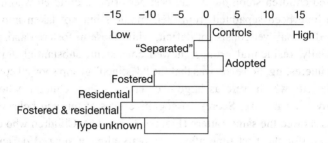

Figure 3b: Standardised Friendly Maths Scores – deviations from the mean

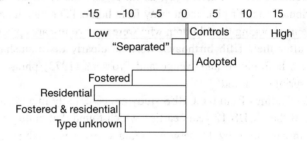

Figure 3c: Standardised Reading Scores – deviations from the mean

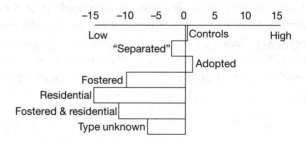

Figure 4

Cognitive outcomes at 10 years and age at first placement

Figure 4a: Standardised Picture Language Scores – deviations from the mean

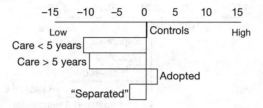

Figure 4b: Standardised Friendly Maths Scores – deviations from the mean

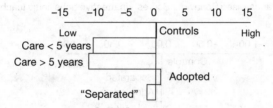

Figure 4c: Standardised Reading Scores – deviations from the mean

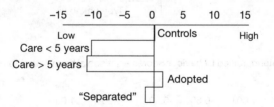

Figure 5

Behaviour at 10 years and type of placement

Figure 5a: Standardised Behaviour Scores – antisocial behaviour: Teachers' ratings

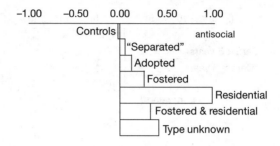

Figure 5b: Standardised Behaviour Scores – inattentive behaviour: Teachers' ratings

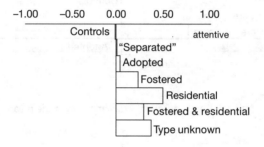

Figure 5c: Standardised Behaviour Scores – antisocial behaviour: Mothers' ratings

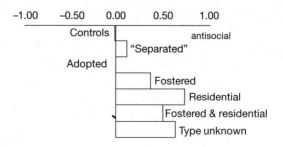

Figure 6

Behaviour scores at 10 years and age at first placement

Figure 6a: Standardised Behaviour Scores – antisocial behaviour: Teachers' ratings

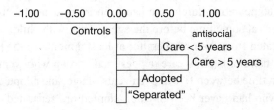

Figure 6b: Standardised Behaviour Scores – inattentive behaviour: Teachers' ratings

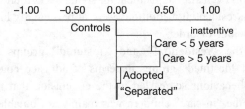

Figure 6c: Standardised Behaviour Scores – antisocial behaviour: Mothers' ratings

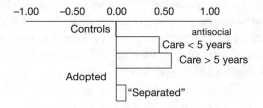

Conclusions

This study was designed to investigate the reasons underlying the association between having been in the care of the local authority and poor achievement and deviant behaviour in young children. The method employed compared children who had been in residential institutions or foster homes at some time before the age of five, with children who had been separated from their mothers for at least a month in the pre-school period but had not been in care, a "destined" group who went into care for the first time between five and ten years of age, and adopted children. Children who had never been in care, adopted or "separated" formed a control group.

Large variations in social background were found between the children in these different groups which accounted for a substantial part of the differences in mean test scores between them. However, the average level of achievement of the in-care groups was significantly lower than that of the controls even after adjustment for social background. Children who had been in residential institutions were at particularly high risk of anti-social behaviour disorder.

Comparing the "residential" and "fostered" groups with the "separated" and "destined" groups in terms of adjusted cognitive development and behaviour scores led to the conclusion that the poorer performance of the "in-care" children was mainly attributable to social background differences, or to pre-existing behaviour disorder contributing to the likelihood that children would be placed in care. Residual deficits attributable to the in-care experience, and which were largest for those in residential care, worsened the already poor developmental prognosis for these children, but such effects were very weak in comparison with those attributed to their social background.

This is not, however, a complacent ending. First, more research directed at understanding the association between any sort of maternal separation and children's cognitive ability and behaviour is clearly imperative. Second, it must never be forgotten that there is no such thing as a foster or residential experience *per se* in real life – the statistical adjustments, which decreased the deficits of fostered and residential groups relative to "separated" and "destined" children are abstract devices which have no bearing on the markedly low scores actually shown by these children. Clearly therefore, concrete policies directed at alleviating social disadvantage of families whose children are placed in care, would be the first, and most probably the most effective step towards helping them.

References

Adamson, G (1973) *The Caretakers*, London: Bookstall Publications.

Butler, N R, Haslum, M N, Barker, W and Morris, A C (1982) *Child Health and Education Study: First report to the Department of Education and Science on the 10-year follow-up*, University of Bristol: Department of Child Health.

Chamberlain, R, Chamberlain, G, Howlett, B and Claireaux, A (1975) *British Births 1970. Vol. 1: The first week of life*, London: Heinemann.

Essen, J, Lambert, L and Head, J (1976) 'School attainment of children who have been in care', *Child Care, Health and Development*, 2:6, pp 339–51.

Lambert, L, Essen, J and Head, J (1977) 'Variations in behaviour ratings of children who have been in care', *Journal of Child Psychology & Psychiatry*, 18:4, pp 335–46.

Jackson, S (1983) *The Education of Children in Care* (published 1987 by University of Bristol).

Mapstone, E (1969) 'Children in Care', *Concern*, 3:23.

Osborn, A F, Butler, N R and Morris, A C (1984) *The Social Life of Britain's 5 Year Olds*, London: Routledge & Kegan Paul.

Rutter, M (1981) *Maternal Deprivation Reassessed*, Harmondsworth: Penguin.

Wedge, P and Prosser, H (1973) *Born to Fail?* London: Arrow/National Children's Bureau.

3 **Failure to escape:** A longitudinal study of foster children's educational attainment

Anthony Heath, Matthew Colton and Jane Aldgate

Previous research has shown that children in care have low educational attainment. The present paper demonstrates that even those foster children in long-term, settled placements, in middle-class environments fail to "escape from disadvantage". Various explanations for this are considered. The notion of "self-fulfilling prophecies" arising from low teacher expectations is rejected, but a history of child abuse or neglect before entering care appears to have lasting effects. The results are compared with French work on adoption, where an escape from disadvantage does seem to occur. The implication is that exceptional educational inputs are required.

This paper has been reprinted from *The British Journal of Social Work*, 24:3, June 1994, pp 241–60.

It is now well established that children in care do not achieve well within the educational system and perform below national norms for their age groups (Essen, Lambert and Head, 1976; St.Claire and Osborn, 1987; Jackson, 1988; Heath, Aldgate and Colton, 1989). This raises important questions about the operation of care and its benefits for the children involved.

The aim of the present study is to explore some possible causes of this low educational achievement. It is based on a longitudinal study of foster children and of a comparison group of children receiving social work support while remaining with their birth families.

Many studies have shown that low educational attainment is associated with social and economic deprivation (e.g. Douglas, 1964; Halsey, Heath and Ridge, 1980; Essen and Wedge, 1982; Mortimore and

Blackstone, 1982). However, we might on these grounds expect children in foster care, if not those in residential care, to perform at around the national average. In terms of environmental factors such as social class, family composition, and so on, foster children appear to be living in relatively "educogenic" environments which might be expected to provide the conditions for "escape from disadvantage" (Pilling, 1990).

Our previous research, based on cross-sectional analysis, did not provide much encouragement for this hypothesis. Longitudinal analysis is preferable, however, as the foster children may have started from a particularly deprived level. The traumas of being taken into care, or other aspects of the children's histories, may have depressed their attainment and it may take some considerable time before the children recover. We might therefore expect the foster children's attainment to improve gradually over time as they become integrated into their foster families.

Another possible explanation for the children's lack of progress may be low expectations, either on the part of the carers or the children's teachers. It has often been suggested that low expectations may become a self-fulfilling prophecy which reinforces lack of achievement (Rosenthal and Jacobson, 1968).

Alternatively the continuing stresses and uncertainties surrounding care, and in particular its open-ended character, may depress performance on a more continuing basis. Research indicates that the impermanence associated with many foster placements may adversely affect a child's development (Triseliotis and Russell, 1984; Aldgate and Hawley, 1986; Berridge and Cleaver, 1987). This has helped to fuel the "permanency movement" in child care, with its stress on promoting lasting relationships for separated children (McKay, 1980; Adcock, 1980; Maluccio, Fein and Olmstead, 1986).

Some of our original foster placements were characterised by a greater degree of "permanence" and legal security than others. During the course of the study, custodianship and adoption orders were made in respect of a number of the foster children. Adoption has been compared favourably with long-term fostering by Tizard (1977) on the grounds that the former involves a greater sense of security for caregivers and children than the latter. It may be interesting, therefore, to compare the overall progress of youngsters who were the subjects of adoption and custodianship orders with that of other foster children.

We begin this paper by comparing the educational progress over time of our sample of foster children with that of the comparison group of children receiving social work support, testing specifically whether the youngsters who were the subjects of custodianship orders or who were in settled long-term placements made greater progress. In the second section we look in more detail at the children in foster care, considering whether aspects of their social work histories could account for their progress. We then consider the role of the schools: did low teacher expectations lead to a self-fulfilling prophecy of low attainment? Finally, we examine the theory of cultural capital, asking whether greater progress was made by children in more middle-class and culturally advantaged environments.

Data and methods

The sample consists of 49 foster children (26 boys, 23 girls) of approximately middle school age (8.14) at the start of the study, in ordinary state schools in one county. Each child had been in care for a minimum of six months, and many had not only been in care but in their placements for several years (mean length of placement = 6 years; median = 7 years). So we have a sample of children in fairly stable long-term foster care – conditions which ought to be propitious for educational progress.

Sixteen of the foster children were in voluntary care at the time the study began, under section 2 of the 1980 Child Care Act. In the case of a further 12 children, the local authority had assumed parental rights and duties (under section 3 of the 1980 Child Care Act) where the child had originally come into care voluntarily. A further 16 children were the subject of care orders under the 1969 Children and Young Persons Act. That is to say, these children had been taken into care compulsorily through the courts.

We thought it sensible to compare our foster children, not with the general population, but with children from similar backgrounds to those of the foster children's birth families (see St.Claire and Osborn (1987) for evidence on the social origins of foster children). We therefore chose a comparison group of children who had never been in care but whose families were receiving "preventive" social work support in the community at the start of the study. We were encouraged in this decision by Packman, Randall and Jacques' (1986) study on the basis, process and outcome of decisions for or against the admission of children to care in two local authorities. They found that there were no sharply identifiable differences between children admitted or not admitted to care.

We recruited 58 children to this social services group, 34 boys and 24 girls within the same age band and attending similar schools. As with the foster children, virtually all were of white European ethnic origin. Five of this social services group were subject to supervision orders (one under the Children and Young Persons Act 1969 and four under the Matrimonial Causes Act). The rest were receiving voluntary support, 35 of them under section 1 of the 1980 Children Act. It was unclear from the social work files what the precise legal status of the remaining 20 children was.

The children's educational attainment was assessed through standardised tests in reading (the Suffolk reading test and NFER's EH2 test for older children), vocabulary (the BPVS) and mathematics (NFER's BM test). The reading and vocabulary tests were administered by a member of the research team in autumn 1987, but the maths test (at the request of the Department of Education) was administered on a separate occasion by the schools. Independent testing on separate occasions both reduced the burden on the children and provided a valuable check on measurement error. It did, however, lead to some missing data on the maths test.

The reading and vocabulary tests were administered in the second round of testing in autumn 1988, and all three tests were administered in the third round in autumn 1989 (the maths test again being administered by the schools). The same tests were administered on each occasion, if they were appropriate for the child's age. Otherwise a new age-appropriate test was substituted. The children scores were then age-standardised. They thus show how well the child was performing relative to the national average for children of the same age.

In any longitudinal study there is bound to be sample attrition (due to refusals, untraceable moves, etc.) and ours is no exception. There is considerable evidence that such attrition tends to be selective and therefore, in order to compare like with like, it is important to compare scores over time only of the children who completed all rounds of the relevant test. That is to say, we employ listwise deletion of missing data.

We also interviewed the carers at the beginning of the study, the children and teachers during the course of the study, and the social workers towards the end of the study. Information was also obtained from the social work files about the children's social work histories. This information was obtained by a researcher who had not been involved with the children's testing or parental interviewing and was therefore "blind" with respect to the individual children's attainment or progress.

Our basic statistical tool in assessing the children's progress is the standard paired-comparison t-test. We should note that there are some problems in measuring progress. Firstly there may be measurement error. On any measuring instrument there is bound to be some error and there will thus be some children whose measured score in the first round was, for example, lower then their "true" score. If measurement error is random (although it often is not random), these children may appear to have made progress by the second round of testing even though their "true" scores may have remained constant. We can overcome this by checking the results on one test with that on another – especially as maths was tested independently by the teachers.

Secondly, there is the problem that a child's performance on all the tests may have been affected by transitory factors, such as ill-health. This is quite distinct from measurement error: the child may have had a genuinely low performance on the first round of testing and may genuinely have made progress by the second round, but if earlier rounds had been available they might have shown that performance had previously been higher and that there had been no long-run progress after all. We can attempt to control for this by including measures of ill-health in our multivariate analysis. (We do not report these analyses as they did not yield any significant effects.) We cannot ever hope to control fully for possibly transitory factors, although we should note that transitory factors which are uncorrelated with our explanatory variable of interest will not affect our conclusions.

Educational progress and placement

Of the 49 children originally recruited to the foster group, ten moved from their foster homes after the first of the three rounds of tests. Five of these children were placed in residential children's homes following the breakdown of their foster placements, and five were reunited with their birth families.

The legal status of a further eight of the original foster children changed between rounds 1 and 3 of testing. Custodianship orders were made with respect to six of these youngsters; the other two children were adopted by their foster parents. Adoption effects a virtually complete and irrevocable transfer of a child from one family to another. By contrast, a custodianship order gives persons other than parents and those entitled to legal custody of a child under the guardianship legislation, legal custody of a child without the final severance of links with the original family effected by an adoption order.

The comparison group was less affected by change. Of the 58 youngsters originally recruited to this group, 53 remained with their families of origin throughout the study. However, five of the original group entered local authority care after round one of testing. Four of these youngsters were placed in foster homes, with the remaining child placed in residential care.

Thus six subgroups of varying size emerged from the original two groups. Four subgroups derived from the original foster group: i) children whose foster placements broke down; ii) children whose legal status changed, giving greater legal security to their caregivers; iii) children who were reunited with their families of origin; and iv) children who experienced no such changes. The remaining two subgroups comprised children from the original comparison group: v) children who went into care; and vi) children who remained at home throughout the study. As noted above, there were some missing data on the later rounds of testing, and in our analyses we restrict ourselves to those children for whom there were no missing data on a given test.

Table 1 compares the average scores of the larger subgroups for each round of tests. We had hoped to find evidence of educational progress among the children who remained with their foster families throughout the study. However, on none of the three tests is there any evidence for relative progress on the part of the "no change" foster subgroup. Thus on the reading test the average score was 94 in the first round, 93 in the second one, and 92 in the third.

We must emphasise that this shows lack of progress relative to national norms for their ages. The children were of course making absolute gains in the their reading ability, vocabulary and maths, and indeed were making much the same absolute gains as the nationally average child. We had, however, hoped to find that they were catching up with the national average; in other words, we had hoped to find that their age-standardised scores were improving. This clearly did not prove to be the case.

The group of foster children who were in perhaps the most favourable circumstances, at least with respect to a sense of permanence, was the group who became the subject of custodianship or adoption during the course of the study. It also seemed reasonable to expect that the increased sense of security for caregivers and children conferred by the making of custodianship and adoption orders might be reflected in the educational attainment of the children concerned. Again, the data give no support to this hypothesis. Indeed, on the maths and vocabulary tests there was a decline in performance.

Our other subgroups are too small to warrant any conclusions and for reasons of confidentiality we do not report their scores. There are hints that the children who returned home improved relative to the others over the course of the study. The improvement occurs on the vocabulary and maths tests as well as on the reading test.

There are also hints that the children who moved into residential care made less progress than the others. On all three tests these children show a decline in their scores. But given the tiny numbers involved, we should draw no firm conclusions. We had also expected that children from the comparison group who were taken into care might show deterioration in performance. However, we have complete data only on three children, and there is no consistent pattern in their progress.

Overall, then, we cannot reject the null hypothesis that changes in placement or legal status during the course of the study were unrelated to educational progress. Where we have reasonably large groups (the

Table 1
Changes of placement

| | Scores on the reading test | | | |
	1st round	2nd round	3rd round	N
Foster Group				
No change	94 (16)	93 (12)	92 (10)	29
Custodianship	92 (12)	89 (9)	91 (10)	8
Residential care				3
Returned home				4
Comparison Group				
No change	89 (16)	90 (15)	91 (15)	39
Went into care				3

| | Scores on the vocabulary test | | | |
	1st round	2nd round	3rd round	N
Foster Group				
No change	94 (13)	94 (15)	94 (14)	28
Custodianship	98 (12)	95 (18)	89 (10)	8
Residential care				3
Returned home				4
Comparison Group				
No change	91 (16)	91 (17)	96 (19)	39
Went into care				3

| | Scores on the maths test | | | |
	1st round	2nd round	3rd round	N
Foster Group				
No change	88 (13)	–	88 (13)	24
Custodianship	90 (9)	–	84 (11)	6
Residential care		–		3
Returned home		–		3
Comparison Group				
No change	94 (13)	–	88 (14)	26
Went into care				3

Figures in brackets give the standard deviations.

"no change" foster and comparison groups), the story is quite clear. The conclusion is also quite clear that the custodianship/adoption group failed to make relative progress, and this finding may have some implications for theories of permanence (see Aldgate *et al*, 1992). However, we should note that this group of children had already been in their foster placements for substantial periods of time. Seven of these eight children had been in their current placements for six or more years. *It is therefore likely that the change in legal status merely ratified an existing state of affairs and did not make a fundamental change in the day-to-day nature of the placement.*

The absence of progress during the course of our study is not, therefore, quite so surprising as it might at first appear to be. On the other hand, these results serve to underline the point that even those foster children who were in the most favourable situations, with settled and long-term placements, were performing well below national norms for their age group.

Social work histories

In this next section of the paper we focus in more detail on the children who were in foster care at the start of our study, and we ask whether aspects of the children's social work histories and planning affected their progress.

We begin with the primary reason for care. Measuring reason for care has been know to be problematic since Gray and Parr's first major survey of children coming into care in the 1950s because a single reason may often mask the complexity of problems beneath the surface (Gray and Parr, 1957).

Since, in many cases, the information we wanted related to events many years previously (and often to many social workers previously), the social work files were our only source of information. There are of course well known limitations to using this medium as a source of data: the information required had not always been collated in a usable form and in some cases we were not able to retrieve the details we needed.

We initially coded the data in the files to a detailed list of categories. In some cases, however, the numbers were too small for separate analysis, and in others cases, we had doubts about the validity of the distinctions. We therefore decided to focus on the cases of suspected child abuse or neglect. We were able to check the validity of this category by cross-tabulating it against the legal status of the child, and we found that no child for whom the files recorded suspected child abuse or neglect was in voluntary care.

As Table 2 shows, there were marked differences between the foster children when we divide them according to the primary reason for care. On all three tests and in all rounds of testing, the children who came into care for suspected child abuse or neglect scored significantly lower than did the other foster children. (The differences, using a t-test, were significant at the 0.01 level on the maths and reading tests and at the 0.05 level on the vocabulary test.)

There was some evidence on the reading test that these children caught up over the period of the study, but this pattern is not replicated on the other two tests and we should not place great reliance on it. The predominant impression is of continuing disadvantage. This finding is sustained when we control for other aspects of the children's social work histories, such as the number of placements, length of time in care, and expectations about the duration of the placement (see Aldgate *et al*, 1992 for further details). In other words, even long-term and settled placements did not seem to have overcome the educational disadvantages of early child abuse or neglect.

In the case of the foster children who had come into care for other reasons, however, the picture was somewhat more encouraging. They were still below the national average in their scores, but clearly were not nearly so disadvantaged. Nonetheless, even these children failed to catch up educationally in the way we had expected over the course of the study.

Teacher expectations

To try to understand the children's failure to catch up we now turn to consider the role of their teachers. The teachers generally had rather low expectations of our children's educational attainment, and teacher

Table 2
Primary reason for care

| | Scores on the reading test | | | |
	1st round	2nd round	3rd round	N
Abuse/neglect	82 (16)	85 (11)	87 (11)	12
Other reasons	98 (12)	95 (9)	93 (9)	31

| | Scores on the vocabulary test | | | |
	1st round	2nd round	3rd round	N
Abuse/neglect	90 (16)	86 (13)	85 (12)	12
Other reasons	96 (13)	98 (17)	96 (12)	30

| | Scores on the maths test | | | |
	1st round	2nd round	3rd round	N
Abuse/neglect	79 (11)	–	81 (9)	11
Other reasons	94 (11)	–	92 (12)	25

Figures in brackets give the standard deviations.

expectations have often been suggested as an important factor in pupil progress. In particular, it has been suggested that there is a self-fulfilling prophecy whereby pupils of whom much is expected improve while those of whom little is expected lose confidence and decline (Rosenthal and Jacobson, 1968; Thorndike, 1968; Claiborn, 1969; Tizard, 1977).

Table 3 shows that the teachers did in general have rather low expectations about the children's educational success. We have defined high expectations as the expectation of obtaining A-levels or A–C grades at GCSE. Medium expectations are defined as some (but not all) A–C grades at GCSE, and low expectations are defined as grades D and E (or lower) at GCSE. These expectations were significantly lower than those of the carers and the pupils themselves, while the children's social workers generally had the most optimistic views of all. (See also Fletcher-Campbell and Hall (1990) on social workers' expectations.)

As we can see, there was a very clear association between teacher expectations and children's reading attainments, both within the foster and the comparison groups. But there is no clear pattern over time. If the theory of the self-fulfilling prophecy were correct, we would expect to see the children's scores becoming gradually more polarised, the children of whom much was expected gradually pulling away from the others. There is no indication whatsoever that this was happening, and all the changes over time are well within sampling error.

This demonstrates the importance of a longitudinal study for investigating causal processes. We felt that, on this evidence, we must reject the theory of self-fulfilling prophecies. In our view, the evidence of Table 3 suggests that the teachers knew their pupils rather well and were making appropriate judgements. We do not think that their expectations can be blamed for the pupils' failure to catch up with the national average.

Table 3
Teacher expectations and reading progress

| | Foster children | | | |
	1st round	2nd round	3rd round	N
High	107 (1)	104 (6)	105 (5)	4
Medium	103 (15)	98 (11)	99 (10)	6
Low	87 (15)	88 (11)	88 (9)	26
	Comparison group			
	1st round	2nd round	3rd round	N
High	–	–	–	1
Medium	98 (13)	101 (12)	101 (12)	6
Low	86 (17)	87 (14)	88 (15)	30

We also had measures of any special help with school work that the child had received, special help with other problems, and the number of schools the children had attended. Table 4 compares the children who had received special help with school work with those who received the usual lessons. As we can see, nearly a third of our children had received special help, and the ones who did so scored markedly lower on the reading test. It appears that the schools were in general rather good at picking out the children who needed help. We would naturally hope that children who received special help would make more progress than the others and that they would tend to catch up. There is evidence for this on the reading tests, where the effect of special help on progress was significant at the 0.05 level. Using a paired-comparison t-test, we found a significant improvement between rounds 1 and 2 on the standardised reading scores of children who received special help whereas the change was not significant among the other children. As we can see, almost identical patterns are found among the foster children and the comparison group.

Special help for other problems, whether the child was "statemented" as having special needs or not, and the number of schools which the child had previously attended failed to show significant effects on progress, once we had controlled for age and special help with school work.

It has sometimes been fashionable to blame schools for their pupils' failings. We do not think that such an interpretation would be appropriate in the case of our data. Rather, we suspect that our teachers knew their pupils well, gave them appropriate help, and did manage to help the pupils who were furthest behind. If the schools were unable to achieve more, we suspect that this was due to their lack of resources.

Table 4
Special help at school and reading progress

| | Foster children | | | |
	1st round	*2nd round*	*3rd round*	*N*
Special help	77 (13)	81 (9)	82 (6)	11
No special help	98 (12)	96 (9)	94 (8)	29
	Comparison group			
	1st round	*2nd round*	*3rd round*	*N*
Special help	74 (10)	78 (10)	77 (8)	13
No special help	98 (15)	97 (13)	94 (14)	28

Educational progress and home environment

Most research on the sociology of education has agreed on the importance of home background, and it is to this that we now turn. Previous studies have focused on a variety of aspects of family environment such as social class (Halsey *et al*, 1980; Heath and Clifford, 1990), cultural capital (Bourdieu, 1977; Heath *et al*, 1982; DiMaggio, 1982; de Graaf, 1986), and parental interest and aspirations (Douglas, 1964, 1968). In particular, St.Claire and Osborn (1987) had found that the low attainment of children in care could, in part, be explained by their disadvantaged social origins. We were therefore interested to see whether the more advantaged current family environments of some of our foster children could help to ameliorate their early disadvantages. Tables 5 and 6 look at the progress of the children divided according to the social class and educational level of the children's carers. Given the small numbers involved we have restricted ourselves to the manual–non-manual distinction. And given the number of single-parent families

Table 5
Social class and reading progress

| | Foster children | | | |
	1st round	*2nd round*	*3rd round*	*N*
Middle class	93 (16)	91 (12)	92 (11)	24
Working class	93 (13)	93 (11)	92 (8)	20
	Comparison group			
	1st round	*2nd round*	*3rd round*	*N*
Special help	96 (22)	98 (21)	97 (22)	6
No special help	89 (16)	90 (14)	91 (15)	36

in the comparison group (36 per cent), we have allocated the family to the middle class if either parent had a white-collar occupation. (That is to say, we follow Erikson's (1984) "dominance" approach to the classification of family social class.) We have investigated class differences using alternative approaches and finer classifications, but have obtained essentially the same results.

Table 6

Carers' education and reading progress

	Foster children			
	1st round	*2nd round*	*3rd round*	*N*
Degree or A-level	110 (12)	100 (10)	101 (9)	1
O-level	88 (14)	88 (11)	89 (10)	13
Below O-level	91 (14)	92 (11)	91 (9)	25
	Comparison group			
	1st round	*2nd round*	*3rd round*	*N*
Degree or A-level	–	–	–	2
O-level	91 (16)	98 (14)	95 (15)	6
Below O-level	89 (17)	88 (14)	90 (14)	34

In the case of carers' education, we have distinguished three levels, namely degree level, O or A-level (or their equivalents) and lower level (or no) qualifications. Again we have classified families according to the "dominance" approach.

The results are rather clear-cut. The differences according to social class are small, are only apparent among the comparison group, and show no sign of increasing over time (see Table 5). A middle-class current environment does not appear to bring foster children the expected benefits.

Much larger differences in attainment are found when we turn to carers' education (see Table 6). If either parent had high-level academic qualifications, the children performed much better on the reading tests (differences being statistically significant at the 0.01 level on reading and at the 0.05 level on vocabulary using the t-test). Interestingly, the differences were smaller on the maths test and did not reach statistical significance.

We should note that this association between attainment and foster parents' qualifications could in theory be a consequence of social workers' selective allocation of children to foster parents. We do not think that this is particularly likely, given that the children had in some cases been allocated before school age and thus before there was any real evidence of their reading ability.

There could also have been more general selective processes based on knowledge about the foster children's social backgrounds. Unfortunately the social work files did not contain the relevant information, but it would be rather surprising if there were enough foster children from highly educated social origins to explain our findings. The evidence provided by Fletcher-Campbell and Hall (1990) rather strongly suggests that the difficulty of finding foster parents is likely to rule out most attempts at "matching".

Selective allocation cannot therefore be ruled out, but the results are also in line with the theory of cultural capital, and it is to this interpretation that we incline. In other words, it is not so much the material advantages present in middle-class homes that are important for reading scores, but the educational skills that the more qualified parents possessed. (Of course material circumstances may come to be important when decisions are later made whether to leave school at the minimum leaving age or not; see Halsey *et al*, 1980.)

However, there is no sign that foster children in educationally advantaged environments made greater progress over the course of our study. On the reading test, indeed, their relative performance appears to decline, the children from the most qualified homes scoring 110 in the first round of the reading test, falling to 100 in the second and 101 in the third. But our interpretation of this result is that there is some measurement error in the first round on the reading test, since those high initial scores were not replicated in the vocabulary and maths tests. These results are sustained when we control for the children's age and gender and for other demographic features of the children's environment (such as single-parent households) in a multivariate analysis.

In addition to these demographic measures, we also attempted to obtain more direct measures of cultural capital, parental interest, and various aspects of activities and aspirations within the home. As might be expected our measures of parental interest, aspirations and cultural capital correlated significantly with social class and parental education and they therefore tell the same story.

We must reject the hypothesis, therefore, that the children in more "educogenic" environments made greater progress over the course of our study. However, the children with highly qualified carers do seem to have made more progress before our study began, and this suggests that early educational intervention may be necessary in order to secure an "escape from disadvantage". In support of this idea we checked whether the young children in our sample made greater progress, and this did seem to be the case. We also found that the two foster children in our sample with the highest scores on the reading test had been with the same, highly qualified foster parents since an early age.

Discussion

This paper has attempted to explore the relationship between the educational progress of a group of 8–14 year olds in long-term foster care and factors in their histories and current home environments.

Our results confirmed previous research documenting the low educational attainment of children in care. Our findings serve to reinforce the message conveyed by research over a period of some 30 years, namely, that children in public care are not well served by the education system (Colton and Jackson, 1993). To be sure, we found that our foster children performed no worse than our comparison group, but our findings are nonetheless disappointing. Our foster children were a particularly favoured group, with the majority having had long-term settled placements with foster parents who showed every indication of providing an environment conducive to educational progress. The comparison between the material and cultural aspects of the foster homes and the homes of the comparison group suggested that our foster children were typically in environments which provided a potential "escape from disadvantage" (Pilling, 1990). It was therefore all the more disappointing that our foster children failed, in general, to demonstrate greater relative progress over the course of our study than the comparison group.

These results are highly robust. They have been demonstrated on three separate rounds of testing, measured on three different tests, and measured independently by the researchers and the teachers. At the very least, then, our study confirms the existence of the problem of the education of children in care. Thus the finding of low attainment among children in care cannot be explained away by the special difficulties of children in residential care or by frequent placement breakdown – it applies to our favoured children in long-term foster care as well. It cannot be explained away by the sense of impermanence affecting many foster homes – even our foster children in long-term placements who became the subject of custodianship or adoption scored no more highly than the comparison group. There was no difference in attainment or progress between children where the eventual outcome was adoption or custodianship and those who would remain foster children.

How then are we to explain the low attainment and lack of relative progress of our foster children? Firstly, one popular explanation for lack of educational progress has been the self-fulfilling prophecy of low teacher expectations. Our data showed that teachers did indeed have rather low expectations of the children's eventual attainment and relatively low evaluations of their current performance (at least as compared with those of the carers and social workers). There is, however, the familiar problem of drawing causal inferences from such correlational data. To test the existence of self-fulfilling prophecies we need the longitudinal data, and here we failed to find any evidence that the children of whom the teachers expected more made greater progress than those of whom they expected less. In this context it is perhaps also worth mentioning that attempts to replicate Rosenthal and Jacobson's original (1968) demonstration of a relation between teacher expectation and pupil performance have signally failed (Claiborn, 1969). Our evidence is consistent with the hypothesis that teachers' judgements are consequences rather than causes of the pupils' performance.

Secondly, the findings suggest that children's early histories before entry to care may have a profound effect on their educational attainment in middle childhood. Children who can be presumed to have experienced poor parenting and had been removed compulsorily from their parents did not appear to recover educationally as easily as those whose care had been necessitated by parental illness or by crises related to economic hardship. What we appear to see here are the lasting effects of early deprivation or maltreatment. However, while the evidence on this point is convincing it does not wholly explain the low attainment of the foster children in general. Thus the foster children who had come into care for reasons other than abuse or neglect were still somewhat below the national average.

Our interpretation of these results is that something more than "normal" family life and "normal" parental interest may be required to compensate for earlier deprivation. Thus, our foster parents were in general an average group in terms of their social class and education. They were not themselves high-fliers educationally, and we would not therefore expect their own birth children to be much different from the national average in their educational attainment. Is it perhaps so surprising if, when "average" educational inputs are given to children with "above average" educational needs they fail to make "greater than average" educational progress? Remember that, given their low starting point, greater than average educational progress would have been needed for these children to have caught up with the national average attainment.

We have also seen that when greater-than-average inputs were provided by the schools, progress was also somewhat greater. These extra school inputs, however, seem to have been allocated to the children who obtained particularly low scores on the reading test, and we may guess that, in view of the scarcity of such resources in schools, they were not continued on a longer-term basis once the worst educational problems had been alleviated.

Our suggestion, then, is that greater-than-average progress needs greater-than-average inputs. In this respect our results are consistent with those of Schiff and his colleagues on the educational consequences of adoption (Schiff, 1980; Schiff *et al*, 1981; Capron and Duyme, 1989). The French team looked at children of unskilled manual parents who were adopted shortly after birth by highly qualified families (described as falling within the top 13 per cent of the occupational structure). The French team compared the cognitive ability of the adopted children with that of their birth siblings who remained with their unskilled parents. Their results showed convincingly that the siblings who were adopted at birth did make substantial cognitive gains. Their mean score was 108 compared with a score of 95 for their siblings.

While the French team did find large gains, we should note that their adoptive families were not average ones but well above average in their social position. And the French team's adopted children were adopted within six months of birth. It is notable that the two foster children in our study who had the highest attainment scores had been with the same highly qualified foster families since an early age, and their reading scores were closely comparable to the scores achieved by the French adopted children. It is quite likely, therefore, that they had made similar education gains to those recorded in the French study.

The majority of our foster parents, however, were around the national average in their occupational and educational attainments and they had not in general been fostering the children since birth. It would therefore be quite unrealistic for the majority of the children in our sample to have made the same gains as the French adoptees.

We do not wish to imply that the answer to the educational problems of children in care is early adoption into highly qualified families. Rather, the point is that gains can be made, but they do not come easily or cheaply. Average inputs are not enough for children with above-average educational needs. Clearly the educational needs of separated children must be given much higher priority.

It is encouraging to note that this is one objective of the Looking after Children Project (Parker *et al*, 1991), which is currently being promoted by the Department of Health. The project rightly seeks to focus the attention of social workers and caregivers on dimensions of children's development that are usually neglected when the parenting role is shared between several adults. Emphasis is placed on the importance of education from the earliest years. Schedules have been developed for each group and are designed to ensure that carers have done those things which well-informed parents would do to promote their children's educational progress.

Naturally, it is important that attempts to use the schedules are supported with adequate resources, otherwise there is a danger of creating unrealistic expectations of social workers and caregivers. Further, it is vital that local authority social services and education departments work together to forge an interdisciplinary approach. Social workers and caregivers require a high level of support from educational psychologists and schools in assessing the special education needs of separated children and in formulating plans that will allow such children to escape from disadvantage.

Acknowledgements

We would like to thank the children and their families, their teachers and the social workers for their patience and co-operation. We must also acknowledge our debt to the ESRC, which funded the study, and to the County's Departments of Education and Social Services which supported our research throughout.

References

Adcock, M (1980) 'The right to a permanent placement', *Adoption & Fostering*, 99, pp 21–4.

Aldgate, J and Hawley, D (1986) *Recollections of Disruption: A study of foster home breakdown*, London: National Foster Care Association.

Aldgate, J, Colton, M, Ghate, D and Heath, A F (1992) 'Educational attainment and stability in long-term foster care', *Children & Society*, 6, pp 38–60.

Berridge, D and Cleaver, H (1987) *Foster Home Breakdown*, Oxford: Basil Blackwell.

Bourdieu, P (1977) 'Cultural reproduction and social reproduction', in Karabel, J and Halsey, A H (eds) *Power and Ideology in Education*, New York: Oxford University Press.

Capron, C and Duyme, M (1989) 'Assessment of effects of socio-economic status on IQ in a full cross-fostering study', *Nature*, 340, pp 552–4.

Claiborn, W L (1969) 'Expectancy effects in the classroom: a failure to replicate', *Journal of Educational Psychology*, 60, pp 377–83.

Colton, M, Aldgate, J and Heath, A F (1991) 'Behavioural problems of children in and out of care', *Social Work and Social Sciences Review*, 2, pp 177–91.

De Graaf, P M (1986) 'The impact of financial and cultural resources on educational attainment in the Netherlands', *Sociology of Education*, 59, pp 237–46.

DiMaggio, P (1982) 'Cultural capital and school success', *American Sociological Review*, 47, pp 189–201.

Douglas, J W B (1964) *The Home and the School*, London: McGibbon & Kee.

Douglas, J W B (1968) *All Our Future*, London: Peter Davies.

Erikson, R (1984) 'Social class of men, women and families', *Sociology*, 18, pp 500–14.

Essen, J and Wedge, P (1982) *Continuities in Childhood Disadvantage*, London: Heinemann.

Essen, J, Lambert, L and Head, J (1976) 'School attainment of children who have been in care', *Child Care, Health and Development*, 2, pp 339–51.

Fanshel, D and Shinn, E B (1978) *Children in Foster Care: A longitudinal investigation*, New York: Columbia University Press.

Fletcher-Campbell, F and Hall, C (1990) *Changing Schools? Changing People? The education of children in care*, Slough: NFER.

Gray, P G and Parr, E A (1957) *Children in Care and the Recruitment of Foster Parents* (Social Survey paper no. 249), London: HMSO.

Halsey, A H, Heath, AF and Ridge, J M (1980) *Origins and Destinations: Family, class and education in modern Britain*, Oxford: Clarendon Press.

Heath, A F and Clifford, P (1990) 'Class inequalities in education in the twentieth century', *Journal of the Royal Statistical Society*, series A, 153, pp 1–16.

Heath, A F, Halsey, A H and Ridge, J M (1982) 'Cultural capital and political arithmetic', *British Journal of Sociology of Education*, 3, pp 87–91.

Heath, A F, Colton, M J and Aldgate, J (1989) 'The education of children in and out of care', *British Journal of Social Work*, 19, pp 447–60.

Holman, R (1975) 'Exclusive and inclusive concepts of fostering', in Triseliotis, J (ed) *New Developments in Foster Care and Adoption*, London: Routledge & Kegan Paul, 1980.

Jackson, S (1988) 'Education and children in care', *Adoption & Fostering*, 12:4, pp 6–11.

McKay, M (1980) 'Planning for permanent placement', *Adoption & Fostering*, 99, pp 9–21.

Maluccio, A N, Fein, E and Olmstead, K (1986) *Permanency Planning for Children: Concepts and methods*, London: Tavistock.

Mortimore, J and Blackstone, T (1982) *Disadvantage and Education*, London: Heinemann.

Packman, J, Randall, J and Jacques, N (1986) *Who Needs Care? Social work decisions about children,* Oxford: Basil Blackwell.

Parker, R, Ward, H, Jackson, S, Aldgate, J and Wedge, P (1991) *Looking After Children: Assessing outcomes in child care,* London: HMSO.

Pilling, D (1990) *Escape from Disadvantage,* London: The Falmer Press in association with the National Children's Bureau.

Rosenthal, R and Jacobson, L (1968) *Pygmalion in the Classroom,* New York: Holt, Rinehart and Winston.

Rowe, J and Lambert, J (1973) *Children Who Wait,* London: BAAF.

Rowe, J, Cain, H, Hundleby, M and Keane, A (1984) *Long-term Foster Care,* London: Batsford/BAAF.

St.Claire, L and Osborn, A F (1987) 'The ability and behaviour of children who have been "in-care" or separated from their parents', *Early Child Development and Care* (special issue).

Schiff, M (1980) 'L'echec scolaire n'est pas inscrit dans les chromosomes', *Psychologie,* 181, pp 51–6.

Schiff, M *et al* (1981) 'Enfants de travailleurs manuels adoptes par des cadres: effect d'un changement de class sociale sur le cursus scolaire et les notes de IQ', *Travaux et Documents,* 93.

Thorndike, R L (1968) 'Review of Pygmalion in the Classroom', *Educational Research Journal,* 5, pp 708–11.

Thorpe, R (1980) 'The experience of children and parents living apart', in Triseliotis, J (ed) *New Developments in Foster Care and Adoption,* London: Routledge & Kegan Paul.

Tizard, B (1977) *Adoption: A Second Chance,* London: Open Books.

Triseliotis, J (1989) 'Foster care outcomes: a review of key research findings', *Adoption & Fostering,* 13:3, pp 5–17.

Triseliotis, J and Russell, J (1984) *Hard to Place: The outcome of adoption and residential care,* London: Heinemann.

4   Children's return from state care to school

Roger Bullock, Michael Little and Spencer Millham

Preoccupation with children's separation from and return to the family should not encourage us to ignore the wider contexts of their experience. Many children rejoining their families have to enter new schools. Sometimes the stigma and insecurities of the past make these negotiations difficult for the young person, particularly if compounded by unease and tensions within the family. As schooling is central to so many aspects of a child's life, its neglect is likely to cause widespread problems for returning children.

This paper is reprinted from *Oxford Review of Education*, 20:3, 1994, pp 307–16.

Introduction

Contrary to popular belief, most children and adolescents looked after by social services eventually go home. Most reunions occur regardless of the reasons for separation or the length of time children are away. Even older adolescents, some convicted of serious offences and long separated from home, will rest in the bosom of their family on occasions. They may not stay long at home; they may use the family as a springboard to or a bolt hole from outside excitements; they may return home only because they have exhausted the tolerance of other benefactors. Whatever the circumstances, the wider family continues to be a vital resource which can be enhanced by social work support and encouragement. Involving parents and sharing care with the family is now recognised as good social work practice.

Not only do most children go home but the majority experience a swift reunion. Nearly three-fifths of all possible returnees are home before six months have elapsed and over a fifth are back in the first week after separation. Nonetheless, regardless of the period away from home, return is stressful for all concerned and much can be done to ease attendant difficulties.

Investigations of the separation and return of children have focused predominantly on leaving and going back to families. The various adaptations necessary for return, such as the negotiations over role and territory, have been charted (Bullock, Little and Millham, 1993). In this paper we shall explore a different aspect of children's restoration, namely their integration into a context outside the family – the school. We shall also see how success in this transition affects reunion generally.

Children's return from care to school

For both short- and long-term care cases, school can provide one element of stability, continuity and belonging in an otherwise disrupted life. It is also clear that the way schools are organised can militate against a child's easy and successful return home. There are a number of ways in which schools can assist a child who returns after a considerable absence. For example, it is helpful if the child is prepared for entry. Although the child's situation may already be known to teachers, peers will be inquisitive and their teasing may be distressing. As an adolescent commented:

Everyone just asked questions. Because you'd been in a children's home they thought you were criminal, they asked 'What did you do?', 'How much did you nick?', 'Did you try to kill someone?'

The recognition of the problems facing such children and the benefits of an induction programme have been highlighted by Fleeman (1984) and Pickup (1987). They emphasise the need for a particular teacher to be available for informal counselling and for senior staff to work in close liaison with social services. They also stress the benefits of close contact between the school and the pupils' families whenever possible

Of the 450 children included in our *Lost in Care* study, we noted that 87 per cent returned home at some stage (Millham *et al*, 1986). Of these, nearly half were of compulsory school age, half of them young enough for primary education and the remainder needing secondary education. In the younger age group, two-thirds of the children left care quickly, that is within six weeks, and only a tiny minority stayed away from home for more than a year. Most of these children fell into the category we shall later call *organised* leavers. They had usually entered care because their parent had been admitted to hospital or was otherwise unable to look after them. For such children there should be no detrimental effects on the child, provided the return from care and entry to school are properly organised. The older children, in contrast, face more complex problems, for, while there were some short stay cases, the majority had been away from home for at least a year.

This emphasis on the importance of school for children in care had not, until recently, achieved much attention in social work literature. Parker (1986) found that foster home transfers were less successful when they were accompanied by changes of school. Kahan's (1979) exploration of ten adults recollecting their growing-up in care showed clearly how their attitude to school reflected their living situations and that few realised how important education would be to their future life chances.

These studies were among a handful which drew attention to the significance of the school experiences of children in care. More recently, however, possibly following the emphasis placed on the issue by the Short Committee (HMSO, 1984), more has become known. Jackson (1987), Heath, Colton and Aldgate (1989) and Fletcher Campbell and Hall (1990) have since undertaken specific studies of the educational experiences of children in care.

However, in social work planning, return to school still has a low profile. Robbins (1990) noted that 'the educational needs of children in care are tackled relatively rarely' and Berridge's (1985) example of the girl who missed her GCE examination because she was not woken by residential staff highlights the indifference that some social workers can display towards the school experience of children in care. In our study of families and children experiencing reunion, we found that return to school rarely coincided with the beginning of term and some older adolescents seemed to be left virtually to themselves to negotiate re-entry to the education system.

Certainly, a number of the social work reports did consider the child's educational welfare and in some cases care placements had been chosen for their proximity to the child's school, so facilitating a stable education career. This strategy was particularly common for children attending special day schools. In addition a number of the older children remained away in care until they had taken their examinations. These efforts to help children attain and gain more from school seem sensible but, despite their significance for children's welfare, when reunion became an issue, few social workers looked beyond the child's family for factors which might influence the adjustment of the returning child. Yet, we know from our interviews that for adolescents, peer relations are a major preoccupation and one would hypothesise that feeling settled at school would be a contributory factor to a child's successful return.

Younger children find return to school easier than adolescents. Primary schools are more child-centred than secondary schools, in that one teacher is responsible for most of the day's activities and learning. There is less streaming by ability, more expressive and group activities, more play, music and drama, all of which encourage in children a sense of membership and group participation. The teaching and nurturing of children is largely the responsibility of one adult; thus the child who is not fitting in, is isolated or is having difficulty stands out much more. In urban areas the schools are more local in intake and likely to be more sensitive to the deprivations and difficulties that accompany childhood in their catchment area. Teachers will be familiar with the child protection register, with the clothing problems and poor nutrition of young children, they will know whose meals are subsidised and so on. The peer group which the child joins on return is less worldly wise and those coming back to school from foster homes or residential care are less likely to be considered delinquent or deviant. In the same way, the prodigal and his or her family situation and wider social structures are likely to be less of a preoccupation with young children than with adolescents.

But return to the secondary school is more difficult. In organisation the school is subject-centred rather than child-centred, and although some teachers have responsibility for age groups and others are delegated to pastoral or special needs responsibilities, the child's experience is not one of closeness to a particular adult but of numerous contacts with a wide variety of teachers. However, children's ability to seek out supportive and sympathetic adults should not be underestimated. As a boy commented:

I hated the place, the big kids bullied you, they pinched everything you'd got and the teachers didn't care much about you at all, except Mrs Johnson, she taught geography and made it interesting with videos and letters from kids abroad. I really liked it, you could talk to her about anything. She wasn't like a teacher at all. She seemed really pleased to see you when you came through the door.

Indeed, with regard to the issue of settling back, the contribution made to the returning child by some sympathetic person within the school cannot be overestimated. As recent studies have shown, a teacher or even older pupils, aspiring apprentices for the caring professions, can ease the adjustment of new arrivals (Cleaver, 1991). Surely it is not beyond the wit of social workers or schools to organise such ways of easing return.

The school's experience of returning children

The educational disadvantages for children in or on the margins of care have been commented on by many. For example, Aldgate, Heath and Colton (1991) found that as many as 91 per cent of foster children obtained a standardised score below average for one or more of the three measures of attainment used, although the performance of another group of "at risk" children known to social services was equally low. The authors also found a strong relationship between permanence in foster home placements and in children's attainments; the longer the duration of the placement, the better children seemed to perform at school. They comment:

The strength of the relationship between educational attainment and permanence deserves emphasis. It suggests that a sense of stability may be an important facilitating factor in allowing children to make progress at school and the longer this stability exists, the more it reinforces chances of success.

Unfortunately, we know that for many children in care, stability and permanence in a placement are rare experiences. Of the children who stay in care for two years or more, 84 per cent move placement at least once and 56 per cent move two or more times (Bullock, Little and

Millham, 1993). Many of these changes also involved transfer to another school, a feature also noted in the studies of children returning home on trial (Farmer and Parker, 1991). Thus, the chances of school disruption for children in care are considerable and the attainments of those who move are likely to be further depressed. However, the picture is not overwhelmingly gloomy and social workers are making efforts to improve the situation. Fletcher-Campbell and Hall (1990), for example, found that a third of children in care experienced a stable school life.

The effects of movement are not only on school progress. Berridge and Cleaver (1987) showed that children in foster homes, whether short or long term, who also changed school were twice as likely to experience a placement breakdown. On the other hand, Farmer and Parker (1991) found that children attending special day schools did better in their home placements than those receiving ordinary education.

In a recent study of children returning home from care, we were able to look at the ways in which schools cope with those pupils who return after a considerable absence (Bullock *et al*, 1993). Children coming back from care are only one group of mobile children needing help. Schools find returning children fall into three main categories. For the first group, which we call organised returners, both departure and reunion are more predictable. For example, children may have to spend time in hospital for repeated treatments. In these cases staff and friends from school are encouraged to visit and frequently do, parents and hospital are given a school work plan and the child's eventual re-entry is carefully organised. Once back, such children usually find school tiring, but their absence need not have detrimental effect on their work. In a school of 1,600 pupils visited during the study of children's return home from care, in the space of a year only two such children returned after a prolonged illness. We can see, therefore, that this category of returnees is small and that, because the absence is usually well managed and the children quickly re-adjust, the return poses relatively few problems.

The second category of returnees common in schools involves pregnant girls. They have greater problems of re-adjustment to school life, and the younger they are the more difficult the return. This is because girls' peer groups can be censorious in such situations and the child

sometimes enjoys considerable notoriety. As one deputy head told us:
The girl can become an outcast. However sympathetic we try to be,
children can be cruel to one another and, once the girl returns to
school, her friends can ostracise her, sometimes with disastrous effects
on her academic attainment.

However, it should be emphasised that even in this inner-city comprehensive, few girls actually returned after a pregnancy but, as with all
exceptional children, whether those with disabilities, severe family
problems or even those with unusual gifts, schools find it difficult to
accommodate their needs.

The final group of children who return to school encounter far greater
difficulties. This group is made up of highly mobile cases. They usually
disappear due to sudden change in family situations, divorce or moon-
light flits to avoid debt and other aggravations. They frequently move to
live with another member of their family or enter the care of social
services. Children who disappear in this way have usually been irregular
attendees and have often been ostracised by peers beforehand, being
seen as odd, sad, dirty or poorly dressed. Their academic performance is
usually lack-lustre and they are often disruptive or withdrawn in class.
Other children shrink from them and their departure can be a relief to all
concerned.

Thus, the return of these highly mobile children to school presents
problems all round. They come back, often unannounced, and try to slot
into routines without much preparation. They are made to feel unwel-
come, acute problems of re-adjustment can arise and they can soon
become disruptive. Their meagre attainments sink rapidly. However, it
is interesting to discover that the number of children leaving and
returning in this way was still low, about ten instances per year in the
largest of the inner-city schools we visited.

Unfortunately, children who have been in care for over a year fall
mostly into this last group of highly mobile cases. Parents often felt they
could not care for the child or cope with his or her behaviour and the
children's school attendance and attainments were poor. Offending and
abuse were often additional complications. Thus, home and school
problems, more often than not, were mutually reinforcing. Yet, when we

scrutinised the return plans for these children, we found that, in nearly every case, return to school was not a considered part of the return strategy and, when included, was only a minor item.

The organisation of schools

The organisation of schools also has a role to play in helping vulnerable young people transfer successfully. A variety of approaches to the problem are possible, either within a particular school or among a group of schools, including further education, within a particular geographical area.

Naturally, one issue of school organisation has long haunted the welfare of children, namely the gulf that exists at all levels between education and social services. While both have the welfare of the child at heart, each tends to view those that return from different perspectives, with consequent problems of communication and lack of understanding.

We were surprised to discover while talking to children's teachers that they find it difficult to conceptualise return to school as an issue. Often there is little notion of the child having a "social" career or that problems in one area could compound problems in another. For instance, following one boy's return to school, we discovered, integration was seen as best promoted by a psychometric assessment of the child's ability and allocation to appropriate sets; the child's social network remained unconsidered and movement within the school aggravated his settlement problems.

Similarly, few attempts were made to build on the child's experiences while away in care. Thus, not only were subject choices dealt with perfunctorily but achievements in sport and art, which had often been used to boost the child's self-confidence while away, were also ignored and, overall, little attempt at continuity was made. One of the children in our study had to cope with a move from one school where he was a "star" athlete to another where sports were not seriously pursued. Indeed, the decline in significance of many non-core subjects in schools, the diminishing of extra-mural activities and sport have disadvantaged many children, not only those who return. Those who seek a role outside the classroom find that the spotlights have been turned off and the stage has gone.

Further limitations on the way schools approach the issue of return to school arise from recent educational changes. As many schools now control their own budgets, governors and senior staff have more power in deciding which pupils to accept and what resources should be allocated to special needs. Policies, therefore, now vary considerably between schools as well as among education authorities. For example, in a school of 1,200 pupils, there was a large special needs unit with nine staff, all of whom were also subject teachers. The school is a model in its approach to children with learning and social difficulties, among whom cluster several children on supervision and some recently returned from care. However, there now exists much insecurity because the cost of this provision is considerable and there is parental pressure to allocate money elsewhere and to ensure that the school comes out well on published assessments. Understandably, the parents of children "in need" do not form a vociferous or influential group within the school.

The local management of schools (LMS) also has implications for the social careers of children who have to spend time away in care. LMS means that the suspension of children is the governors' decision and can only be rescinded after negotiation with parents. Children from deprived families are again at a disadvantage in such situations as they have limited legal power, few people pursuing their cause, and parents who are poor negotiators; they are also likely to have had minimal home tuition.

An added problem for children who change schools arises from the introduction of the National Curriculum. Although major revision to the content of courses is likely, the structure will probably remain. At present in secondary schools there are two key stages of return, at 11 and 14 years of age. From 11 to 14, and from 14 to 16, the National Curriculum runs in blocks. Although the same subject areas are covered in every school, the stages reached in each subject could differ and the content may vary locally creating problems when compulsory testing occurs.

It is easier, therefore, for a child to enter a new secondary school at the beginning of either the first or the fourth year. In addition, as one head teacher said:

Recent changes have reduced our flexibility. I used to be able to tuck these children under the wing of Mr Jameson in design and techno-logy. He was marvellous with them but now he's not only too tied up to bother but also worried about the effects of such kids on his appraisal.

Unfortunately, the moment of return from a separation is not influenced by these considerations.

At the level of immediate responsibility for the child, the contact between teacher and carers can most charitably be described as variable. Indeed teachers and social workers can hold quite contrasting views on the importance of education for children in care. As children are likely to move around while away in care, teachers tend to emphasise the stability offered by schooling while social workers feel that other issues, such as who should care for the child, are more important.

Generally, whatever their professional ideologies, both teachers and social workers have low academic expectations of children in care. It is believed that such children will attain little and as young adults experience unemployment or, at best, take unskilled jobs. Some of the social workers we interviewed happily viewed regular school attendance as sufficient and communications with teachers more often than not concerned children's behaviour rather than their educational progress or vocational preferences. Aldgate *et al* (1991) comment:

Recent educational research has emphasised the importance of parents' and teachers' expectations. Our results so far suggest a similar situation for children in care and we expect further analysis on social workers' and carers' expectations to add confirmation of fairly low expectations. The question remains as to whether higher aspirations and more remedial input could raise levels of attainment as Jackson (1987) has suggested. Hazel (1981) found that the com-bination of these factors had a distinct effect on the final educational attainment of adolescents placed in professional foster homes and compensated markedly for earlier educational disadvantage.

We did encounter several conscious efforts to counteract the negative effects of being in care. Two of the residential units we studied had a policy of keeping the children at their original school whenever possible. This was partly a necessity due to the fact that local schools were reluctant to accept children from community homes but, nevertheless, the policy was costly as the minibus journey to schools took an hour. It was felt that the benefits of maintaining continuity in education outweighed the disadvantages of distance. It also provided some security and sense of belonging for children going through considerable upheaval at home.

Missing from our discussion so far is the child's experience of going back to school. The study of returning children previously cited included an intensive follow-up of 20 children going home from care, 11 of whom went to full-time schooling. While most of these children found the transition easier than their previously expressed anxieties would suggest, they were still terrified of "getting it wrong". We should remember that the smallest things worry children and not knowing what to do or feeling unable to trust others exacerbates these difficulties.

Indeed, our theoretical perspectives on return were brought down to earth when we interviewed children about their new schools. Children confirmed few of our wider anxieties over return but expressed surprise at things such as size, buildings, racial composition and unfamiliar routine. 'I didn't think we'd have to take our shoes off before going in the gym' was typical. But such worries should not be underestimated by teachers; they need to appreciate that these trivial anxieties are often the expression of wider and inexpressible unease. Indeed, the smallest fears can have considerable effects. One lad, for example, refused to eat school dinners simply because he was afraid that, in public view, he would not be able to operate the tap on the water urn correctly.

Many apparently routine things fill children with high anxiety when they are unaware of the required behaviour. Insecure children find the clatter, noise and enforced bonhomie exhausting and disorienting. They trek along endless corridors, dropping precious pencils, seeing alien faces in distant rooms. Such an experience is even worse if you don't know which way the corridor leads and, as the last familiar companion disappears behind the sagging Nissen hut, you realise that you are not late but lost.

The newcomer, as she or he enters through the school gate, is an object of considerable interest, something bright on an otherwise sepia landscape. Everything they do is public, scrutinised by an audience of peers anxious for a laugh, particularly at someone else's expense. There is competition and jostling for position besides which scholastic achievement takes second place. Thus, taking off one's clothes for gym, the chilly trip to the swimming bath, grabbing a seat at lunch time, waiting for the bus, all anxiously loom in the child's mind long before the bell rings, like a morning on the Somme, a trill that signifies you are going over the top, alone and without a comforting swig of rum.

Any return involves negotiations over role and territory and those features which were once familiar to young people present new challenges. The successful establishment of a role takes time and diverts attention from anxiety but, once again, children returning to school from care face difficulties. Their return can follow a long sojourn in care and the questions of peers require a well-prepared story. Children who suddenly appear are objects of curiosity to classmates; mystery and fantasy will naturally abound. The problems of self-presentation for children in care are considerable. Even factual misunderstandings can defeat the struggling returnee. As one child said, 'I came from Shrewsbury. It had been the centre of my life but no one had the remotest idea where it was'.

Several studies have stressed the importance of influential peer cultures in schools (Coleman, 1961; Hargreaves, 1967; Ball, 1981; Corrigan, 1979; Willis, 1977). One of the problems we found was that even the most astute staff were not always familiar with the dynamics of the pupil world. The use of the wrong slang, for example, immediately indicates to others that the newcomer is "different". While being "different" may not worry young adults, at least in some areas such as leisure and taste, it is very important for younger children and adolescents to feel part of the group and to be the same. Coming from a strange background, being a welfare case and struggling to find a niche in the leading crowd were all significant to the children we interviewed. The use of sympathetic peers to ease entry seems to be helpful and children seemed happier when there was a specific teacher in whom they could confide. Positive staff attitudes also seemed to help parents to overcome their depressed situation.

A child's return to school is only one of several transitions that have to be made when a child returns from care. Older children, in particular, have to fashion peer-group relationships, find employment and cope with the vagaries of accommodation and social security. Nevertheless, school is central to many aspects of the child's life and its neglect is likely to cause widespread problems.

Conclusion

In this paper, we have explored children's returns from care to a context outside the natural family. We have seen that in education the scope for helping children return successfully is considerable. For example, it lies in administrative arrangements for schooling, in co-operation between teachers and social workers, and in developing sensitivity to children's needs. While the education of children in care is important, for the reasons we have explained, it is still given too little significance in social work planning, a situation which, it is to be hoped will change following recent legislation, government guidelines and research findings.

It is also the case that children in care are often cleverer and more capable than professionals like to think. They are seen as "dim" or "unreliable" and are rarely encouraged to apply themselves at school, in work or in the pursuit of personal relationships. As we wrote in *Locking up Children* (Millham, Bullock and Hosie, 1978), 'because we cannot envisage the Sistine Chapel being nurtured in the art room of a secure unit, we act accordingly'.

Innate intelligence apart, however, the experiences of children in care can be defeating because of the situations we put young people in. To return from a child-centred, supportive care placement to a large structured day-school or unsupportive work situation and to expect children to cope without money, accommodation and friends all add up to a recipe for failure. The children will get things wrong and adapt accordingly, either by the well-tried strategy of withdrawal or by manipulating professions, friends and relatives against one another.

We were surprised in our intensive studies by the low educational, employment and social expectations put on children returning from care and at the ways, many of them very subtle, that care experiences militated against academic and other achievements. One school report stated, 'the trouble is he's not educationally motivated'. True as this might be, the fact remained that without the sensitivity we have described, he was never going to become so.

This conclusion re-affirms many of the points about continuities and transitions established by a number of research studies of children in care (DHSS, 1985; DH, 1990). A successful reunion reflects not only the child's reintegration within the family but also his or her ability to make progress in other settings, most notably school. In the light of this evidence, it is important for a successful return that, once at home, the child establishes a role outside the family which does not undermine his or her role within it.

Note

The schooling of young people returning home from care or accommodation has benefited from general efforts to improve the education of all looked after children. Education is salient in the Looking After Children materials, the Assessment Framework and the Quality Protects initiative. In addition, the guidance on the Education of Young People in Public Care requires that a school place be found within 20 days of changes in living situations. School selection should, therefore, be an immediate concern rather than an afterthought to other decisions. However, there is no evidence to show whether the quality of negotiations over school placements and the academic and social support offered to children have changed since the original study. The adjustment difficulties found by returning children may not have diminished despite better administrative arrangements for ensuring education.

Roger Bullock, January 2001

References

Aldgate, J, Heath, A and Colton, M (1991) *The Educational Progress of Children in Care*, Report to ESRC, Oxford University.

Ball, S (1981) *Beachside Comprehensive*, London: Cambridge University Press.

Berridge, D (1985) *Children's Homes*, Oxford: Blackwell.

Berridge, D and Cleaver, H (1987) *Foster Home Breakdown*, Oxford: Blackwell.

Bullock, R, Little, M and Millham, S (1993) *Going Home: The return of children separated from their families*, Aldershot: Dartmouth.

Cleaver, H (1991) *Vulnerable Children in Schools*, Aldershot: Dartmouth.

Coleman, J S (1961) *The Adolescent Society*, Glencoe: Free Press.

Corrigan, P (1979) *Schooling the Smash Street Kids*, London: Macmillan.

Department of Health (1990) *Patterns and Outcomes in Child Placement: Messages from current research and their implications*, London: HMSO.

Department of Health and Social Security (1985) *Social Work Decisions in Child Care: Recent research findings and their implications*, London: HMSO.

Farmer, E and Parker, R (1991) *Trials and Tribulations: A study of children home on trial*, London: HMSO.

Fleeman, A M F (1984) 'From special to secondary school for children with learning difficulties', *Special Education: Forward Trends*, 11:3, Research supplement.

Fletcher-Campbell, F and Hall, C (1990) *Changing Schools? Changing People?: A study of the education of children in care*, Slough: NFER.

Hargreaves, D H (1967) *Social Relations in a Secondary School*, London: Routledge & Kegan Paul.

Hazel, N (1981) *A Bridge to Independence*, Oxford: Blackwell.

Heath, A, Colton, M and Aldgate, J (1989) 'The educational progress of children in and out of care', *British Journal of Social Work*, 19:6, pp 447–60.

HMSO (1984) *Second Report of the House of Commons Social Services Committee 1983–4*, London: House of Commons, HC 360–1.

Jackson, S (1987) *The Education of Children in Care*, Bristol Papers in Applied Social Studies, No. 1, University of Bristol.

Kahan, B (1979) *Growing Up in Care*, Oxford: Blackwell.

Millham, S, Bullock, R, Hosie, K and Haak, M (1986) *Lost in Care*, Aldershot: Gower.

Millham, S, Bullock, R and Hosie, K (1978) *Locking up Children*, Farnborough: Saxon House.

Parker, R A (1986) *Decisions in Child Care*, London: Allen & Unwin.

Pickup, M (1987) *A Critical Analysis of a Research Study by AMF Fleeman (1984)*, M.Ed. Thesis, University of Exeter.

Robbins, D (1990) *Child Care Policy: Putting it in writing*, London: HMSO.

Willis, P (1977) *Learning to Labour*, Farnborough: Saxon House.

5 Leaving care, education and career trajectories

Mike Stein

This paper is Reprinted from 'Oxford Review of Education', 20:3, 1994, pp 349–60; special issue on The Education of Children in Need. It explores the career trajectories of young people aged 16–19 years who were looked after by local authority social service departments. It includes a discussion of four substantive areas: first, the educational attainment of young people at the minimum school-leaving age; second, the perceptions of looked after young people of their educational experiences; third, young people's further education, employment and training routes; and finally, some of the influences connected with their career trajectories as well as policy and practice recommendations. The paper is based substantially upon three 'leaving care' research studies carried out at the University of Leeds (Stein and Carey, 1986; Stein, 1990; Biehal et al, 1992). Table 1 presents a summary of these studies.

> *Well, it makes it harder to get a job now, with having no qualifica-tions . . . I wish I'd sat 'em now . . . I just wish I'd one . . .* (Unemployed care leaver, Stein and Carey, 1986, p 92)

Educational attainment

> *Children in care, and in particular those who remain in care over a long period are put at a further disadvantage in respect of their general educational progress and achievement compared to other children of similar age and background . . . it would appear that few children in care attain educational qualifications and that fewer still go on to further and higher education.* (House of Commons, 1983–1984, p 340)

Completed research in this area has confirmed the Short Report's observations concerning the poor educational attainment of young people

Table 1
Summary of leaving care research studies 1981–92

Prepared for Living? (Biehal *et al*, 1992)
First publication of a four-year study, 1990–94, of leaving care schemes funded by the Department of Health.

Sample data:
Total = 183, male = 52.5%, female = 47.5%, black/mixed origin = 13.5%

Methodology:
Information was collected by social worker-completed questionnaire in respect of 183 young people, aged 16–19 (91% response rate) from three different local authority areas, who either legally left care or moved to independence during the last six months of 1990.

Living out of Care (Stein, 1990)
A three-year evaluation of the Leeds Leaving Care Scheme funded by Barnardo's.

Sample data:
Total = 65, male = 51%, female = 49%, black/mixed origin = 12%

Methodology:
The main focus of the research was an account of the project careers of the young people aged 16 and 17. Interviews were carrried out with 32 young people, their project workers and their social workers on three occasions. In addition, basic quantitative data was collected in respect of a total sample of 65 young people who were part of the project from February 1986 until February 1989.

Leaving Care (Stein and Carey, 1986)
A three-year study of young people who left care in 1982 funded by the Economic and Social Research Council.

Sample data:
Total = 45, male = 55.5%, female = 45.5%, black/mixed origin – only one young person in the exploratory study.

Methodology:
A qualitative follow-up study based upon semi-stuctured interviews with young people aged 16–19 who left the care of a social services department in 1982. The were interviewed on four occasions between 1982 and 1985.

in the care system (Jackson, 1988–9; Heath, Colton and Aldgate, 1989) and this includes the three studies carried out at the University of Leeds.

In *Leaving Care* and *Living out of Care*, 90 per cent and 54 per cent respectively possessed no qualifications when they left school. In our most recent survey, *Prepared for Living*, two-thirds of the young people had no qualifications at all and only one of the 183 had an A-level qualification; 19.5 per cent of social workers did not know whether their young people had any qualifications (see Table 2).

The *Prepared for Living* findings of low educational attainment are also broadly consistent with Garnett's (1992) findings that over three-quarters of care leavers had no qualifications. The educational attainment of care leavers compares poorly with national figures on the qualifications of 16–19-year-olds. In the Economic and Social Research Council's (ESRC) "16–19" study of 5,000 young people, it was found that 18 per cent of young people had not taken any GCSE or equivalent qualifications and 40 per cent of young people had poor GCSE or equivalent qualifications, compared to an average 70 per cent of the care leavers in our three studies who had no qualifications at all (Banks *et al*, 1992).

Table 2
Young people by qualifications* (n = 180)

	n	*%*
No qualifications	120	66.5
GCSE	22	12.0
City and Guilds	5	2.5
B Tech 1st Dip	2	1.0
A level	1	0.5
Don't know	35	19.5

*Some young people would have obtained more than one qualification.
Source: *Prepared for Living?*, p 20

Research findings in relation to the educational attainment of young people who have lived in care in both Canada and the United States are consistent with the results of British studies. Festinger (1983) in her study of 250 young people who had been in care in the New York

metropolitan area and a same age comparison sample from the population at large highlights educational achievement as a key difference.

> *Although in most respects foster care graduates were more alike
> than different from others of their age in the general population, our
> results showed that they lagged behind in scholastic achievement.
> During their placement many fell behind in school, and once a lag
> developed it was difficult to make up for lost time.* (p 297)

Raychaba (1987) reviews the evidence from a number of Canadian
studies in concluding:

> *Due to numerous reasons related to their initial home life, cultural
> background, reasons for coming into care, as well as their experience
> in care, child welfare youth are noted for their general lack of success
> in school.* (p 6)

Some of the factors leading to poor attainment that have been identified
in research studies include damaging pre-care experiences, non-attendance, emotional stress experienced prior to and during care, inadequate
liaison between carers and schools, the low expectations of carers and
teachers, the prioritisation of welfare above education concerns, the
disruption caused by placement moves and the low priority given to
education when social workers are organising moves (Stein and Carey,
1986; Jackson, 1987, 1988–9) In *Prepared for Living?* we found an
association between movement in care and poor attainment. Three-
quarters of those who had experienced four or more moves in care had
no qualifications compared to only half of those who had made no moves.
We also found that a higher proportion of young people leaving residential care had no qualifications (72.5 per cent) than those leaving
foster care (52 per cent). Poor educational attainment has also been
ascribed to the fact that the experience of care does little to ameliorate
the educational problems children bring with them into care (Heath *et
al*, 1989). The fact that almost a fifth of the social workers in *Prepared
for Living?* did not know whether the young people had any qualifications seems to add further weight to the assertion that social workers
often give low priority to education.

Young people's perceptions of education

Being in care? It's not the same. You look at somebody else and they've got a mum and dad, a proper mum and dad . . . they don't know what it's like for somebody who hasn't any parents. (Stein and Carey, 1986, p 68)[1]

We know from the voices of young people who have left care that many experienced difficulties at school. In *Leaving Care*, nearly all the young people reported feeling they were different, the "odd one out", the subject of curiosity, of teasing or even abuse. This is partly linked to the centrality of "the family", in ideology, policy and practice, to the education process. No longer are parents just transporters of children but increasingly are involved inside the school, for example, by assisting children in reading or numeracy particularly in their early years, by giving talks about their work or hobbies, by helping with sports and leisure activities or by becoming parent governors or belonging to the local parent–teachers associations. Not only that, "the family" also looms large within the curriculum itself, in reading schemes or thematic project work. Schools in part reflect the meaning and status of "the family" in society at particular points in time and although there may be shifts and changes – such as the current attack upon lone parents and the popularity of the two-parent nuclear family – the presence of "the family" remains constant and the impact upon those young people living part from their families is enormous.

If you haven't got a mum and dad you're a bastard – you know. And I didn't like that at school. If anybody said that to me I used to bray them . . . All kids started making fun of you. 'Oh where's your mam, where's your dad?' And I used to end up in quite few fights 'cos of that. (Stein and Carey, 1986, p 46)

Having to cope with feeling different and manage the ubiquity of "the family" is, however, only the first learning hurdle for young people in care. A second hurdle is the labelling of young people.

---

[1] All quotations are from young people except when otherwise indicated.

Oh 'she's one of children's home lasses her, keep away from her, she's got nits' and things like that. And you'd let it go so far and then you'd lash out at 'em. And then they'd wonder why you were on report all time.

I can remember my foster parent telling me that headmaster came round and said 'Are you bringing another handful into my school, more troubles?' (Stein and Carey, 1986, p 46)

When I went to school there was a music teacher and the least little thing that I used to do wrong these were his very words: 'You're all the bloody same you lot'. (Page and Clark, 1977, p 17)

Perhaps, not surprisingly, young people come to accept the stigma themselves:

When I first went to my school there was some money being pinched and I felt so guilty because I knew I was from a children's home and I felt I was picked on, and I knew it wasn't me, but you can't tell anybody that. (Page and Clark, 1977, p 16)

A third learning hurdle is that of movement and disruption in care.

I've been in three homes, other places too, but I can't remember, six months is the longest I've stayed anywhere. (Page and Clark, 1977, p 13)

In *Leaving Care,* just over three-quarters of the young people had experienced three or more placements in care and just over 40 per cent

Table 3
Movement in care (n = 180)

Number of moves	n	%
No moves	16	9
1–3 moves	72	40
4–9 moves	56	31
10+ moves	18	10
Don't know	18	10

Source: Prepared for Living?, p 10.

five or more placements, or an average of 4.4 placements per person. In *Living out of Care*, over half of the young people had between seven and 12 placements by the time they were 16 years of age and the average for the sample was six per young person. And in our most recent survey *Prepared for Living?* fewer than one in ten of the sample remained in the same placement throughout their time in care. Nearly one-third made between four and nine moves and one-tenth moved more than ten times (see Table 3).

A high proportion of these young people came into care as teenagers and therefore these moves have been compressed into a relatively short time period. The association between movement in care and poor educational attainment has already been outlined but the impact of what is referred to as "multiple placements" is much wider, especially following successive placement breakdowns. As the present author has commented:

> *Such an objective description as "multiple placements" cannot capture the emotional impact upon young people of changing carers, friends, neighbourhoods, schools, on several occasions, with little constancy in their lives. Neither, despite the resilience of young people, can it capture the emotional energy and strength required by these young people to meet changing expectations derived from new relationships and different social situations – those very same young people whose own developmental stages have often been impaired or damaged by their pre-care experiences. A rare convergence of sociological, psychological and psychiatric perspectives would conceive being in care, under these conditions, as an assault on personal identity.* (Stein, 1993, pp 238–39)

Education as a developmental process is therefore likely to have little meaning given the disruption to syllabuses, course work and examination preparation. There may also be additional practical learning hurdles, particularly for young people living in children's homes.

> *There is absolutely no privacy. To do homework, you had to sit among 14 or 15 little nippers bombing about, you know, booting the table or coming up asking what you were doing, and there was just no privacy at all.* (Page and Clark, 1977, p 26)

Finally, expectations of staff may also play their part.

They said, 'Well, what are you going to do now you are leaving school next year?', Leaving school was a foregone conclusion. I had no say . . . I asked my housefather about going on to college and he just said, 'If you're in care you don't go to college – who's going to keep you? (Page and Clark, 1977, p 55)

It is perhaps not surprising, linking these different points, that for many young people in care in our three studies there was little interest in school or school subjects and, by the time they were 16, many saw exams as pointless and education as a whole a 'waste of time'.

Further education, employment and training routes

I was in a bed-sit on my own . . . I couldn't handle it . . . being on my own, being lonely . . . no family behind me, no friends. I didn't like my Youth Training Scheme so I was stopping home, being bored, watching TV all day. I got into financial difficulties and was evicted in January. (Stein, 1990, p 60)

It is clear that the low level of educational attainment of most of the care leavers in our three studies left them ill-prepared to compete in an increasingly competitive and shrinking youth labour market. A similar connection is made by Raychaba (1987) in his review of Canadian research.

While the rate of youth unemployment, nationally, runs at about 17 per cent, the rate calculated in a sampling of Winnipeg teenage Crown wards was approximately 70–80 per cent . . . Given their difficulties in school they are effectively handicapped. (p 41)

Returning to our research, in *Prepared for Living?* the young people were vulnerable to periods of unemployment punctuated by training schemes and short-term employment (Table 4). Only 13 per cent were in full-time employment and very few remained in full-time education. Over one-third were unemployed within a few months of moving to independence or being legally discharged from care. It is surprising that only 13.5 per cent were on training schemes at the time of the survey, when unemployed 16- and 17-year-olds have, since 1988, lost their general entitlement to income support. However, if we take into account the post-school experience of our sample of young people, nearly two-thirds (60 per cent) have been on training schemes at some stage. Although it is the Government's stated policy that training places will be "guaranteed" to unemployed 16- and 17-year-olds, there has been recent evidence of a failure to provide sufficient training places (National Association of Citizens' Advice Bureaux, 1992; Social Security Advisory Committee, 1992).

In *Prepared for Living?* we found that there was a connection between a final placement in a Community Home with Education (CHE) or an independence unit, and unemployment. Just under half (48 per cent) of

Table 4
Young people by current education/employment status (n = 182)

Status	n	%
School/FE	16	8.5
Training	25	13.5
Employed (full-time)	24	13.0
Employed (part-time)	4	2.0
Unemployed	66	36.5
Caring for own child	19	10.5
Custody	8	4.5
Casual work	1	0.5
Other	4	2.0
Don't know	15	8.0

Source: *Prepared for Living?*, p 21.

those leaving CHEs and nearly two-thirds (65 per cent) of those leaving independence units were subsequently unemployed. It is not possible for us to comment on whether this is due to the fact that these young people were particularly ill-prepared by their experience in care to enter and survive in a highly competitive labour market or whether they were already the most disadvantaged young people in the sample when they entered care. However, it is interesting to note that Festinger (1983) in her American research identified the "group settings" sample as more likely to be dependent upon public assistance than those who had lived in foster care, the latter whose rates were similar to the general population sample.

In *Living out of Care*, 60 per cent of the young people were unemployed by the end of the study. Only 20 per cent were employed which meant that the majority of these young people (80 per cent) were living on or near the poverty line, being dependent upon some form of benefit – income support, Youth Training allowance, social services top-up grants or social services educational maintenance grants. Perhaps unsurprisingly there was a clear association between employment status and those who were managing and those who had broken down in their own tenancies, the latter all being unemployed. Two young women from the sample went on to higher education and, as with employment status, this was generally associated with a positive managing outcome. In *Living out of Care*, this was defined as:

> . . . *young person able to manage very well, good practical skills and able to handle personal relationship, friends and support networks likely to be outside of project. Minimal level of project support.*

A similar picture emerges from *Leaving Care*. With few qualifications, young people who had been in care were poorly equipped for a contracting labour market and its scarce rewards. Throughout the project they inhabited a world of benefits, work schemes, casual labour, and other practices (legal or otherwise) on the margin of employment. A "proper" job, full-time and permanent, was a rarity few could hope to obtain.

As was the case with their accommodation, the picture was one of ever-changing circumstances involving job schemes, temporary work and unemployment. However, there was a discernible pattern as early Youth Opportunities Programmes gave way to the dole or seasonal work, and later more advanced schemes vied with prolonged unemployment; a minority, throughout, clung to their valued, if not enjoyed, work.

By the second interviews, nearly 60 per cent of the young people were unemployed, which for most of them had been the case for six months or more; a further six young men were working on schemes provided by Community Industries, Youth Opportunities (YOPs) or National Association for the Care and Resettlement of Offenders (NACRO). From other's previous experience, these were unlikely to lead to proper jobs. Of the remainder, only three had full-time permanent jobs, none of which were highly paid. Any changes had been in the direction of unemployment or temporary work.

At the third interview, five of the 30 young people we spoke to were employed, but again only three of these were in permanent full-time jobs. Another four had been employed at some time since the last interview, the longest period having been for five months. YOPs had now been phased out, and only one young person was still young enough to be eligible for the new Youth Training Scheme; other schemes, run by NACRO and Community Industries were, as at the second interviews, only taken up by males. Those who were unemployed (over half the group) formed the majority, although half the young women were not looking for work because they had babies.

By the final interviews, over 80 per cent were unemployed. Only two of the group had permanent full-time jobs, one young man had just joined the army, and two more young men were employed in temporary part-time work. Most of those who were unemployed were seeking work, with the exception again of the women with very young children who, however, usually talked of working in a few years' time (although one had recently had a Saturday job in order to have money to 'spend on the bairn').

At the centre of our discussions in *Leaving Care* was the issue of unemployment: its weariness, boredom and frustration.

> *My biggest problem is being bored . . . I've been trying to get a job. But I can't get one . . . Think I'm gonna crack up.* (Stein and Carey, 1986, p 135)

As regards further education, the findings from *Leaving Care* were consistent with our other studies. Only three young people, all women, completed courses by the end of the project: one course was a Diploma in Social Care and the other two were pre-nursing courses. The value of educational qualifications for obtaining employment was a subject forced into the consciousness of most of the group and reactions were varied.

Some young people continued to dismiss it as irrelevant or a waste of time and some had not even bothered to go back to school to find out their examination results. However, this scepticism was not universal and for some young people there was a distinct feeling of regret and frustration.

Well, it makes it harder to get a job now, with having no qualifications. With being on them government schemes I've got a certificate like, but I haven't done much really. (Stein and Carey, 1986, p 92)

Often it was their own lack of motivation and determination they regretted, but they referred also to their sense of having missed out by being in care: the syllabuses and appropriate levels of work had been disrupted, and they had lost track of examinations just at the crucial time.

Career trajectory influences

Drawing upon our three studies the common career trajectory for the great majority of care leavers is: leave school at 16 without qualifications, employment training and unemployment. However, this basic categorisation oversimplifies the complexities and connections of pre-care, care and after-care careers. These are illustrated by two examples.

Mary Y experienced ten different placements from first being taken into care when she was four years old following parental abuse and neglect. Before she was 17, she had lived with two different sets of foster carers, in two children's homes, in two assessment centres, in a specialist residential school and in a community home with education, as well as being returned unsuccessfully "home on trial" on two different occasions. Her shortest placement was three months and her longest just over four years. Perhaps not surprisingly she left school without any qualifications. She moved into accommodation supported by a leaving care project and started a youth training scheme. However, she failed to attend regularly most weeks and lost her place. She is currently unemployed.

Jack S came into care when he was 13 following difficulties at home with his stepfather and non-school attendance. He lived in three different children's homes and with foster carers for a short time before moving to his own tenancy. Although "non-school attendance" was one of the main legal reasons for him coming into care, he did not attend school regularly whilst in care and left with no qualifications at all. He moved to his own tenancy at 17 years of age supported by social services but has been unemployed since leaving school. He found it very difficult to manage living on his own and within 12 months he was in debt, all his services were cut off and he moved into lodgings. In his own words:

I didn't want to be on my own. I just felt lonely, I didn't stop at the house very much . . . I got into difficulty paying bills . . . I've not worked since joining the project, I wanted to pack up and go . . . I wanted to leave. (Stein, 1990, p 59)

But what are the influences upon this, including the societal contexts? One way of addressing this area is by looking at pre-care, care and post-care careers. As regards pre-care careers, the findings of several studies support the Short Report's (1984) observation (for a discussion of these studies see Frost and Stein, 1989):

There is a well-established link between deprivation and children coming into care. Put crudely the majority of children in care are the children of the poor. (House of Commons, p xxi)

Given the accumulated evidence on education and inequality, it follows that the disadvantaged social class position of the families from which young people enter care will have a major influence upon their low educational achievement (Halsey, Heath and Ridge, 1980; Coleman, Hofler and Kilgore, 1981). In addition to the empirical evidence of class differences in educational opportunity and achievement in the UK and the USA, theoretical studies of language codes (Bernstein, 1975) and cultural reproduction (Bourdieu, 1988) identify barriers to educational achievement to children from low socio-economic backgrounds. Research has also shown that black Afro-Caribbeans in Britain fare considerably worse in the education system than whites and this cannot be simply explained by class background (Craft and Craft, 1985).

Patterns of gender inequality are somewhat different from those associated with class and ethnicity. In terms of academic performance, girls fare better than boys in primary school and up to and including GCSE level in secondary schools. The differences become more marked in post-16 education, choice of subject areas reflecting traditional gender divisions and boys achieving better results than girls (Spender, 1983; Stanworth, 1983).

In terms of pre-care careers, children and young people possess class, gender and ethnic identities which will have already greatly influenced their educational opportunities. However, in addition to these structural identities and influences we will need to add the impact of damaging intra-family relations including physical, sexual, emotional abuse or neglect and the consequences of this for primary socialisation, including emotional and intellectual development and educational experience.

Ideally, the second stage, the care career, should provide stability and compensatory experiences and for some young people this is the case. But for far too many young people, their care career adds to their educational difficulties. Family and neighbourbood links including education are often weakened and thus identities derived from class, family and ethnicity further fragmented. The challenge for the care system is to offer a positive care identity but as has already been discussed, "looked after" young people often *feel* different by living apart from their families and this is compounded by labelling, movement and disruption as well as practical learning difficulties and low carer expectation. The work of Roy Parker and colleagues on *Assessing Outcomes in Child Care* may provide an opportunity for rethinking the contribution of care to education (Parker *et al*, 1991). This is surely overdue for it is unsurprising that the cumulative impact of the pre-care and care careers of many "looked after" young people in our three studies leads to a post-care career of training schemes, often disrupted, and unemployment. This career trajectory cannot simply be explained theoretically in terms of structural identities (Banks *et al*, 1992), labour power reproduction (Bowles and Gintis, 1976) or, more imaginatively, cultural reproduction (Bourdieu, 1988; Willis, 1977). For "looked after" young people there are additional disadvantages derived both from damaging intra-family relations and their care experiences which contribute to a cluster of poor life chances: poor educational attainment, unemployment, young single parenthood, accelerated independence, over-representation among the homeless and the offending population and in custodial institutions (for a summary of this data see NCB, *Childfacts*, 1992).

Policy and practice recommendations

It is in response to the derivation of these disadvantages that social services "could do much better", and the studies discussed in this paper point to a number of policy and practice recommendations. Overall, education should be given a far higher priority in relation to pre-care, care and post-care careers.

At the pre-care stage educational links and performance should be a key part of supervision plans, preventive work and any assessment process, including the decision as to whether a young person should be "looked after" by social services. The prioritisation of welfare above educational concerns should be challenged and replaced with specified outcomes as part of individual pre-care planning.

At the "looked after" (substitute care or accommodation) stage, placement stability must be seen as a pre-requisite for educational development, as must maintaining positive pre-care school links. Educational development and performance should be clearly identified in care planning outcomes. Close carer–school links should be maintained so that young people are not disadvantaged through non-attendance at parents' evenings, curriculum meetings and other forums involving parents. Children and young people in substitute care should be encouraged, expected and supported to achieve at school. This will involve challenges to the non-achieving welfare culture of many children's homes dominated by low expectations and in some homes even a lack of private study facilities. In addition, teachers should be far more aware of the care process, its impact upon young people, and the role of the personal social services so that they avoid labelling or inappropriate over-compensation and can be more sensitive in their curriculum planning around "the family". It was ten years ago, in 1984, that the Short Report recommended:

> ... *that a basic understanding of the wide range of circumstances which can lead to children coming into care should form part of every teacher's training.* (Social Services Committee, 1984, p cli)

But this has still not been acted upon.

Finally, at the post-care stage a lot more could be done – not only ensuring that young people receive the financial assistance which social services are empowered to provide under the Children Act 1989 in connection with further education, employment and training, but also in encouraging young people to return to learning. It is often later that complacency turns to regret.

> *I work my way through newspapers and go down and have a look at the Job Centre to see if there's owt, and nowadays it's just those that's qualified.* (Stein and Carey, 1986, p 95)

Career advice, including the compensatory opportunities of post-compulsory education (e.g. Access, resits, new opportunities, vocational routes), should be an essential part of care planning with young people. My experience as an adult educator suggests it's never too late 'to sit 'em now'.

Note

Care leavers continue to fare worse in their educational and career trajectories in comparison to other young people in the general population. Also, the theoretical analysis outlined in the 1994 article is still relevant. Their poor educational and career outcomes are a result of the complex inter-relationships between structural and cultural factors, intra-family relations and care experiences.

What has changed since 1994 is the greater recognition of the problems faced by care leavers. This has included increasing support for care leavers as a funded priority under the Quality Protects Programme *to ensure that young persons leaving care, as they enter adulthood, are not isolated and participate socially and economically as citizens*; the National Priorities Guidance target for social services to improve the level of education, employment and training for care leavers *to at least 60 per cent of the level amongst others of the same age group in the area*; and the introduction of the Children (Leaving Care) Act 2000 (from October 2001) to improve the life chances of care leavers.

In addition, wider government initiatives to combat social exclusion, especially through the introduction of the Connexions service, and also in respect of under achievement in education should impact upon the education and career paths of care leavers.

Overall, this represents a more comprehensive strategy than hitherto to address the causes identified in my theoretical analysis and assist the achievement of citizenship status for this highly vulnerable group of young people.

Mike Stein, January 2001

References

Banks, M, Bates, I, Breakwell, G, Brynner, J, Emler, N, Jamieson, L and Roberts, K (1992) *Careers and Identities*, Milton Keynes: Open University Press.

Bernstein, B (1975) *Class Codes and Control*, London: Routledge & Kegan Paul.

Biehal, N, Clayden, J, Stein, M, Wade, J *et al* (1992) *Prepared for Living? A survey of young people leaving the care of three local authorities*, London: National Children's Bureau.

Bourdieu, P (1988) *Language and Symbolic Power*, Cambridge: Polity Press.

Bowles, S and Gintis, H (1976) *Schooling in Capitalist America*, London: Routledge & Kegan Paul.

Coleman, J, Hofler, T and Kilgore, S (1981) *Public and Private Schools*, Chicago: National Opinion Research Centre.

Craft, M and Craft, A (1985) 'The participation of ethnic minority pupils in further and higher education', *Education Research*, 25.

Festinger, T (1983) *No-one Ever Asked Us: A postscript to foster care*, New York: Columbia University Press.

Frost, N and Stein, M (1989) *The Politics of Child Welfare*, London: Harvester.

Garnett, L (1992) *Leaving Care and After: A follow-up study to the Placement Outcomes Project*, London: National Children's Bureau.

Halsey, A H, Heath, A and Ridge, J (1980) *Origins and Destinations*, Oxford: Oxford University Press.

Heath, A, Colton, M and Aldgate, J (1989) 'The educational progress of children in and out of care', *British Journal of Social Work*, 19:6, pp 447–60.

House of Commons Social Services Committee (1983–1984) Second Report *Children in Care* (The Short Report).

Jackson, S (1987) *The Education of Children in Care*, Bristol Papers in Applied Social Studies, No.1, University of Bristol.

Jackson, S (1988–9) 'Residential Care and Education', *Children & Society*, 2:4, pp 335–50.

National Association of Citizens Advice Bureaux (1992) *Severe Hardship–CAB evidence on Young People and Benefits*, London: CAB.

National Children's Bureau (1992) *Childfacts: Young People Leaving Care*, 25 June.

Page, R and Clark, G (1977) *Who Cares?* London: National Children's Bureau.

Parker, R, Ward, H, Jackson, S, Aldgate, J and Wedge, P (eds) (1991) *Looking After Children: Assessing Outcomes in Child Care: The report of an independent working party established by the Department of Health*, London: HMSO.

Raychaba, B (1987) 'Leaving Care – Where?' *Ontario Association of Children's Aid Societies*, 31:9.

Raychaba, B (1988) *To be on your own . . . with no direction from home*, National Youth in Care Network.

Social Security Advisory Committee (1992) Eighth Report.

Spender, D (1983) *Invisible Women, Schooling Scandal*, London: The Women's Press.

Stanworth, M (1983) *Gender and Schooling*, London: Hutchinson.

Stein, M (1990) *Living out of Care*, Ilford: Barnardo's.

Stein, M (1993) 'The abuses and uses of residential care', in Ferguson, H, Gilligan, R and Torode, R (eds) *Surviving Childhood Adversity*, Dublin: Social Studies Press, Trinity College.

Stein, M and Carey, K (1986) *Leaving Care*, Oxford: Blackwell.

Willis, P (1977) *Learning to Labour*, Farnborough: Saxon House.

6 Time to care about those in care

Peter McParlin and Eric Graham

Reprinted from *The Times Higher Education Supplement*, 13 October 1995.

Panic levels have been soaring with the capture of another year's worth of undergraduates. Tutors have outdone each other in displays to attract unqualified adult learners, administrators have chased the funding attaching itself to students from ethnic minorities and admissions officers have broken out the bubbly at their new crop of female engineering undergrads.

But for one group of potential students higher education is, practically speaking, out of the question. Suffering already from many forms of disadvantage, this group has additional problems which are unique and very specific and it requires specialised and finely targeted support.

We are talking about people who have spent time in residential or foster care – children who have been "looked after", to adopt the latest nomenclature. Even where carers are dedicated, patient and imaginative, the trauma of even a relatively small part of a childhood (a year, reckon psychologists) spent in care cannot be over-estimated.

Already scarred by the experiences which have brought them into care, "looked after" children suffer bewilderment, loss, guilt, resentment, loneliness, a sense of worthlessness in the best of homes, to which may be added the bullying and abuse by their peers in the homes and classmates at school, if not by their carers.

In many cases the statistics tell a grim tale. Care-leavers make up 54 per cent of the prison population aged under 25, half of all London beggars and 66 per cent of male prostitutes. Fifty per cent of care leavers are homeless and half of all women care users are pregnant within 18 months of leaving. Seventy per cent have health problems due to inadequate or inconsistent attention in childhood. Eighty per cent experience destitution and poverty.

Education will not solve all the problems but it will give these young people some self-esteem, a chance to dream and aspire, and an entry into other worlds than the painful and chaotic one of their childhoods. But education is often the last item on the agenda. Young people in care may be bundled from school to school and are more likely to be bullied or labelled by teachers and contemporaries. Truanting is endemic and an estimated 60 per cent will be excluded from school at some time. A child who has been in care for just one year will fall one year behind in mathematics and two years in reading.

By the time examinations loom the chances of doing well are small. Three per cent may pass the five or more GCSEs at C or above that up to half of their fellows are confidently predicted to obtain. In 1994 when 37 per cent of all school children reached the NVQ attainment target (thus able to qualify for a university place), for the in-care population the figure was between 0.4 and 1 per cent. In other words, only one in 200 "looked after" young people may be qualified to enter university or a college of higher education.

Even this tiny minority are unlikely to proceed further. These youngsters usually have no natural family to supplement grants, nowhere to live between terms, and no way of affording all-year-round accommodation given the reduction in government housing allowances. There is also a dearth of emotional support; after all, no one expects care leavers to go to university. What can be done?

In the past year no fewer than five national conferences have attempted to highlight this problem and delegates have argued for extended grant provision and for trained support and advocacy. Care leavers should be entitled to this help regardless of their age – they have been robbed of this access for three decades. Flexible time limits should be implemented, given the extra difficulties likely to be experienced by care leavers.

Staff awareness and training, advertising which targets residential homes, open days to which foster parents and residential social workers are specifically invited are required. A member of staff with particular responsibility for care users and leavers could work with them and develop colleagues' insight into their particular problems. Lecturers could help recover the shattered self-confidence of care leavers and help them to establish good learning patterns.

Education professionals may argue that there are no more special privileges to be handed out; advantage must be taken of what already exists. This is a smug and insensitive position when the nation's most vulnerable and abused young people are denied access to opportunities that are open to the rest of us. The onus is on deliverers of higher and further education to act and on the Government to take seriously its role of "corporate parent" and to, at least, free the funds.

Note

I am grateful to BAAF and Professor Jackson for kindly including this article in this very much needed book. As someone with 18 years experience of some 30 odd children's homes and foster homes, I know how much young people's views have been left out or paid lipservice to in the past. We now need to be genuine in our inclusivity policies – including young people and care leavers in all aspects of education. I will know that this objective has been attained when the 0.4 per cent of children are represented by ex-care leavers in high office throughout such walks of life as MPs and DfEE officials. My hope was that there should be a care leaver on the government task team 2000 – but alas there was not. Maybe next time. However, the hope for jam tomorrow can be hard to sustain.

Peter McParlin, January 2001

7 Transforming lives
The crucial role of education for young people in the care system

Sonia Jackson

This paper was delivered as the Tory Laughland Memorial Lecture at the *Royal Society of Arts* on 29 June 1995.

It is a great honour to have been asked to give this lecture in memory of Tory Laughland, the founder of the Who Cares? Trust. I have chosen a subject on which I know she felt strongly as she did about most things to do with young people in care. She wanted a care system that would recognise and celebrate the talents and creativity of young people and open up opportunities for them. She wanted them to aim for success, not just get by, and *Who Cares?*, both the organisation and the magazine, is the expression of that philosophy.

Anyone who reads *Who Cares?* must be struck by its unique combination of realism and optimism. It doesn't attempt to deny the difficulties that its readers face every day. They are there to see in the letters, the problem page and the photostories, but the emphasis is always on how people can overcome those problems and move on.

Tory saw that young people in care desperately need positive role models and she had the brilliant idea of arranging for *Who Cares?* readers to interview well-known people, many of whom had been in care themselves, the celebrity interviews that continue to be a feature of the magazine.

I think this illustrates one of the paradoxical things about Tory. She was extremely modest and even rather shy, but on behalf of children in care she had no inhibitions about asking anyone to do anything, no matter how important or famous they might be. Not only did they nearly always say yes, but often went on to become personal friends and supporters. No one could resist Tory's enthusiasm and humour and commitment to children. She was a person who inspired immediate and lasting affection, one of the most lovable people I have ever met.

Why education matters

Why is education so important for children and young people in the care system? Firstly because it is the only reliable route to escape from disadvantage, especially for girls (Pilling, 1990). We know that the 60,000 children and young people looked after by local authorities mostly come from families struggling with poverty, poor housing, ill-health, isolation (Bebbington and Miles, 1989). They have often suffered abuse, rejection or bereavement. Too often their problems are made worse by their experiences in care and that is reflected in the shocking figures highlighted by Who Cares?. Over half of care leavers are unemployed after a year, more than a third of homeless young people have a care background and so do 23 per cent of the adult prison population. One in four young women leaving care between 16 and 18 is pregnant or already has a child. Without education these young people run a high risk of repeating the pattern that brought them into care in the first place.

It is through school that children earn passports to different kinds of futures. That is one of the reasons why parents care about it so passionately, why they move house and take out insurance and fight like tigers to send their child to the school of their choice. Those who don't get the passport lose out in all sorts of ways. Their path to post-school education is blocked, and increasingly their employment prospects are restricted or non-existent.

But education does not just matter for practical reasons. There are two other reasons why education is specially important for children who are separated from their families. First, education gives you access to other worlds than the one you currently live in. You can escape into books, you can read about other countries, other times, other places, different ways of life. You can find out how to sew or make models, paint, grow vegetables, play music. It makes you less dependent on the people around you, and for children who have little control over their lives and often no choice about who looks after them, that is crucial.

Secondly, education enables you to look beyond the personal and immediate and see your own situation from outside as well as within. That's a hard thing to do, but at best it means that, instead of reacting to the unfairness and cruelty of life with the kind of unfocused rage that psychologists call behaviour or conduct disorder, you can think about your situation objectively and plan how to take control. Perhaps one of the best ways of doing that for people in care is to write about their experiences, as Fred Fever has done so movingly in his book *Who Cares?* (Fever, 1990).

Putting education on the care agenda

Isn't all this obvious? But when I first started thinking and writing about this subject it was very difficult to get anyone interested. I found that there was not a single book in the English language about the education of children in care and only one or two short articles. Most books about foster and residential care did not even include school or education in the index. I was in despair. Then it occurred to me that this was a discovery in itself. The explanation was that the whole subject had dropped down the gap between care and education, a gap that runs right through the system from the top of the civil service down to the smallest village playgroup.

At the policy level that gap is at last beginning to be bridged but it may be a long time before that filters down to the level of local authority social workers, placement finders and residential care staff, too long to help young people in the care system now unless we do something urgently about it.

What is the effect of the neglect of education in the care system? All the research shows that children in care, even good stable foster care, are on average two years behind other children in reading and one year behind in mathematics (see Chapter 2). By the time they get to take public examinations, if they ever do, their chances of success are very small. Three-quarters of care leavers still have no educational qualifications. Why should this be?

The most popular explanation among professionals, one that I have heard over and over again, is: it is because of what happened to them before they began to be looked after by local authorities. What can you expect from children who come from such disadvantaged backgrounds?

I believe that this is an explanation that we can absolutely reject: it is defeatist nonsense. If you talk to some of the young people who are here today you can make up your own minds about it. For a start many people come into care before school age and have spent their whole childhood within the care system. The only parent you can blame if they fail to do well in education is the local authority that was supposed to be looking after them.

But even when children come into the care system later and have suffered damaging experiences, surely that is a reason to give them more intensive help and support, not to give up on them. When we have eliminated all the obstacles which prevent young people in residential or foster care from fulfilling their potential, we shall find that there are very few who cannot reach a much higher level than they do at present.

Succeeding from care

How do we know? Well, for a start we might look at people with a care background who *have* been educationally successful and ask how they did it. This is the subject of some research I did with support from the Leverhulme Trust, a project which is called "Successful in Care".[1] It started with an article about my work in *The Sunday Times* which ended with an appeal for people who had been in care as children to write to me about how they had managed to succeed. I had about 30 replies and gradually I collected more names and contacts, but it was very slow work.

It was Tory who really got the project off the ground. She suggested putting a leaflet in *Who Cares?* magazine linked with an interview by a young person and a photostory focusing on education. Tory was always very keen on prizes and, again at her suggestion, I offered a prize to anyone who returned the leaflet and agreed to complete a questionnaire. The prize was a rather nice Parker ballpoint pen. Tory also wanted to offer a balloon flight to the person who sent in the best story, but I

---

[1] This research and the "High Achievers" project that followed it are reported in Jackson, S and Martin, P (1998) 'Surviving the Care System: Education and resilience', *Journal of Adolescence*, 21, pp 569–83.

thought that might be an invitation to fantasy.

The criterion of success was not very demanding but people needed to have five O levels or GCSEs at Grade C or above or to have gone on to further or higher education. That meant only small numbers of readers of *Who Cares?* would qualify – many would be too young. But 250 leaflets were returned, and of those eligible nearly three-quarters later completed questionnaires. That is an exceptionally high return for a postal survey, and many respondents explained that they had taken the trouble because they so much wanted to help other young people who were having to face all the obstacles and difficulties they themselves had been able to overcome.

My hope was that their accounts would provide valuable pointers to good social work and educational practice and that hope was fulfilled to the extent that many of their ideas have contributed to my later work and writing (see Jackson and Martin, 1998).

What was different about these people from the majority of those who have been through the care system? The most obvious difference was in their current life situations. Almost all of them were in full-time employment or education, only one described himself as homeless, over a third owned their own homes, most of the over-30s said they were in stable relationships. The range of occupations was quite wide, with a bias towards social work and the caring professions, but including writers, accountants, computer analysts, teachers, librarians and a photographer. One person wrote from the Cabinet Office, adding a P.S. 'thank you for the pen'.

None of these people had had easy lives. I expected at least to find that a high proportion had lived in the same residential unit or foster home for long periods and there were some like that (one is now a university lecturer in social work). But mostly they had gone through a succession of placements, just as we know happens to most children looked after by local authorities. The average number was 5.6 and the record for placement changes was 36, a young woman who now has a psychology degree from London University. One man now managing a large company had had 30 placements. Both these people had come into care at under one year.

Now obviously placement changes are not desirable, and those must have been people of extraordinary resilience to survive such a degree of turmoil in their lives. But it underlines the point that, with the right support from a sympathetic adult, educational progress can go on even when the other parts of children's lives are in a mess.

In other ways, too, these successful people were not untypical of other "looked after" young people. Many of them had been abused, their parents were sick or had died, and some had lost touch with all their relatives. They had many complaints about their care experiences: the lack of interest and support for schoolwork that they experienced from social workers and residential workers, low expectations, poor facilities for study. One woman had to do her homework on a plank between two lockers in the cloakroom. Another used to work between one and four in the morning, the only time she could get any quiet. A few had had a lot of help from foster carers, but often they felt that their carers, even if well meaning, simply did not have enough education themselves to be able to advise them.

Their hardest fight was against the prejudice and discrimination they encountered just from the fact of being in care, bullying and name-calling from other pupils, the low expectations of teachers:

Being good at sport was my saving grace – nobody seemed particularly interested academically. They were shocked when I passed my 11 plus, shocked when I passed my O levels. Teachers made a judgement of my ability based on their expectations of a low grade student, which they thought was the norm for someone in care.

As the only black child in a school of 900 and the only one in care I was usually blamed for any trouble and frequently accused of theft and searched.

Because of being in care I was always treated like dirt, as someone who would never achieve anything academically.

We will need to do more work before we can say with any confidence why these people did so well despite all their problems. Some of the things they thought had helped them were learning to read early, a sympathetic teacher, foster carers who acted as advocates for them. But for me there was one thing that stood out above everything else.

All these people went to mainstream school. Only one of the 150 had been out of school for more than a week except through illness. This contrasts dramatically with research over the past two years which shows that more and more looked after children are being excluded from school, sometimes for quite minor reasons. A recent Scottish survey calculated that the chance that a child in residential care will be excluded is 80 times as high as the chance that the same thing will happen to a child living with his or her own family.

Local surveys and government reports consistently show between 40 and 60 per cent of looked after children excluded from school on any one day. Some of these exclusions are technically temporary, but can last for a very long time, a year or more.

What has happened is that two aspects of government policy are in conflict with each other. The Children Act 1989 makes the local authority as a whole responsible for promoting the well-being of looked after children, not just the social services department. But the Education Reform Act 1988 and the Education Act 1993 have set schools in competition with each other and at the same time switched power from the LEA to individual schools. The result is that schools are reluctant to accept pupils who may cause trouble and are unlikely to improve their score in the exam league tables. The reduced power of local authorities combines with the stigmatisation which being in the care system still carries to deny looked after children their right to education. Many of them have to make do with a token five hours a week home tuition. Many get nothing at all. How can they learn if there is no school for them to go to? They do learn of course, they learn that they are of no importance and nobody cares about them.

And because school defines children's present and future lives, exclusion from school can often mean exclusion from society. The long-term costs both for individuals and society are incalculable. Both the Department of Health and the Department for Education recognise the problems and are trying to do something about them.

The Department of Health and the Social Services Inspectorate are attempting to improve the educational chances of children in residential and foster care through the Looking After Children Assessment and

Action Records. They ask a series of searching questions about the quality of care provided and the outcomes achieved on a number of developmental dimensions of which education is one (DoH, 1995). The Department for Education has issued circulars attempting to stem the rising tide of exclusions. But, with some exceptions, discussion of education in official circles still tends to be problem rather than achievement oriented. Children in the care system are at best seen as children with special needs, a source of trouble, not as ordinary children and young people who have had to contend with special difficulties and therefore need very intensive educational help and support if they are to achieve success.

What would make a difference?

It must not be left to individual social workers or foster carers to have to fight the system to get a school place or return a child to school after a temporary exclusion. The scandal of residential units where none of the children go to school, of children who are locked out of school for years at a time, should be ended at once. The legal right of all children to full-time education should be enforced. If necessary, the denial of that right to children looked after by local authorities should be challenged by judicial review.

There must be a clear expectation that all children in public care attend mainstream school. Some local authorities have shown that this is an achievable aim. It needs changes in attitudes among teachers and social workers and a specialised support service on the lines of those that already exist in Manchester and Hampshire.[2] It needs to be staffed by teachers who carry credibility within schools and know their way around both the education and care systems.

The Children Act should be amended to lay a duty on local authorities to promote the education of looked after children by all means in their power. Any person who has spent a year or more in the care system and whose family is not able to support them at the time of leaving care should be entitled to financial help from the local authority up to the

---

[2] This point is further addressed in Chapters by Hetcher and Firth, and Walker respectively.

completion of their full-time education, including higher education, and to assistance to return to education at any time up to their 30th birthday. This is necessary because young people who have had painful and chaotic childhoods are sometimes not ready to start seriously learning until they have been able to get their lives in perspective, which may not be until they are at the point of leaving school. Local authority grants should be mandatory for ex-care people who need to make up for the education they missed earlier. We have got to the point where according to the Council for Industry and Higher Education, six in ten of today's 18-year-olds can sooner or later expect to enter universities or colleges. We need to make sure that looked after children have the opportunity to be among the 60 per cent.

Foster carers and residential workers should see themselves as partners in the educational process and educational qualifications should count for a lot more than they do at present in the selection of carers.

But most of all, social workers who share parental responsibility for children and young people living away from home must come to see education as the key to a good quality of adult life and be prepared to fight for the rights of those children and the opportunities they are entitled to, just as they would for their own children.

Who Cares? has already made a vital contribution by enabling young people's voices to be heard in this debate. Back in 1993 Tory organised a panel of young people to speak at the first conference in England (the Scots were ahead) on the Education of Children in Need, which made a great impression on everybody who heard them. The young people left no doubt of the importance of education in their lives. At an early stage in the Who Cares? organisation, Tory set up a Who Cares? educational advisory group which has generated a host of ideas now coming to fruition.

For example, the Who Cares? Trust carried out a survey with the National Consumer Council, and published a report written by Barbara Fletcher under the title, *Not Just a Name*, in which 600 young people told us what was right and wrong about their educational experiences. This is the most substantial piece of evidence ever published on what young people themselves think about their education and is constantly quoted. Last month, Who Cares? organised a very successful conference,

"Seen and Heard: Educated and Employed" and published a practical self-help guide for young people, *Who Cares About Education?.*

Another practical initiative is the Who Cares? bookbuying scheme, which has enabled many young people in Manchester and Leeds to buy and own books for the first time. Literacy is the essential foundation for educational success but how can we expect children to learn to read and love reading if we don't provide the means? It was sad to hear of the residential worker who said, 'What's the point of giving these children books – there'd be nowhere quiet enough here to read them'. But others found the scheme provided a much-needed incentive to sit down and give close attention to an individual child.

In education as well as the other target areas of health, employment and counselling, Susanna Cheal and the Who Cares? team have been able to keep up their momentum despite the grievous loss of Tory's vision, inspiration and wonderful creative energy. But I think Tory would have been most pleased by the fact that young people who know at first hand what it's like to be in the care system remain at the heart of the Who Cares? enterprise.

References

Bebbington, A and Miles, J (1989) 'The background of children who enter local authority care', *British Journal of Social Work*, 19:5, pp 349–68.

Department of Health (1995) *Looking After Children: Assessment and Action Records*, London: HMSO.

Fever, F (1990) *Who Cares? Memories of a childhood in Barnardo's*, London: Warner.

Fletcher, B (1993) *Not Just a Name: The views of young people in foster and residential care*, London: Who Cares? Trust.

Jackson, S and Martin, P Y (1998) 'Surviving the care system: education and resilience', *Journal of Adolescence*, 21, pp 569–83.

Pilling, D (1990) *Escape from Disadvantage*, London: National Children's Bureau.

Part III

Changing the picture

8   Current educational initiatives
What value have they for looked after young people?

Felicity Fletcher-Campbell

Introduction

It is salutary to pause and reflect on what has happened in an area over a period of time, not only to note the successes and failures but also to consider what past events can suggest for the future. It is timely to do this with regard to the education of "looked after" young people, i.e. those in the public care system. The combination of scarce resources, good will, a very broad spectrum of practice, a shifting context with competing priorities, and vulnerable young people is one which can either move things forward positively, with mutual benefits to all concerned, or perpetuate the structural weaknesses which have spawned and nurtured the problems up to now. Time does not stand still for the young people in the midst of this: they weave their lives in and out of our structures and if the final tapestry finds favour with no one, we have only ourselves to blame.

In the decade since the seminal literature review by the editor of this present volume (Jackson, 1987), which identified the lack of attention to the area, the education of children in care (or latterly, children who are looked after) has seen rapid, albeit patchy, development. At the beginning of the 1990s, research established that this was a problem area and the causes of the problem were delineated (Fletcher-Campbell and Hall, 1990). In the middle of the decade, a number of initiatives to address the problems were implemented and described, and practitioners were able to give their reflections on the process and outcomes (Fletcher-Campbell, 1997). We learnt much about direct case work.

Recently, at the end of the decade, we have begun to gain a deeper understanding of the necessary and sufficient elements of "corporate parenting" and the relevant processes which have to be enacted to ensure that all young people who are looked after have an equal chance of having a positive educational experience. Furthermore, there is now empirical evidence to confirm the symbiotic nature of the interaction between education and care plans: it is now acknowledged by many practitioners working with young people who are looked after, that care plans cannot succeed without attention to education plans and *vice versa*.

What we know is that the education of children who are looked after is blighted by:

- ignorance (of the importance of education, of the nature of care, of what goes wrong);
- fragmentation (of domestic, social and school lives/careers/ biographies);
- low expectations of academic performance (without any evidence to suggest a necessarily disproportionate number of young people with learning difficulties in this group).

Approaches to the education of looked after young people

Three points need to be made about the issue of the education of young people who are "looked after": these are fundamental to understanding the way in which approaches to the issue have been formed and the way in which they need to develop in the future.

First, the issue is, essentially, one of inclusion; all that we know about effectiveness for this group accords with what we know about the inclusion of other minority groups – namely, that what is needed is systemic reform. This systemic reform involves changes in attitudes and practice; and, underpinning this, the systematic collection and appropriate dissemination of evidence and information. It may include discrete provision and/or positive discrimination for young people who are looked after.

Second, it is equally clear – both practically and theoretically – what the issue of the education of young people who are looked after is *not* about. It is *not*, essentially, about remedial or therapeutic approaches or the changing of individuals. *Education* changes people – all people – and the challenge is to bring young people who are looked after in touch with the education that is their entitlement and which they can share with their peers. In the vast majority of cases, they have lost touch because of tensions in the care system itself – and, in some cases, domestic situations obtaining prior to care.

Third, what is currently "the problem" is soluble, given systemic reform. There is sufficient evidence, albeit collected on a local rather than a national scale, that young people who are looked after can have positive educational experiences and outcomes. But this position is only achieved with multi-agency co-operation in a context in which professionals are not frightened of dismantling policies and practices which, while they may have served valid purposes at some stage, may now be obstructive.

These three points give rise both to considerable optimism – optimism which is reflected in a range of initiatives that have developed over the past decade or so – and highlight the inappropriateness of the model which implies that there is something badly wrong with the individual who is looked after and that the individual needs "treatment" in order to assimilate him/her into normality. That this model prevails in places is borne out by empirical evidence: for example, perceptions that young people who are looked after necessarily "mean trouble" or have committed some offence or are bound to achieve little at school (see Fletcher, 1993; Fletcher-Campbell, 1997).

Accepting that addressing the problem of the education of looked after young people involves systemic reform is, undeniably, professionally threatening insofar as it means recognising that welfare systems may not be entirely beneficent and may have a malevolent effect on "the client". This is uncomfortable for "the caring professions" – and it should be said that there is negligible evidence of any illwill towards young people who are looked after, even if there is evidence of poor understanding and procrastination. Yet alongside the threat there should be encouragement for, as with other inclusion issues, no special initiatives or discrete legislation are needed. What is needed is to ensure that the interests of the minority group (here, the tiny proportion of the school-aged population who are in the care system) are firmly on the agenda for any current initiative for the general population of which they are a part.

Considering interests means, in some cases, ensuring access and, in others, disaggregating data to compare trends and performance. Both of these may need discrete measures. But we need to be very clear about the nature of these measures: it has become clear that they are, essentially, about access to what is there normally and only rarely about *replacing* what is there normally. This is something that has been learnt over the past decade. Previously, residential children's homes sometimes had education units on site. This practice was extremely limiting in that a small group of children of various ages, with very different needs and abilities were educated together by a small number of staff a few yards from where they lived together. Not only were the curriculum opportunities far from the "broad, balanced and relevant" programme to which pupils were entitled when the national curriculum was introduced under the terms of the Education Reform Act 1988, but there were also serious drawbacks in the stultifying social environment. Again, the residential children's homes that are at the forefront of effective practice as regards education now advocate, on the basis of experience built up over several years, using a wide range of local schools for residents so that the young people have the opportunity to make their own friends independently and have space away from those with whom they have to socialise in the evenings and at weekends.

It is thus increasingly important that young people who are looked after are involved as much as possible within ordinary mainstream provision. This chapter considers some examples of recent general education initiatives which have the potential to support young people who are looked after and considers the extent to which they are inclusive *per se* and also promote inclusion. Some of these initiatives are structural – encouraging inter-agency collaboration, for example – while others are directed towards individuals.

The sufficiency of recent initiatives

It should be stressed that none of the initiatives reported below is in any way a substitute for a coherent authority-wide policy for the education of looked after young people (see Chapter 9 for a discussion of how such a policy might be achieved) nor for specific strategies for identifying educational needs and putting in place an action plan (see Chapters 10,

12 and 13 in this volume). It is important to bear this in mind, for general, non-discrete initiatives, if presented as evidence of a strategy sufficient to meet the needs of looked after children, have three fundamental flaws.

First, the initiative may be piecemeal: the eligibility criteria may mean that some looked after children will be excluded; or it may be in the nature of a limited pilot or project, only available in certain areas. On its own, it could reinforce, rather than ameliorate, the fragmentation which characterises the lives of these pupils.

Second, it may not be appropriate to meet the specific needs of looked after young people. For example, it could sustain low expectations or ignorance: alternative curricula by way of work-based packages are appropriate and valuable for thousands of pupils at Key Stage 4 (years 9–11) but they are not the answer for a young person who, given the right encouragement and support, should be setting his/her sights on higher education.

Third, it may be transient: many initiatives for vulnerable young people are enabled by short-term, project-specific funding. While the best of these look for sustainability, some yet fail to ensure this, with the result that continuity and progression for individual young people are endangered and the ubiquitous fragmentation gains further hold.

Unless these flaws are acknowledged, there is the danger of perpetuating the excuse which has often been given as regards the educational needs of looked after pupils: 'we have education social workers, we have behaviour support teams, we have pastoral care in schools, so what is the problem? Young people who are looked after can latch into these resources as can any other pupil.' There is considerable empirical evidence that while these resources may be helpful, yet on their own, without particular attention to the unique needs of looked after children as a group, they will not address the structural barriers. Thus, all such provision needs to be regarded in the main as complementary – a resource which should be available to those providing for the educational needs of looked after young people and used if and when appropriate. Clearly, in some cases, such provision may be sufficient but this should not be regarded as inevitable.

There are, thus, unique management issues lodged within many mainstream initiatives if the potential of these initiatives to enhance the educational experiences of looked after young people is to be realised: this requires focused action.

The New Start programme

One of the challenges for corporate parenting – and for the repair of the fragmentation that characterises the lives of looked after young people – is that the multiple agents concerned are often unaware of each other's strengths and of the opportunities offered elsewhere in the authority. Corporate parenting involves equipping those making decisions about provision and support with the relevant information as to what is available. Thus there needs to be scrutiny of the way in which information is exchanged and of the procedures for monitoring and evaluating it and keeping it up-to-date.

One of the outcomes of the multi-agency partnerships formed under the Government's New Start programme has been the compilation of area directories of local provision for young people who are disaffected from mainstream education or for whom the normal curriculum at Key Stage 4 (ages 14–16) is inappropriate or unacceptable. In one region, there were hundreds of small schemes which few people knew about other than those intimately involved. The systematic collection and dissemination of information about provision has informed decision-making on various levels. Not only can providers get a grip on the overview and thus both avoid duplication and see where gaps need to be plugged but those helping young people to make choices or plan the next move in their educational careers have an additional resource.

Another outcome of the New Start programme has been greater attention to the management of data exchange. Those trying to take a multi-agency approach to provision for vulnerable young people have audited data management systems in different agencies and found incompatibilities in software, storage mechanisms, formatting and retrieval systems, cycles of data collection and processing, dissemination and accessibility; all of these have occurred both inter- and intra-agencies. Much has been learnt that is directly applicable to the education of looked after young people and there is some evidence of remedial action being taken – for example, common software protocols to protect confidentiality. However, the key issue underpinning all this is that the purpose of data collection must be clear to all and the interaction of these purposes must be equally transparent and understood. None of this activity will benefit vulnerable young people, not least looked after children, unless corporate parenting extends to all operational practices: the overall vision must inform the apparently mundane.

Furthermore, there is a challenge as regards awareness-raising. There is evidence that professionals will be reluctant to prepare data for exchange or respond to requests for data, where there are no mandatory requirements, unless they see the purpose in doing this. Thus the awareness-raising which is the first step in the development of an authority's strategy for the education of looked after children needs to be maintained (as new colleagues come into post, for example) and extended (as new initiatives come into operation). This is particularly important given that effective multi-agency partnerships are rarely static. In order to be responsive to needs as and when they arise, partnerships must be flexible and change their shape according to their particular function at any time (for example, whether they are strategic, advisory, operational, consultative or for the purposes of delivery).

There is evidence that looked after young people are significantly represented in projects which fall under the New Start programme. Interestingly, New Start Partnerships have themselves identified the fact that looked after young people are a distinct subgroup within those who are broadly labelled as "disaffected". The challenge for those specifically involved with looked after children is to judge the degree to which they should be transparent within these projects and the degree to which data sets should be disaggregated to show participation and outcomes for looked after young people. At a very pragmatic level, the authority concerned should be able to locate the education or training placements of all the young people whom it looks after. Equally, it should be interrogating these data. For example, is it satisfied with the proportion represented – is it too high or too low and what baseline data help to answer this question? What are the outcomes (if they are negative – that is, if the young person "failed" in the alternative provision – was this because he/she was given insufficient support or the placement was inappropriate)?

There are also challenges for the providers. Are they aware of the way in which the provision affects looked after young people? Should they be? Decisions here depend on there having been effective awareness-raising within an authority (see above). This should include awareness of needs as well as awareness of the sensitivity of the area: singling out looked after children within a group can be harmful and contrary to anything that that young person would wish for. On the other hand, there is evidence from work on alternative provision at Key Stage 4 (see Cullen *et al*, 2000) that apparently tiny factors can cause a young person to reject the offer of a placement which might be of immense value to him or her. Often, these factors are related to the young person's confidence or self-esteem. As looked after young people are often vulnerable in terms of social skills, it is critically important that there is adequate counselling from the appropriate person for these young people, in order to ascertain that the young person is not erecting barriers which, with support, could be eliminated.

Learning mentors

The Learning Mentors scheme, which is part of the Government's strategy of action directed towards the inner cities (DfEE, 1999), will focus on secondary-school pupils in six urban conurbations. Pupils will have access to a trained Learning Mentor responsible for identifying and removing any school or home-based barriers to an individual's learning. The mentor will be able to act as a one-stop shop for access to specialist support – something that research has shown is highly valued in existing support services for the education of looked after children (Fletcher-Campbell, 1997). The issues with which the mentor might deal include literacy, bullying, racial harassment and ensuring that a high achiever is challenged.

The aims of the initiative are fully in harmony with all that is known about effective practice for young people who are looked after: in particular, the stress on removing barriers, on meeting individual needs, and on multi-agency collaboration. Furthermore, it is intended that mentors support young people who are moving between secondary schools – something that often happens to young people who are looked after. However, these mentors need to be acquainted with the particular needs of looked after young people. Who will ensure that this is done, particularly in areas of the country where little has, as yet, been developed as regards the educational needs of looked after children?

Pastoral Support Programmes

Another initiative which may well support pupils who are looked after is the proposed Pastoral Support Programme; it is a planned and agreed intervention which is put into place if a pupil is at serious risk of exclusion, disaffection or involvement in criminal activity. It depends on assessment and a record of prior action, including the involvement of external agencies such as social services, health, careers, probation, youth and leisure. The guidance stresses that account should be taken of curricular, social and behavioural issues. Again, those responsible for initiating a programme (it is anticipated that this will generally be the school special educational needs co-ordinator) need to be aware of the particular needs of pupils who are looked after. Furthermore, there is the danger that pupils who are often "invisible", because of high levels of mobility or poor attendance, may not be eligible for interventions: for example, a pupil may not have been in a school for a sufficient length of time for there to be an adequate record of prior action.

Target-setting for schools

As part of the Government's programme to raise standards of attainment in schools, The Education Act 1997 required all schools to set and publish pupil performance targets annually. Detailed guidance was available (DfEE, 1997) on the target-setting process and this was later applied to pupils with special educational needs for whom the national targets might be inappropriate (DfEE, 1998). One of the messages that has come from experience of target-setting (and all other value-added measures) is that effective practice involves looking at the performance of both individuals and sub-groups within the broad age cohort so that there is no unidentified underachievement despite overall targets having been met. Some subgroups have long been recognised, for example, pupils for whom English is an additional language. Others may be appropriate only for certain schools. It is suggested that the performance of looked after young people should be routinely scrutinised in those schools for whom this is relevant and, moreover, that performance should be challenged in order to identify underachievement. It may be that extra attention and time needs to be given to the performance of looked after pupils as, in some cases (until the data collection required by Quality Protects becomes more firmly established), baseline data may be missing.

Again, what is required here is that schools consider the specific needs of their looked after pupils *within* what is a well-established exercise.

Initiatives led by other agencies

Recently, attention has been paid to the learning needs of young people who are looked after, as a consequence of an organisation's desire that their work be inclusive. Two examples are programmes sponsored by, respectively, the Basic Skills Agency and the Community Education Development Centre (CEDC); both are focused on basic skills. In both cases, the work draws on the substantial and proven experience of the agencies in working in the area of basic skills; thus the actual content of the programmes (such as the approaches to literacy or the materials used) are not under question, having been evaluated in other contexts. What is new is that both agencies have independently identified that there are barriers caused by low levels of basic skills among both young people who are looked after and their carers. This attention harmonises with the Who Cares? Trust *Book of My Own* project (Bald, Bean and Meegan, 1995), which has been replicated in various ways in other locations, and with a later initiative, *Breaking Their Fall*, in partnership with the National Literacy Association (Griffiths, 1999).

Such projects are particularly interesting for they have the potential to produce much needed evidence about the specific needs of the looked after population when addressing literacy and numeracy difficulties. While there is anecdotal evidence about low levels of literacy skills among looked after young people and this would seem to accord with such evidence as there is on the attainment of the population, there is less evidence about the extent to which general initiatives to improve literacy, for example, home–school partnership schemes, need to adapt to be inclusive for all holding the parental role and those living away from home.

Extension of the concept of corporate parenting

As pointed out above, we have learnt much about corporate parenting over the last decade and valuable developments have taken place and are taking place under Quality Protects (DoH, 1998). However, the concept has, in the main, been applied to collaboration between multiple services providing for individuals or groups of individuals – thus, social services, health, probation, education must collaborate around looked after young people. There is now evidence that the concept needs to extend even further so that all providers, whatever their over-riding brief, bear in mind the needs of the looked after population and examine their provision in terms of its accessibility, just as they might in terms of its applicability to young people from a particular ethnic group or with particular disabilities. This presents challenges in terms of awareness raising, for it means that considering the educational needs of looked after young people becomes a broad equal opportunities issue rather than something to be addressed by case work. But if these young people are to be looked after, corners cannot be cut. Previously, the problem was that the corners were not recognised. Now, they are clearly identifiable: negotiating them is not resource intensive but it does require that they are firmly on a range of maps.

References

Bald, J, Bean, J and Meegan, F (1995) *A Book of My Own*, London: Who Cares? Trust.

Cullen, M A, Fletcher-Campbell, F, Bowen, E, Osgood, J and Kelleher, S (2000) *Alternative Education Provision at Key Stage 4*, Slough: NFER.

Department for Education and Employment (DfEE) (1997) *From Targets to Action: Guidance to support effective target-setting in schools*, London: DfEE.

Department for Education and Employment (DfEE) /Qualifications and Curriculum Authority (DfEE/QCA) (1998) *Supporting the Target-setting Process: Guidance for effective target-setting for pupils with special educational needs*, London: DfEE.

Department for Education and Employment (DfEE) (1999) *Excellence in Cities*, London: DfEE.

Department of Health (1998) *Quality Protects: Transforming children's services*, *LAC(98) 28*. London: DoH.

Fletcher, B (1993) *Not Just a Name: The views of young people in foster and residential care*, London: Who Cares? Trust.

Fletcher-Campbell, F and Hall, C (1990) *Changing Schools? Changing People? The education of children in care*, Windsor: NFER-Nelson.

Fletcher-Campbell, F (1997) *The Education of Children who are Looked After*, Slough: NFER.

Griffiths, C (ed.) (1999) *Breaking Their Fall*, London: National Literacy Association in partnership with Who Cares? Trust.

Jackson, S (1987) *The Education of Children in Care*, University of Bristol: School of Applied Social Studies.

9 Developing equal chances
A whole authority approach

Howard Firth and Barbara Fletcher

Introduction

The educational experiences of children in public care throw a very harsh light on the systems and services which should be there to protect them and to help develop their potential. Getting it right for looked after children is about improving services for all children – because their experiences highlight how robust and inclusive policies and practice really are for all children.

The education of looked after children has moved steadily, and more recently speedily, up the policy agenda because of the welcome emphasis upon raising standards and tackling the causes of social exclusion. Broad policy themes of particular relevance to looked after children include:

- raising standards and tackling underachievement;
- an emphasis upon target-setting and planning;
- the recognition that particular groups are at risk of disaffection and social exclusion, and a range of policy initiatives aimed at promoting inclusion;
- an integrated approach to service provision;
- delivering efficient services which represent value for money.

The legislative framework is also clear. Local authorities have a duty under s22(3) of the Children Act 1989 to safeguard and promote the welfare of all children and young people who are looked after. One critical dimension of their welfare is their education. The School Standards and Framework Act 1998 places a duty on local education authorities to promote high standards and produce Education Development Plans (EDPs) setting out key targets and how they will be met.

The Government's Review of the Safeguards for Children Living Away from Home, undertaken by Sir William Utting in 1996 and reported on in *People Like Us* (1998), drew attention to the continuing educational underachievement of looked after children. The Government's response to the Children's Safeguards Review was unequivocal:

The Government is convinced that the quality of the public care system in which children are looked after by local authorities is unacceptably low.

A major three-year programme, Quality Protects, was launched in September 1998 (now extended by a further two years) to 'tackle problems of attitudes, standards, management, service delivery and training'. One of the programme's eight national objectives is:

To ensure that children looked after gain maximum life chance benefits from educational opportunities, health care and social care.

The work of the Social Exclusion Unit on Truancy and School Exclusion (1998) also emphasised the need for joined up solutions, especially for children in care, and recommended that 'effective education should be considered a key outcome of relevant social services work involving school age children'. It established an overarching target of reducing by one-third the numbers of permanent and fixed term exclusions by 2002, and a similar reduction in time lost to truancy.

These then are some of the policy drivers for local authorities set out in joint Government *Guidance on the Education of Children and Young People in Public Care* (DFEE/DH, 2000) supported by LAC (2000) 13. They are informed by and build upon the earlier research and inspection evidence outlined in Chapter 8. Together they provide a climate which is conducive to achieving measurable improvements for looked after children.

Better corporate parenting

If looked after children are to benefit from this positive climate, local authorities – their corporate parent – must be effective champions and ensure that they gain access to and benefit from the opportunities on offer.

This chapter sets out some of the essential steps local authorities, as corporate parents, need to take to improve the educational experiences and outcomes for children in their care. In doing so it draws upon collective experience of devising and developing a national initiative aimed at improving corporate parenting in relation to education, the Equal Chances Project, and the long-term experience of Hampshire's Education Support Service in providing a strategic framework as well as day-to-day support for looked after young people. It also draws heavily upon the views and ideas of looked after young people about what works best for them, and what gets in the way of them having an equal chance.

The Equal Chances Project was developed in response to growing evidence and concern about the serious underachievement of children in public care, most notably the findings of the joint inspection by the Social Services Inspectorate and OFSTED in 1995. The report concluded:

> If the standards of achievement of the children are to be improved, individual schools have to assume, in conjunction with the LEA, a greater responsibility for fostering and maintaining the partnership with the Social Services Department and developing strategies which promote achievement of the children. (SSI/OFSTED)

The project was developed by the Who Cares? Trust in collaboration with the Calouste Gulbenkian Foundation and supported by a consortium of Trusts and Foundations. It worked with two authorities, Bradford Metropolitan Authority and Brighton and Hove Council, to develop some key features of better corporate parenting, and to offer model processes to other local authorities.

A "whole authority approach" is a logical response to the demands of "corporate parenting". It recognises the collective responsibility of local authorities to achieve good parenting. Once a local authority has taken the difficult decision to remove a child from his or her family, it is the duty of the whole local authority to 'safeguard and promote his welfare' (Children Act 1989, s22(3)(a)). The whole local authority includes local education authorities.

Who is involved?

The range of individuals involved in corporate parenting, from a child's point of view, is potentially overwhelming. They include: elected members, senior officers and managers of the LEA and social services department; head teachers; school governors; social workers; residential social workers and foster carers; education social workers; teachers and learning support assistants; educational psychologists and education support personnel; fostering and family placement personnel; and parents and relatives. Local authorities may also have a Children's Rights Officer, and there may be mentors, guardians *ad litem* and independent visitors involved in the lives of looked after children, as well as other health professionals.

The extent of the involvement of these professionals will vary according to the needs and circumstances of the child. Some, like primary carers, teachers, and social workers will more directly influence a young person's educational progress than others. But all need to be aware of their collective responsibility in promoting and supporting educational opportunities and achievement. Corporate parenting is about articulating the actions and efforts of all those involved so that children and young people receive as seamless and non-stigmatising a service as possible.

A whole authority approach also recognises that fragmented services damage children's life chances. The case for more integrated services for children and families has been consistently made. The Audit Commission's (1994) report, *Seen but not Heard*, called for social services, health and education to publish joint plans to help improve services for children and families in need. Numerous subsequent inquiries, particularly in the field of special educational needs and mental health, have came to a similar conclusion.

Ownership and champions

Effective practice and research evidence demonstrate that effective collaboration and intervention cannot be achieved without a truly corporate effort – political ownership and leadership from senior management across the authority are essential.

Existing structures and decision-making arrangements within local authorities will affect the pace at which inter-agency working will progress. How informed are councillors about the experiences, needs and aspirations of young people in the care of the authority? The Equal Chances experience was that the interest and involvement of elected members proved critical to developing a whole authority approach. At the time a joint Education and Social Services sub-committee facilitated sharing of information and provided a forum for speedier decision-making. As local authorities modernise their committee structures it is to be hoped that opportunities to integrate services will be enhanced rather than diminished.

Practice experience has also shown that inter-agency working is best promoted by having someone working at the "interface" – across education and social services and forging positive relationships with schools. Research undertaken by NFER (Fletcher-Campbell, 1997) documents a wide range of practice examples, from discrete services to lone individuals with little power or influence to shape lasting change and improvement. This is perhaps the key: a champion for looked after children at local level has to have sufficient authority and corporate support to persistently challenge attitudes and practice, and effect change and sustained improvements. The project status of many valuable initiatives, combined with short-term funding, has meant that important gains in many authorities have not resulted in measurable improvements for young people and have failed to bed in to the system.

Corporate parenting principles

A whole authority approach should be underpinned by some key principles now set out in joint DfEE/DH guidance (2000):

Prioritising education

This is the message for all involved in corporate parenting. Education, and all that regular schooling offers, can help change lives. It is somewhere to develop self-confidence and skills, to receive praise and encouragement, to learn about and build relationships, and to achieve. It must be a central part of care planning and post-placement support.

Inclusion

Changing and challenging negative attitudes about looked after children is critical to improving outcomes. This means developing a whole authority approach which ensures that all looked after children are included within policy and practice developments that embrace all children at a service level. It also means ensuring that, wherever possible, looked after children's educational needs are met within the mainstream, and that assumptions are not made that they require separate and different provision. Children in public care are likely to span the full ability range. Their care experiences do not automatically mean that they will have behavioural and emotional difficulties. Many children have achieved educational success while suffering abuse prior to being looked after. However, children who do experience separation and loss – of any kind – are likely to have difficult feelings to resolve and will need understanding and support. They need adults who consistently value what they are good at and stress how important their education is whilst offering that support.

Achieving continuity and stability

School can provide an important source of stability in an otherwise turbulent and uncertain life. Numerous, and often unplanned, moves of placement are known to contribute to underachievement. Quality Protects has set targets to reduce placement moves and promote stability. Effective inter-agency working is critical to achieving these targets.

High expectations

Research has identified low expectations as one of the key barriers to achievement. It is partly a reflection of the low priority accorded to education in care planning. High expectations need to translate into: regular attendance; securing a school place without delay; homework and study support; and behaviour support where appropriate. It is also about the authority having explicit aspirations for the children in its care.

Early intervention

Avoiding delay and taking positive action quickly should be a shared objective of all involved in corporate parenting. Early intervention is preventive. Long periods out of school and unmet need are damaging. Early intervention also means that carers and Early Years providers should prioritise the education and learning opportunities of young children in their care.

Listening to children and young people

Much of what is known about the impact of care upon education comes from the young people themselves. They know what care feels like, they know what motivates and interests them, and what works best in terms of supporting their education.

Structures and policies: the key players in effective multi-agency working

The drive towards "joined-up services" moves the agenda away from discrete departmental functions to seeing social inclusion as a corporate responsibility. This is underpinned and enshrined within Best Value, Children's Services Plans, Education Development Plans and Quality Protects Management Action Plans. Together these provide a corporate framework which safeguards the interests and unfulfilled potential of looked after children.

In practice, shared commitment should be built around corporate parenting principles and set out in a policy endorsed by local authority departments and councillors. This gives a clear signal of authority-wide ownership.

The development of policy in Hampshire is based upon explicit statements, detailing how educational objectives are to be realised. First and foremost is an entitlement to full-time mainstream education. Policy needs to set out clearly the respective roles of all involved, including the designated teacher (see joint Guidance, Dfee/DH, 2000). It needs to also set out authority-wide targets which reflect local priorities and aspirations and clear strategies and protocols for ensuring equal access and monitoring arrangements for children who are placed outside the authority. An integral part of this is the development of Personal Education Plans (PEPs).

> *Every looked after child needs a personal education plan which ensures access to services and support; contributes to stability, minimises disruption and broken schooling; signals particular and special needs; establishes clear goals and acts as a record of progress and achievement.* (joint Guidance, DfEE/DH, 2000).

This plan is an essential tool in raising achievement and improving attendance and provides a basis for real dialogue between social workers, carers and schools and underlines the importance attached to the young person's education by everyone involved in corporate parenting.

Policy into action

Making it happen operationally is the ultimate challenge. Improving attendance and achievement is not simply a tracking exercise made possible by sophisticated databases. Local authority progress in this area is about the added value contributed by corporate action.

Hampshire is developing equal chances for its looked after young people by:

- challenging low expectations and negative stereotyping;
- supporting achievement and attendance through specific departmental strategies;
- developing and maintaining a corporate approach;
- engaging and retaining schools within the corporate parenting partnership;
- collating and celebrating success.

Of these, Hampshire's greatest challenge as a local authority is engaging and retaining schools within the corporate parenting partnership. We need to use all our corporate powers of persuasion as well as statute and guidance to ensure that children in our care have access to equal chances. The mechanism to help us achieve this is through designated teachers.

> *Schools should designate a teacher to act as a resource and advocate for children and young people in public care. LEAs and SSDs should*

co-ordinate suitable training for them and maintain an up-to-date list of designated teachers in schools in their area. (DfEE/DH, 2000, p 33)

It should ensure that every school:
- has a teacher with sufficient authority to make things happen;
- provides an advocate to access services and support;
- shares and supports high expectations;
- helps prevent unnecessary moves of school and minimises the chances of exclusion, through liaison with other agencies.

In putting the Guidance into practice, Hampshire regards the involvement of schools in corporate parenting as its greatest success. This has been achieved by the development of multi-service social inclusion partnerships within the county's seven social work areas. Initially created to improve communication between social services and schools, these groups have developed into a forum consisting of head teachers, social work managers, LEA and health authorities representatives, practitioners and young people, with the remit of promoting school and social inclusion at a local level. The critical elements in the success of these groups have been a joint commitment to preventive services and a corporate commitment to looked after young people which is specified within a service level agreement. A senior social work manager has chaired the forum.

The value for schools has been: the development of seven social work posts focusing on a joint approach to preventing exclusion from school; a regular newsletter keeping them in touch with developments and with each other; and the provision of multi-agency training for social services and education.

The value for children in care has been: jointly funded buddying and mentoring projects across all key stages; joint training opportunities in which looked after young people have participated; and a corporate carers' and children's home policy which sets out social services' commitment to schools and carers' expectations from education.

Consulting young people

Central to creating a culture that promotes equal chances is genuine consultation with "care users".

I moved around so many schools; the older I got the harder it was . . . in the end I hated school and left without GCSEs. (Participant in Big Mac consultation day for care leavers, Hampshire, July 1999)

If we are really serious about including young people in creating better services we need to utilise their first-hand experience, their insights and their common sense. Within the Equal Chances Project piloted in Brighton and Hove, a questionnaire devised by young people from a number of local authorities was sent out to all looked after children who were over five years old. Their responses told us that the majority of them liked school and attended regularly, that they had friends at school and parents who were proud of their achievements, but there was also a high incidence of bullying reported.

As a direct result of this pilot, an anti-bullying peer support scheme has been established in a local secondary school. If the scheme is effective it will be extended to all schools. Equally important, the findings of the questionnaire and process of developing it has led to the formation of a young people's reference group. They meet every three to four weeks and their views have been fed into the Quality Protects Management Action Plan. The group is in the process of making a video based upon their experiences of education and what they think needs to be done. They hope this can be used for training social services and education staff.

In Hampshire a similar group exists: the Care Action Team. Twelve young people aged between 13 and 18 are using their collective experience and excellent communication skills to make radical changes in perceptions of how children in care are viewed. They meet monthly (after school or college) to support one another and to plan ways of helping make school better for all young people in care. This group has:
- addressed the Who Cares? Trust Equal Chances Project launch alongside the Chief Inspector of Social Services, Denise Platt, and Sir William Utting, author of the Safeguards Review (Utting, 1998));

- worked as members in the county's Literacy Summer School;
- become core members of the county's Quality Protects Steering Group;
- provided training on key issues that affect young people in care;
- helped other local authorities establish user groups;
- promoted a positive image for children in care with head teachers and governors.
- helped launch the Draft Government Guidance on the education of children and young people in public care in June 1999.

The group has demonstrated the enormous value which looked after children's insights provide, and challenged the culture of negative stereotyping and low expectations. Their views have informed councillors and officers and have enabled Hampshire to set more challenging educational targets in both the Quality Protects and the Education Development Plan.

Information – on which to act

Lack of reliable information has prevented local authorities from having an overview of the needs of looked after children as a discrete group, and planning effectively for their needs. To achieve a whole authority approach, corporate parents need to be well informed about the progress, experiences and needs of children in their care, and have ways of sharing information effectively. Information at a strategic and individual level fuels improvements: 'Evidence once collected and presented is too powerful to ignore' (Fletcher-Campbell, 1997). Routine collection of evidence should also be part of how a local authority evaluates whether the strategies it has adopted are working.

In Hampshire sharing and celebrating improved test scores of looked after children has been an important part of achieving corporate ownership and of having high aspirations for the young people.

Parents know that attending school regularly improves children's life chances; that reading to them and hearing them read regularly improves their confidence with all their school work; and that regular contact with school helps parents to provide support and ask for additional help

167

when it is needed. Importantly, they remember the educational milestones in their child's life, the achievements, the problems and how they were overcome. This level of detail is needed in corporate parenting. It can only be achieved by social services, LEAs and schools sharing information which will help primary carers to supply the quality of day-to-day support that good parenting provides. It involves collecting baseline information needed to meet national targets. For each authority this includes:

- how many looked after children there are;
- what type of placement they are in;
- how many placement moves they have had;
- how many attend school regularly;
- how many are excluded from school;
- what their test scores and examination results are (SATs and GCSEs);
- how many do not have a school place;
- how many have a Statement of Special Educational Needs;
- how many are in mainstream school;
- how many young people over 16 are in education, training and employment.

Information should lead to action. Improved data should allow authorities, children's homes and schools to review policies and practice in the light of evidence. For instance, significant variation in admission difficulties or attendance rates should be immediately investigated. Many elected members are shocked to find that a disproportionate number of children in care are not educated in mainstream provision, and that no one has questioned why (see Chapters 12 and 13). Regular reports to elected members and school governors will form part of this process. As corporate parents they need to be informed and know the correct questions to ask.

The information needs of corporate parents

Gathering data on individual children only meets part of the information needs of corporate parents. A local authority needs to know where it is starting from in improving services for children: what is the level of knowledge of key corporate parent personnel involved in improving education. The Equal Chances Project piloted a corporate parenting questionnaire which was administered to a wide range of personnel in the two pilot authorities in order to establish what they knew about the children in their care; how they assessed and met their needs; and what they needed to do differently to improve services for them. The additional benefits of such an exercise are in building a whole authority approach, raising awareness, providing vital information and increasing ownership of the improvement process.

Similarly, the project piloted questionnaires for young people and for foster carers. The Young People's Questionnaire was drawn up by children in the care of different local authorities and gathers information about how being looked after affects education, views about school, and about whether you get the support you need. The information, once collated, is powerful and useful evidence with which to plan improvements and can be presented to elected members and officers by young people themselves. Local authorities need to establish methods of hearing from the young people in their care, either through questionnaires or by bringing groups of young people together regularly and involving them in the process of improving services.

Consulting carers and establishing their information, training and support needs in supporting the education of the young people in their care is another important piece of the information jigsaw. Joint training for social services and teachers, seminars for elected members, and training for school governors can all provide important information gathering as well as information giving opportunities for the local authority, and help build a whole authority approach.

Raising attainment

Hampshire has set the most exciting target of any local authority – we have done this because our children told us what they needed to achieve. (Andrew Seber, County Education Officer, 1999)

In the same way that good parents encourage their children to succeed, the whole authority needs to have clear aspirations for the children in its care.

The whole authority approach is not simply about putting policy and structures in place which make professionals feel better about working across departmental boundaries. It is also about achieving measurable improved outcomes for young people. Some ways in which this is done are: advertising and celebrating how well children do in their academic, recreational and vocational pursuits; developing strategies to raise literacy and numeracy; holding annual prize-giving or achievement days; initiating study support groups and homework clubs in children's homes and Family Centres; securing a school place in all cases without delay; and devising a corporate training programme for all employees which reinforces the commitment to raising standards for all children, including the children in the care of the authority.

Hampshire's Education Support Service has developed a range of strategies for raising attainments of looked after children. These include a Looking After Literacy Strategy which is a partnership with the National Literacy Association. The strategy for improving reading skills of children in residential and foster care includes:

- literacy targets included in the Quality Protects Management Action Plan;
- addressing poor literacy levels identified by specialist support teachers for looked after young people;
- providing a specialist teacher to support homework clubs in children's homes;
- providing additional books donated by the National Literacy Association to children's homes and foster carers;
- a week-long literacy summer school for 25 looked after children aged ten to 13 years;
- a training day for carers and children's home staff on literacy;
- a research project to raise the literacy levels of the two parallel groups of children in foster care and residential care.

Conclusion

The measures needed to raise the attainment of looked after children strengthen the system for all children, particularly those who may lack parental advocacy.

Valuing and supporting the education of children in public care is the single most important contribution a corporate parent can make to their lives, because it is about investing in and caring about their future, and recognising that education is their passport to better chances in life. (DfEE/DH, 2000)

References

Audit Commission (1994) *Seen But Not Heard: Co-ordinating child health and social services for children in need*, London: HMSO.

Department for Education and Employment (DfEE) and Department of Health (DH) (2000) *Guidance on the Education of Children and Young People in Public Care Local Authorities*, LAC (2000) 13, London: DfEE/DH.

Fletcher-Campbell, F (1997) *The Education of Children who are Looked After*, Slough: NFER.

Social Services Inspectorate (SSI) and Office of Standards in Education (OFSTED) (1995) *The Education of Children who are Looked After by Local Authorities*, London: SSI/OFSTED.

Social Exclusion Unit (1998) *Truancy and School Exclusion*, London: The Stationery Office.

Utting, Sir W (1998) *People Like Us: The report on the review of safeguards for children living away from home*, London: The Stationery Office.

10 Directing social work attention to education: The role of the *Looking After Children* materials

Tricia Skuse and Ray Evans

Introduction

The *Looking After Children* project is a long-standing research and development programme. It began in 1987 and has since passed through a number of stages. These have been extensively documented elsewhere (Parker *et al*, 1991; Ward, 1995, 1998a, 1998b; Jones *et al*, 1998). Briefly, the first stage (1987–91) was theoretical and resulted in the development of the Assessment and Action Records, a series of six age-related practice tools designed for use with children who are looked after. These records are made up of seven developmental dimensions along which children need to progress if they are to reach long-term well-being in adulthood: health, education, identity, family and social relationships, social presentation, emotional and behavioural development and self-care skills. Each dimension sets out a range of aims, activities and behaviours that any parent might expect a child to achieve. The purpose of the Records is to encourage awareness of outcomes for children in routine social work practice and to highlight, to those responsible, the probable consequences of different "parental" actions or omissions.

The second stage of the *Looking After Children* initiative (1991–95) involved the extensive piloting and revision of the Assessment and Action Records. A key finding from this stage of the project was that the Assessment and Action Records were unlikely to be routinely used if they were not embedded within a comprehensive system of information gathering, planning and review. The Essential Information Records, Care Plans, Placement Plans and Review Forms were subsequently developed which resulted in the full *Looking After Children* package that is currently available. All local authorities in England were then invited by the Department of Health to participate in a series of implementation cohorts aimed at introducing the materials into daily practice within children's services. Authorities also received a substantial package of financial and practical support during this transitional period (Jones *et al*, 1998). The implementation stage of the programme lasted three years (1995–98) with the result that all but four English authorities and all Welsh authorities have now adopted the *Looking After Children* (*LAC*) materials. There are also initiatives to develop, pilot and implement the materials in Scotland and Northern Ireland, as well as in a number of countries outside the United Kingdom (Ward, 1998b).

The fourth and final stage of the project is concerned with using the *LAC* materials to assess outcomes and developmental progress for looked after children. Following close consultation with managers, senior practitioners and information technology staff within a number of local authorities a number of key questions from the *LAC* forms have been identified for regular monitoring. A much wider group of questions from the *LAC* materials has also been selected for use in a research project conducted by Dartington Social Research Unit and Loughborough University. The objective of this study is to investigate how information recorded on the materials can be used by both managers and policy makers. The research study covers a wide range of developmental outcomes although the focus of this discussion will be education.

The research project comprises two databases:

i) Two snapshot samples of children looked after in six local authorities. This study is designed to explore how local authorities can tailor their services better to meet children's needs. The first snapshot took place on 1 April 1998; the second on 30 September 2000[1].

ii) A three-year follow-up of the first snapshot sample. The aim of this study is to track the care careers and psychosocial development of children who enter long-term care. Children who leave care or accommodation in the first year are also being followed up by interviews with the research team.

This chapter will highlight some of the main findings from the first of the two snapshot samples. Criteria for inclusion in the first sample were

---

[1] The date for data collection was changed from 1 April to 30 September in order to align with recent Government requirements for the returns from local authorities.

that children began their current care episode on or after 1 April 1996, they had been looked after for 12 months or more and were still looked after on 1 April 1998. That is, children had been looked after for between 12 and 24 months. These particular criteria were chosen to ensure that, as far as possible, like was being compared with like. It would have been inappropriate to compare children who had been looked after for many years with children who had only been looked after for 12 months. As the *LAC* materials were not fully implemented in all authorities until April 1996, this was agreed as the earliest admission date that would qualify for inclusion in the study. The authorities involved were chosen to be a representative sample of local authorities in England, both in terms of geography and level of urbanisation. Thus, findings presented here are considered to be a fair reflection of what is occurring in authorities more generally.

The Quality Protects Programme

Launched by the Department of Health in September 1998, the Quality Protects Programme is a three-year initiative (recently extended by a further two years) aimed at improving the management of services and the outcomes for children and young people in need. Based upon the ideology and theoretical constructs of *Looking After Children*, Quality Protects identifies eight objectives intended to improve all aspects of children's care experience including the stability of placements, child protection, health care, education and aftercare. For the purposes of this discussion we shall refer only to Objective Four which relates specifically to the education of looked after children:

Objective Four:

Children looked after gain maximum life chance benefits from educational opportunities, health care and social care.

Associated with this objective is a National Priorities Guidance target which sets out precisely the level of improvement local authorities are expected to achieve:

Improve the educational attainment of children looked after, by increasing to at least 50 per cent by 2001 the proportion of children leaving care at 16 or later with a GCSE or GNVQ qualification; and to 75 per cent by 2003.

As a consequence of these new measures, authorities are now obliged to submit to the Department of Health data regarding the National Curriculum attainment levels and GCSE/GNVQ results for all their looked after children. This would appear to be an important step forward in promoting the educational development and progress of children looked after away from home. The unsatisfactory education of this population of children and young people has been well documented (Berridge and Cleaver, 1987; Fletcher-Campbell and Hall, 1990; Jackson, 1994; Ward, 1995; Flynn and Biro, 1998). Ward (1995) notes that at a time when the focus for non-looked after children is upon educational progress and subsequent employment, the emphasis for many looked after children is upon the relationship with their families. Whilst appropriate contact with families is clearly an important area and should remain so, it is unfortunate that children's education often remains a substantially lower social work priority. Flynn and Biro (1998) conclude that 'children in care need earlier, more intensive, and more effective educational assistance both to prevent the development of problems and to improve their chances for success' (p 232). Without this support, educational outcomes for looked after children are likely to continue to lag behind their non-looked after peers. The Quality Protects Programme for the first time raises monitoring the educational development of children in need to a statutory level. Authorities which have implemented the *LAC* materials should, theoretically, already have the information available. GCSE and GNVQ attainment levels should be recorded in the Essential Information Record and SATs results should be annually noted in the Assessment and Action Record.

While indicators such as those required under Quality Protects provide information concerning children's educational progress, and offer useful targets for improvement, they remain a relatively crude measure of outcome. In particular, they cannot be interpreted fully unless set alongside other contextual information concerning both the vulnerabilities or needs of this group of children and the extent to which the service they receive is likely to meet those needs. That is, in order to make a comprehensive assessment of whether children are making progress commensurate with their age the following other information also needs to be gathered:

i)   Background data regarding children's innate or acquired vulnerability (for example, the prevalence of learning disabilities or developmental delay, the numbers of children with behavioural problems which might impede satisfactory progress, the proportion of children for whom English is not their first language, whether they have a history of abuse).

ii)   The extent to which an authority is able to compensate for such vulnerabilities via the provision of statements of special educational need, mental health support or special language tuition.

iii) The extent of organisational risk factors which impede satisfactory service delivery (for example, frequent changes of social worker, frequent placement change, the relationship between placement change and school change, school exclusion).

Results[2]

Sample

The sample comprised 249 cases; 139 (56 per cent) males and 110 (44 per cent) females. The mean age at entry into the current episode of care/accommodation was 7.00 (s.d. 5.26). The age of the children was much younger than first anticipated, perhaps reflecting the fact that teenagers tend not to stay in care/accommodation for extended periods but rather come in and out of the care system on shorter episodes.

Implementation of the *LAC* materials and the recording of educational outcomes

Before any analysis and discussion of the findings can be undertaken, it is necessary to examine the extent of implementation of the *LAC* materials (see Figure 1).

---

[2] This paper was submitted in August 1999. During subsequent waves of data collection, the construction of the sample was altered slightly. Results presented here reflect the data as they stood at submission. There may be some discrepancy with findings reported elsewhere.

Figure 1
Implementation of *LAC* materials

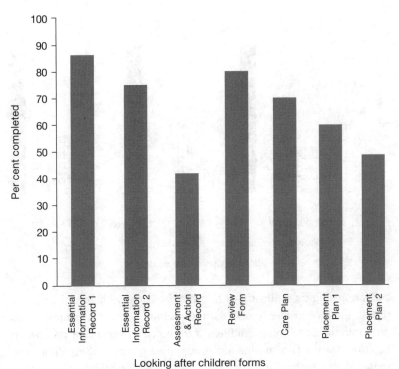

Looking after children forms

As can be seen in Figure 1, the use of the records varied. The Essential Information Records yielded a much higher level of completion than did the Assessment and Action Records. This is an important finding as information regarding children's SATs results are contained in the Assessment and Action Records and without these forms on file it was extremely rare that details regarding children's educational progress had been recorded at all. However, the presence of an Assessment and Action Record on the case file did not necessarily mean that all sections had been completed. In many cases the questions regarding National Curriculum attainment levels were left uncompleted. The end result of this was that there were substantial missing data in this first year of

Figure 2

Recorded SATs results in English, Maths and Science for children aged 5–9 years

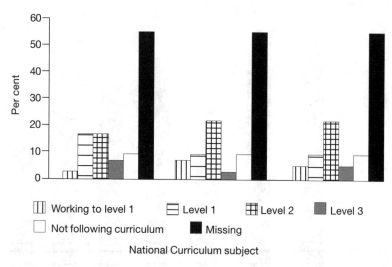

collection. Figure 2 illustrates this more clearly with regard to SATs results for five to nine year-olds. Information on 53 per cent of cases was unavailable. Similar findings were noted in other age groups. In addition, for the five to nine age group, nine per cent of children were reported not to be following the National Curriculum, presumably because of a disability.

Information regarding the GCSE results for the over 16s is recorded in the Essential Information Record 2. Figure 1 might suggest that there should be less of a problem with missing data given that most case files contained this form. Unfortunately this was not the case. Much of the information covered in the Essential Information Record 2 requires regular updating; for example, immunisation history, GCSE results, criminal convictions and cautions, and in many cases records had not been attained. Of the 27 young people aged 16 or above who had sat their GCSEs, there were missing data for 30 per cent of them. According to the information provided, only eight (30 per cent) in this age group had attained a GCSE grade C or above (see Table 1). It is possible that

Table 1
GCSE results for young people aged 16 years and over

	Frequency	*Percentage*
No GCSEs	6	22
Some GCSEs but none above grade C	1	4
1–4 GCSEs grade C or above	4	15
5 or more GCSEs grade C or above	4	15
Not following curriculum	4	15
Missing data	8	30

this figure is higher and closer to the 50 per cent target set by Quality Protects but without information from the missing cases it is difficult to draw any conclusions.

Vulnerability factors

Findings for the contextual data were more illuminating. There was much less missing data, to the extent that it was statistically acceptable to omit the missing data from the analysis and base percentages upon the information that was available. While for the first year's data it has not been possible to examine how children's vulnerability factors relate to attainment, it has been possible to get a much clearer picture of the nature and extent of need across the looked after population and speculate how this might influence educational progress targets.

Children with ongoing health conditions or disabilities

If children's educational progress is to be accurately monitored, a key piece of contextual information that also needs to be gathered is the presence of ongoing health conditions or disabilities. Children with chronic conditions may perform less well at school than their healthy peers. As can be seen from Figure 3, learning disability represents the largest single health-related obstacle, affecting 18 per cent of the sample. This represents a sizeable percentage of the looked after population that may require specialist support. Moreover, the high prevalence of learning disability is likely to affect local authorities' ability to meet the Quality Protects targets set for the educational achievement of children looked after as children will be likely to progress at a slower rate. It is worth noting that the definitions of a learning disability used here are those of the social workers recording the original information. Such definitions are, of course, open to a wide variety of interpretations and another research study investigating interpretations of terms regularly used in social work practice is currently under development.

Figure 3

Ongoing health conditions or disabilities (not discrete)

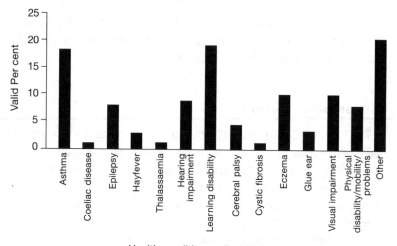

Health condition or disability

Hearing disability and visual impairment each affected nine per cent of the sample – conditions which may also influence children's educational attainment, especially if adequate support and intervention are not provided. Unfortunately, further details regarding the severity of conditions such as asthma or ezcema are unavailable. If extreme these conditions may also impede schooling.

Many children were suffering from more than one condition: 13 per cent of children had two health conditions that were ongoing when they entered care/accommodation and 14 per cent of children were experiencing three or more conditions. It would be reasonable to suppose that educational progress is likely to be much more difficult for these children than it is for children without health problems.

First language

A child's ability to achieve educationally will undoubtedly be affected by their familiarity with the language in which they are being taught. If a child is learning in their second, third or even fourth language that they only get to use when at school, it is likely that they will progress at a much slower pace than their peers for whom English is their mother tongue. From this analysis, however, language barriers do not appear to be a widespread problem. Findings indicate that 97 per cent of the sample had English as their first language. Bengali, Punjabi and "other" accounted for the remaining three per cent.

Behavioural problems

A high percentage of children in the sample displayed some kind of behavioural problem. As of 1 April 1998, the case files of 50 per cent of

Table 2
Type and prevalence of behaviour problems (not discrete)

Problem behaviour	Frequency	Percentage noted at 1.4.98 (not discrete)
Conduct problem (not related to ongoing health condition)	78	33%
Conduct problem (related to health condition)	4	2%
Conduct problem (unclear if related to health)	1	0.4%
Self-harming behaviour	19	8%
Inappropriate sexual behaviour	19	8%
Relationship problems	18	8%
Anxiety	14	6%
Bedwetting (related to anxiety)	14	6%
Bedwetting (related to health)	4	2%
Concentration problems	7	3%
Other problem	8	3%

children (for whom data were available) indicated behavioural patterns that had been of concern, with many children displaying multiple problems. The types of behaviours and the rates of occurrence as noted by the research team are indicated in Table 2. As can be seen conduct problems (temper tantrums, aggressiveness, offending, absconding, defiance) were the most prevalent.

Protective factors

Authorities' ability to compensate for some of the vulnerabilities listed above were also investigated. It is encouraging to note that 84 per cent of children with learning disabilities were either pending or had already been made the subject of a statement of special educational need. Nevertheless, 16 per cent of learning disabled children had no assessment or statement or their statement had now expired. It is unclear from this analysis whether these children were receiving any additional educational support.

While not all behavioural problems recorded necessitated mental health intervention, children with problems which present the greatest amount of difficulties to local authorities did appear to have access to mental health support. Children with conduct problems (lying, defiance, absconding, temper tantrums), inappropriate sexual behaviour (pre- cocious behaviour, prostitution, promiscuity) and self-harming behaviours (cutting, scratching, substance abuse, suicide attempts, severe eating disorders) were all significantly more likely to be seeing a mental health professional than children not exhibiting these behaviours (Fisher's Exacts 0.004; 0.036 and 0.001 respectively) (Ward and Skuse, 1999). Despite these findings 57 per cent of children with inappropriate sexual behaviour and 36 per cent of self-harmers were not receiving any support from mental health services. Fortunately this only applied to a relatively small number of cases. Nevertheless, one must question whether, without such intervention, these children were going to be able to make full use of the educational experiences available to them.

Risk factors

Just under 20 per cent of over five-year-olds had been excluded from school either permanently or temporarily in the preceding term. Obviously this will have implications for their educational progress. If children are not in school they are unlikely to do as well as their school attending peers. Both temporary and permanent exclusions entail disruption and discontinuity in school work and often indicate other more fundamental problems with children's behaviour.

School disruption is also often associated with placement change. While parents of children living in the community can try to ensure that a change of address does not necessarily entail a change of school, this strategy is often unavailable to social service departments which are restricted by the availability of suitable foster carers or residential units. An analysis of the number of placements experienced in the first 12 months of the care episode showed that, while most children had only experienced one or two placements since admission, nearly 28 per cent had experienced three or more placements (Ward and Skuse, 1999). For this group of children especially, the potential for duplication or omission of key material on the National Curriculum seems large, as does the risk of children becoming detached and withdrawn from the educational process.

Implications for local authorities

The findings presented above produce a mixed picture. While information regarding the vulnerabilities of looked after children does seem to be available on children's case files, details regarding National Curriculum attainment levels were scant. Reasons for the omissions were varied. In many cases completion of the Assessment and Action Record did not appear to have been attempted. In other instances, Records were completed but unavailable, being stored in a separate cupboard or with the foster carer. Essential Information Records usually held information with regard to family history, legal status or reason for being looked after but details about young people's qualifications were often left blank. It does not appear to be the case that the information was recorded elsewhere on the children's files. Where information was unavailable on the *LAC* forms, the research team examined the whole case file in the event that details had been filed separately. Thus, findings for educational attainment reflect a review of the whole case file not just the *LAC* materials. The sparsity of information may suggest that the low priority for education amongst social workers indicated by Ward (1995) is continuing, or it may simply be a problem of co-ordination between education and social service departments. Whichever it may be, the Quality Protect initiative will require a change in practice. In some authorities this has taken the form of re-training social work staff on the timings, content and results of assessment in school: what is a SATs result?; when do they become available?; what do the different levels mean? Other authorities have taken a broader approach and introduced a comprehensive system of co-ordinating information that not only allows them to meet their Quality Protect targets but also permits a much fuller understanding of the education of children looked after away from home. One of these authorities is Coventry and an account of their experiences of implementing such a system is given below.

Monitoring the education of children looked after in Coventry

Research into the education of children looked after in Coventry began during 1996. This was in response to the joint report by the Social Services Inspectorate and the Office for Standards in Education (SSI/OFSTED, 1995). At that time, as in most local authorities, there were almost no hard data about the educational attainments and progress of children in care. Anecdotal information, however, suggested that they were likely to be poor. Alongside the quantitative research, therefore, was a drive to establish effective alliances between the Social Services Department (SSD), the Local Education Authority (LEA) and schools. This was to take purposeful action to improve the educational outcomes for this group of disadvantaged young people.

The research plan
The plan was to include all children looked after, for any length of time, in the month of June 1996 and repeat this process in the following three

years. The data gathering would include: school placement details such as type (e.g. mainstream, special school for children with emotional or behavioural difficulties); academic attainments (Standard Assessment Tasks or GCSEs); the extent of any special educational needs (Stage of the Special Educational Needs Code of Practice); plus attendance and exclusions data. Information on current care status and placement was also included, as were some historical data, for example, the number of changes of school and care placements, and the total duration in care.

The starting point

A major hurdle in the early years of the research was establishing an accurate list of looked-after children. The SSD database did not contain the names of every child who was actually being looked after, and many that were listed had left the care of the local authority. Once a relatively accurate list had been determined, together with other essential information such as date of birth, gender and ethnicity, the LEA was asked to provide the educational information listed in the research plan. It was necessary to go through this process as the SSD was not in a position to provide any educational information. There was not even a "field" on the SSD database for the name of the school. Similarly, the database held by the LEA had no indication as to which young people were looked after and, therefore, could offer no analysis of the attainments and progress of children in the care system.

This approach resulted in less than 50 per cent of the required data being made available. There were a variety of reasons for such a poor return from the LEA, for example: children being recorded under different names; errors in dates of birth; frequent changes of school (resulting in no school providing the LEA with information); and a significant number (16 per cent) being placed in schools outside the City. Other databases held by the LEA, such as that held by Special Education, were examined to find out, at the very least, the name of the school the young person attended. Finally, if all else failed, individual social workers were asked for the name of the school. Missing data were then requested directly from the school by fax, often accompanied by a telephone conversation with head teachers.

This whole operation proved to be extremely time consuming and expensive. Nor was this situation unique to Coventry. Other researchers have drawn attention to similar difficulties, e.g. Berridge and Brodie (1996), Fletcher Campbell (1997) and Christmas (1998).

Small steps to improvement
The difficulty in collecting information, and the implications inherent in this lack of focus on education, began to be more widely recognised within the local authority, and an inter-departmental working group was established. One outcome was a change in the Statutory Review Process. From that time Reviewing Officers were given the responsibility to collect a basic data set of education and health information, and to ensure that plans were made to address any identified problem areas. This basic data set included the name of the school attended; its type and address and whether it was out of the City; attendance and exclusion information; and Stage on the Special Educational Needs Code of Practice. In effect, this was a sub-set of the *LAC* materials.

The next significant development in Coventry took place in September 1997 when the SSD directly employed a specialist teacher. One of the responsibilities of this post was to monitor the educational progress of looked-after children in residential accommodation.

Bigger steps
Following the publication of a second report by Sir William Utting (1997), resources were made available to establish a service, Education Access, dedicated to raising the achievements, and promoting the inclusion, of all looked after children. The service came into existence in September 1998 and consists of an educational psychologist, three teachers and an education welfare officer. The service has a role in developing policy, improving professional practice, and working directly with individual children. Work on developing policy has, for example, resulted in a substantial section on looked after children being included within the LEA's Educational Development Plan.

Schools have been encouraged to identify a 'Co-ordinator for Looked-After Children' who is then trained alongside nominated colleagues from the local SSD office. Responsibilities of these new posts include raising awareness amongst the whole staff group, monitoring the performance of looked after children, and taking positive steps to ameliorate some of the difficulties they experience.

The introduction of the Quality Protects initiative in September 1998 re-emphasised the need for collecting and reporting data within the whole authority. The Education Access Service now has an interim role in the process of monitoring the progress of all children in the care system, while helping the local authority develop more efficient methods for achieving the same ends.

It is likely that the difficulties in data gathering that have been encountered in Coventry will feature in most authorities across the country. Coventry's experiences lead one to suggest that a possible solution would be for authorities to establish a co-ordinating group with a senior officer representing each arm of the organisation. This group would be aware of all the reporting requirements and ensure that actions were taken to capture the necessary data in a form that would be useful. Moreover, the transfer of information from education to social services would be made considerably simpler if each database had some common elements. One possibility would be the "Unique Identifier" given to each child by the Department for Education and Employment (DfEE) in Autumn 1999. This would assist in tracking children within and between local authorities, and overcome some of the problems, such as changes of name. However, there are still some unresolved issues between the DfEE and the Data Protection Registrar about the acceptability of using a unique identifier and the transfer of information between agencies. Unfortunately, this matter was not addressed within the draft guidance on looked after children published by the DfEE in June 1999. Although, the statutory Guidance on the Education of Children and Young People in Public Care issued in 2000 does require all local authorities to establish and maintain a protocol for sharing relevant information about care, placements and education (DfEE/DH, 2000). Whatever proves to be an acceptable way forward with respect to data protection, there will always be human factors to consider in establishing and maintaining an accurate information base. Fundamentally, the database will have to be useful to the personnel inputting the data, otherwise it will be received as an additional burden rather than a helpful management tool.

Conclusions

Having considered some of the findings from the *Looking After Children* study and examined how one authority has endeavoured to improve the monitoring of the education of looked after children, what conclusions can be drawn? The *LAC* materials would appear to represent an important tool in directing social work attention towards the education of looked after children. Nevertheless, evidence from this first wave of data collection has revealed significant gaps in the recording of educational progress. While authorities appeared to have a reasonable level of information regarding the extent of children's needs and the services designed to meet these needs, without accurate recording of children's educational progress they will not be able to examine the relationship between the two. Without regular recording of children's attainments it will be impossible to determine the value of intervention. Does the provision of mental health support lead to better outcomes for children? Do children whose first language is not English perform less well than their peers? Does access to additional language tuition improve their attainment? Do children with certain health conditions or disabilities get their GCSEs? Findings from subsequent follow-ups are, however, beginning to answer some of these questions.

Some authorities are endeavouring to meet their Quality Protects targets by submitting *en bloc* statistics regarding attainment received from education departments. While this meets the formal requirements of the authority, it does mean that the potential for promoting the education of individual children is lost. Without records of children's achievement on case files, education will remain a low priority in social work practice. The *LAC* materials allow authorities the opportunity not only to monitor if they are reaching their Quality Protects targets but also permits them to investigate why they may not be. The materials are currently under revision. The revisions are being developed alongside a range of assessment materials which together will provide a streamlined programme for monitoring children from the point of referral. Such a programme will provide a more co-ordinated system of care provision and will also allow authorities to record baseline data against which children's progress can be assessed.

The Guidance referred to above (DfEE/DH, 2000) following consultation in May 2000 encourages a greater collaboration between social service and education departments. In future every school should have a designated teacher to liaise with social services and every child will have an individual education plan which outlines both long and short-term goals and aspirations. Experiences within Coventry would appear to support this kind of approach but also indicate the need for co-ordination to be taken one stage further. Having a team of people dedicated to improving the education of looked after children, without competing demands on their time, appears to have moved the local authority forward more rapidly than would otherwise be the case.

References

Berridge, D and Brodie, I (1996) *The Education of Young People in Residential Care*, Luton: University of Luton.

Berridge, D and Cleaver, H (1987) *Foster Home Breakdown*, Oxford: Blackwell.

Christmas, L (1998) 'Looking After Learning: making a difference for young people in care', *Education and Child Psychology*, 15:4, pp 79–90.

Department for Education and Employment (DfEE)/Department of Health (DH) (2000) *Guidance on the Education of Children and Young People in Public Care Local Authorities*, London: DfEE/DH.

Fletcher-Campbell, F (1997) *The Education of Children who are Looked After*, Slough: NFER.

Fletcher-Campbell, F and Hall, C (1990) *Changing Schools? Changing People?: The education of children in care*, Slough: NFER.

Flynn, R and Biro, C (1998) 'Comparing developmental outcomes for children in care with those for other children in Canada', *Children & Society*, 12:3, pp 228–33.

Jackson, S (1994) 'Educating children in residential and foster care', *Oxford Review of Education*, 20, pp 267–79.

Jones, H, Clark, R, Kufeldt, K and Norrman, M (1998) 'Looking After Children: Assessing outcomes in child care – the experience of implementation', *Children & Society*, 12:3, pp 212–22.

Parker, R, Ward, H, Jackson, S, Aldgate, J and Wedge, P (1991) *Looking After Children: Assessing outcomes in child care*, London: HMSO.

Social Services Inspectorate/OFSTED (1995) *The Education of Children Who are Looked After by Local Authorities*, London: Social Services Inspectorate/ OFSTED.

Utting, Sir W (1997) *People Like Us: The report on the review of safeguards for children living away from home*, London: The Stationery Office.

Ward, H (1995) *Looking After Children: Research into practice*, London: HMSO.

Ward, H (1998a) 'Assessing outcomes in child care: an international perspective', Editorial, *Children & Society*, 12:3, pp 151–54.

Ward, H (1998b) 'Using a child development model to assess the outcomes of social work interventions with families', *Children & Society*, 12:3, pp 202–11.

Ward, H and Skuse, T (1999) *Looking After Children: Transforming data into management information, Report for first year of data collection*, Totnes: Dartington Social Research Unit.

11 The effects of trauma on childhood learning

Kate Cairns

The intense stress of attachment deprivation, abuse and other childhood traumas causes brain and body injuries, which give rise to physical, emotional, cognitive and behavioural symptoms. Children can present difficulties which perplex and frustrate teachers and carers. Knowing about trauma does not solve the problems, but it does provide a robust theoretical model from which to develop more effective and appropriate ways of living and working with children who have suffered such harm.

First thoughts: a day in foster care

For children who suffer the disorders which follow infant and childhood trauma, nothing, absolutely nothing, is easy or straightforward. Today breakfast has come and gone and he has not appeared. Yesterday, our day of rest, he arrived in our room at 5.00 a.m. with mugs of coffee. 'I wanted to do something for you. Aren't you pleased?'

Struggling to sit up in bed, I remember when we used to sleep naked, limb against limb, the friendliness of it. Those days ended with fostering, which could be sponsored by the makers of flannelette nighties. Struggling, too, to find a calm voice, knowing he truly means well, has no access to the same basic understanding of others that most of us happily take for granted. 'It's a good thought, but we still need to sleep, Shane. You go back to bed, and we'll have a drink together later.'

Slam. Crash. Coffee and mugs meet wall and carpet. A meeting which will lead to a permanent relationship if I don't get up and do something about it. And I have to get him to help me, get him to stay connected and take responsibility for what he has done. At five o'clock in the morning. Please can I have an easier job in my next lifetime? Wrestling bears or breaking rocks come to mind.

This morning is a not-getting-up day, however. It is also a visit-from-my-social-worker and a finding-out-my-mum-still-doesn't-want-to-see-me day. Perhaps these things are connected. Tim offers to go and wake Shane. I think his usual method, as regularly applied to older brother David, of six ice cubes down the back of the neck, while effective, might not be quite what Shane needs today.

Stern compassion seems to be closer to the mark. 'Shane!' I yell from the bottom of the stairs, 'I've made your sandwiches, ironed your shirt, and if you're not up and about in five minutes there'll be consequences!' I'm good on consequences. Sounds horrible, means nothing, and judged properly is nearly always effective. My father, a headmaster, used to threaten there would be 'blood on the moon', but I take after the less violent side of the family.

Colin puts his arms round me. 'Do I need to shout at him?' 'No, I think that will have done the trick,' I say, listening to the morning litany of swearwords moving towards the bathroom. 'Then I'll take the dog for a walk,' he says, matching the actions to the words as she enthusiastically endorses the idea. On a morning like this, it would not do to leave Shane and the dog in the same space. He will fall over her, drop scalding tea on her, "accidentally" tread on her, in any case she will end up hurt and he will protest vigorously, and for all I know accurately, innocence of any intention to do harm.

David, ringing home at lunch time, 'There's been some sort of fight in the school yard. I think you might need to ring school and sort something out.' 'Do you know what it's about?' 'I think Shane might be in some sort of trouble.' Tactful, this one. Not about to drop anyone in anything they haven't stirred up for themselves.

I ring Janice, the school secretary, a regular contact after all these years. She won't make mountains out of molehills, I know I can trust her judgement. 'I'm glad you've rung. The head of year was wondering whether to bring you in or deal with it himself. I think he'd like you to come in.'

We meet in a classroom, the tutor, the head of year and Shane gathered around a table at the front of the room as I arrive. Shane is wearing his blank defiance look. Uh oh. This does not bode well. The story is that Shane has stolen a pencil case belonging to another boy. The boy demanded it back. Shane denied all knowledge of the theft, the pencil case and anything else relevant or irrelevant to the matter under discussion. A fight ensued.

Once the tutor became involved, he asked Shane to turn out the contents of his bag. There the missing pencil case was found. Shane, however, was adamant that the pencil case was his, and that he had stolen nothing. Since the pencil case had the name of the other boy inside it, as well as a dozen pens with his initials and a calculator with his name stamped on it, Shane's story sounds a little thin. Except that he is so convincingly certain that this pencil case belongs to him, and so evidently bewildered that anyone fails to believe him.

Thank goodness David rang me. The school staff, to their great credit, are patiently continuing to exercise reason and rationality with Shane. I know that they could do this forever and it would take them no further. I pick up the pencil case and look at Shane until I am sure he is making eye contact with me. 'Shane, this pencil case belongs to . . .' quick check inside to get my facts right 'Daniel. It is blue. Your pencil case is red. Where is your red pencil case, Shane.' 'I think it's on my dressing table.' 'Right. You can put it in your bag tonight and make sure you have it for tomorrow. Now we'll give this one back to Daniel and you can say sorry. Then perhaps Mr. Johnson will lend you a pen for today.'

I look at the teachers. They look surprised, but seem prepared to go along with this solution. The "fight" was really a scuffle, and no one has been hurt. Shane gives the pencil case back to Daniel, and apologises so pleasantly that I should think I am the only one who knows he still has no real idea of what he's done.

Shane arrives home cheerful. 'Have you had a good day?' I ask, interested. 'Yeah, great. We watched a video in English.' He looks back at me with a face innocent of all guile. He genuinely has construed this as a good day, and that is how he will remember it. We have some work to do on this, I make a mental note, but not right now.

His social worker is due to arrive at any moment. I suggest we put the kettle on to make tea and biscuits for him, and Shane takes up the task with enthusiasm. He likes seeing his social worker. This is one of his most successful and comfortable relationships. He is central to it, and is clearly the focus of care and concern within it, yet it remains occasional and therefore superficial and, most importantly for Shane, it is a relationship in which his actions do not have evident consequences.

I am grateful for this on his behalf. Grateful, too, that here we have a local authority still able to provide some service to the children it looks after.

After they have gone off to the burger bar, or pizza palace, or wherever else is serving its turn as a social work office, the rest of us gather for the evening meal. These occasional breaks allow us to have meals together without the continual jolting reminders of the painful gaps in Shane's understanding of the most basic things about the ways human beings relate to one another. He is intelligent and sensitive and loving. And at some very early stage of his development he missed out on vital and fundamental learning.

Day by day he makes us aware of the basic relational skills which otherwise we would take entirely for granted. Non-verbal signals and simple relational sensitivities are nearly all missing for him. Trust is missing. Fun and playfulness are missing. Curiosity and interest in the world around him are missing.

In place of all these he is left with a massive defensive egocentricity, and a divided self which simply cannot take responsibility or make plans since the left hand has no idea what the right hand has done, is doing, or may be going to do. Yet with strangers he appears open and friendly and trusting. His beautiful spaniel eyes gaze adoringly at anyone who might let him call them his friend. We, who love him, are afraid for him.

Now he arrives bouncing and spluttering with excitement. He has, by agreement, gone on from his meeting with his social worker to play in the park. There he has met up with a friend. Wants to go back to his friend's house. Wants us to lend his friend a bicycle to make the journey easier. 'Who is your friend, Shane?' 'Oh, he lives up the other side of the estate. He's in my class at school.' 'What's his name?' He looks at me blankly. 'I forgot to ask him. Oy!' he shouts towards the front door 'What's your name? The old dear wants to know!'

'Shane,' I begin, thinking I ought at least to try, 'friends are people we know well. People we like and trust. Not just . . .' I give up. This is a time for decision not explanation. 'No,' I say, 'the answer's no. But you can bring him in and introduce him to me, and he can stay here for a while if you like.' Happy enough with this, he brings in a bedraggled waif, and proudly introduces him, having checked his name afresh in the hallway. I give them both drinks and biscuits, and Colin takes them off for a game of snooker.

Bedtime brings tantrums. The social worker had brought news of fresh rejections, as we knew he would. Now, at last, in the peace and quiet of the ending of the day, the message sinks in. 'Come on, Shane, time you were thinking of bed,' I suggest. 'You shut your face,' he explodes, 'leave me alone. You're not my mum. I hate you. Just leave me alone.' Colin steps in, his quiet voice almost always effective in this situation. 'That's enough, Shane. Go to your room. We'll talk about it later if you want to.' Shane stamps upstairs, slams one door, two doors, turns on his radio at full volume. We wait, look at one another, wait a little longer. Sigh thankfully as the music is turned down. Now Colin will go and see if Shane wants to talk. 'Remember to make sure he packs his pencil case in his bag,' I say, as I wander off to find my own quiet corner of the household.

The nature and effects of traumatic stress

Any threatening or demanding event will cause us to generate stress hormones. This instant physiological response to our recognition that demands are to be made upon us enables us to function most efficiently and to survive in a difficult environment. The stress hormones thus produced tone up our brains and bodies to respond rapidly and effectively to challenging stimuli and increase our capacity to notice, engage with and respond to others of our kind who may be enlisted as allies in our struggles. Moderate amounts of stress heighten our effectiveness physically, psychologically and socially (Goleman, 1996).

Traumatic events generate stress of quite a different order. These are events which are, or are perceived to be, so threatening to the life or physical integrity of self or others that the person confronted with them reacts with fear, helplessness or horror (Kinchin, 1998). Horrific events in our environment produce an intense stress response in us. This automatic response to terrifying events, known as traumatic stress, is so intense that the levels of stress hormones produced are toxic. Under the impact of traumatic stress we are poisoned by our own physiological survival response. The brain and body are injured at this level of toxicity, producing permanent and irreversible alterations in physical, psychological and social functioning.

Traumatic stress causes serious injuries to brain and body. In the developing child these injuries are even more serious and pervasive in their effects than in the mature adult. Most children who suffer trauma, however, will recover spontaneously. To do so they need three conditions to be met. They must be in a safe place with people they trust and to whom they are securely attached; that allows for the first phase of recovery – stabilisation. Then they must be able to communicate what has happened to them, and the distress it causes them – integration. And finally, they must be able to experience the joy and delight of social reintegration – the phase of post-integrative development or adaptation.

Children in public care are very likely to have suffered traumatic stress. In infancy, separation from the primary caregiver may in itself be enough to constitute trauma. Developmentally the infant is utterly dependent on the care of adults, and will be forming the attachment relationships which are the foundation of so many vital structures for the adult personality by placing trust in those adults to provide nurture and comfort. If the adults disappear, the bereft child suffers severe stress, even though new adults step in to fill the gap.

In later childhood, many looked after children have suffered some form of abuse or serious neglect. Children may be abused physically, sexually or emotionally, or they may suffer neglect which is also life-threatening to the dependent child. All these abuses are traumatic experiences for children. Often they suffer more than one form of abuse, and often the abuses are repeated over long periods.

Unfortunately the events which bring children into public care also indicate a high probability that the children will have lacked the conditions necessary for spontaneous recovery from trauma. They may have spent a long time in chronically unsafe environments. They are unlikely to have experienced secure social networks with well-formed attachment relationships. They may have had little opportunity to develop good communication skills through play or through conversation.

When people are unable to recover from traumatic stress, they may adapt to their now chronic state of arousal, learn to live with some symptoms of disorder, and thus develop a reasonable level of social functioning. Often in these situations, the natural amnesia for the trauma persists, and the person establishes a lifestyle in which the trauma is locked away in a corner of their lives, with the rest of life being relatively untroubled. Although unstable, this is a tolerable situation. Others who are subject to more of the vulnerability factors develop post traumatic stress disorder (PTSD).

Post traumatic stress disorder and child development

When the victim of traumatic stress lacks the social and personal conditions for recovery from, or containment of, symptoms the solution becomes the problem. The normal process of recovery is an alternating cycle of intrusive re-experiencing of fragments of the traumatic events, and periods of rest and integration in which all reminders of the trauma are avoided (Joseph, Williams and Yule, 1997, pp 69–86). Since this is an entirely automatic process of recovering health it tends to be set in motion even when important bits of the recovery equation are missing.

These abortive attempts at integration and recovery, for that is what they seem to be at the beginning of the disorder, lead to disaster instead of health. The brain is automatically triggered to release a fragment of traumatic memory for processing and transfer, as it were, to the safety of narrative memory; but the victim, unable to deal with this still over-whelming bit of recalled trauma intruding into everyday life, becomes terrified. Now the trauma memory has become a new trauma event. The victim is beginning to be retraumatised by their own memories. The avoidance part of the recovery cycle also comes adrift. Stress hormones are never really dropping to levels less than toxic, so that avoidance, which would otherwise provide periods of rest and recuperation, now becomes phobic behaviour and compulsive thoughts and activities accompanied by denial and minimisation. These symptoms of intrusive re-experiencing and avoidance are among the defining criteria for PTSD.

Children will respond to all this pain by becoming locked into a state of frozen terror from which they cannot escape without help. In this state of terror, and the uncontrollable rage which often accompanies it, they will begin to develop patterns of behaviour which the rest of us will find difficult to accommodate. Nightmares, night terrors, disorders of sleeping and eating, learning difficulties, memory problems, aggression, violence, hyperactivity, inattentiveness, phobias, compulsive behaviours, self-harm, and later, self-medication through abuse of drugs and alcohol are all common symptoms of post traumatic distress.

If there are associated attachment difficulties we could add in a long list which would include, for example, stealing, meaningless compulsive lying, destructiveness, cruelty to animals, self-stimulating behaviours such as head-banging or masturbation, self-soothing behaviours such as rocking or thumb-sucking, and so on (Fahlberg, 1994). These are all symptoms of the pain and distress suffered by children whose brain and body development has been interrupted and harmed by stress injuries.

What happens to these vulnerable, troubled and troublesome children will then depend on when they come to the notice of a professional service, and which service notices them. Here gender, "race", culture, age, and perceived disability make a significant difference to outcome. Boys are treated differently from girls; in general terms, boys are more likely to suffer from hyperarousal and thus to act out, while girls suffer more from dissociative conditions and are more likely to be seen as at risk and in need of protection or mental health provision following traumatic stress. These differences combine with different societal expectations about gender to result in boys being more likely to end up being looked after and less likely to find permanent carers through adoption than girls (Ivaldi, 1998; PIU Report, 2000), and boys also being more likely to enter the criminal justice system. Black children are over-represented in the public care system (Barn *et al*, 1998), and once there they are less likely to find permanence through adoption than white children. Young children who act out sexually are likely to be seen as in need of care and treatment, while older young people sexually acting out are more likely to be seen as offenders (Farmer, 1998). Disabled children are both more vulnerable to abuse and more likely to be overlooked as victims of trauma, and services they receive are more likely to be health based than services offered to their peers.

Broadly speaking it is fair to say that the results of the response of our community to children who have suffered trauma are at present exclusion rather than inclusion. Children in the looked after system are more likely to be excluded from school than their peers, and less likely to go on into further education. As young adults they are much more likely to be unemployed, to be homeless, to be in prison, or to be recipients of mental health care than other people of the same age. Victims of trauma, locked in the grey and terrifying world of PTSD, feel themselves cut off from others; our social structures seem only too ready to make this self-image a reality.

The effects of traumatic stress on learning

The functional changes produced by PTSD are extensive, and are even more global in effect following childhood trauma than for people already adult when first traumatised: 'The [DSM-IV][1] field trials confirmed that trauma has its most profound impact during the first decade of life' (van der Kolk, McFarlane and Weisaeth, 1996, p 202). Brain and body functions, emotional functioning and social functioning are all likely to be seriously impaired. Cognitive processing will be distorted, and the sufferer will be preoccupied with trauma-related affect and cognition.

Out of the global harm caused by unresolved trauma, each victim will generate a unique constellation of symptoms and responses. The complex interactive system of individual and social networks, which is the locus of response to traumatic stress, creates an intricate interplay of vulnerability and resilience which will determine the outcome for the course of the disorder. Children who have suffered or are suffering much the same precipitating trauma may attract very different assessments of need.

Let us consider some of the functions which may be impaired and the learning difficulties which may occur as a result.

Brain

Language: areas of the brain in which several language functions are located are significantly altered under the impact of traumatic stress.

---

[1] DSM IV: *Diagnostic and Statistical Manual of Mental Disorders* (ADA, 1994).

Language and the symbolic representation of events and feelings are central to the functioning of human intelligence. Impairment in this area of functioning will lead to a range of learning difficulties.

Memory: victims are likely to suffer partial or complete memory disturbance for the traumatic events. This may take the form of amnesia or hypermnesia, in which the victim is unable to forget – the trauma, or fragments of it, endlessly replay in the victim's awareness. Changes in the brain also lead to significant short-term memory loss or distortion. Children with impaired memory find it very difficult to learn.

Physiology

Autonomic hyperarousal: the permanent arousal of the autonomic nervous system which controls bodily functions and physiology, and kindling of the limbic system which provides regulation of emotional states leave the child unable to concentrate or to string thoughts together cohesively. Preoccupation with trauma-related affect and cognition, and the pressing need for a permanently high stimulus environment, will lead to inattentiveness and disruptive behaviour.

Hypervigilance: perpetually scanning the environment for threat, interpreting neutral stimuli as traumatic stressors, subject to exaggerated startle responses so that they jump to every sound, these children are exhausting to be with. When not distressed and hyperactive, they will also be exhausted themselves. There is no middle ground at this level of arousal.

Altered perceptions: perceptual fields alter under the impact of traumatic stress. Peripheral vision sharpens, scanning the environment, and concentration on focused visual tasks such as reading becomes very limited. Auditory field selection changes, as the innate preference for the human voice is superseded by the need to notice danger. Non-threatening sounds are tuned out, and children may be thought to be deaf. They will certainly be thought to be inattentive.

Physical functioning

Lack of co-ordination: hyperarousal of the long muscles leads to problems with physical co-ordination and clumsiness, as well as stiffness and pain in the joints. This has an impact on many educational activities, and also contributes to the poor self-image which follows traumatic stress and again reduces educational attainment.

Numbness: overloaded with self-generated pain relievers (endogenous opioids) which are part of the traumatic stress response, the child cannot experience pain appropriately and is at risk of injury. These endogenous opioids are addictive, and this may lead to self-harming behaviour which positively seeks out injury to generate an added dose.

Psychosomatic conditions: stress hormones alter many bodily functions. Persisting over time these alterations in digestion, breathing, heart function, circulation, and muscle tone are likely to give rise to problems. The immune system is also challenged by the toxic levels of stress hormones. Moreover, children who are unable to experience feelings, but instead experience physical changes of function (somatisation), are often subject to illnesses when other children would experience emotions. Poor health may cause absences from school, and inattentiveness when in school.

Emotional functioning

Numbing: it is very difficult to engage with children who are suffering emotional numbing, or to engage them in any activity requiring emotional responsiveness. Aesthetic appreciation, a vital part of learning, is absent or impaired.

Extreme reactiveness: the same perpetual arousal which produces numbing also produces a hair-trigger reactivity to neutral or trivial emotional stimuli. The reaction will be one of terror or rage or both combined. This has a significant impact on the capacity to learn. Schools often find it difficult or impossible to contain the behaviour, which may be actually dangerous to self and others.

Somatisation: the inability to experience feelings as anything other than alterations in physical functioning, and the absence of language for feel-

ings, may severely limit the capacity to understand concepts, or participate in activities, which require emotional sensitivity and recognition.

Anhedonia: the loss of the capacity to experience joy will severely
circumscribe all educational activity which relies on appreciation,
wonder and awe.

Social functioning

Loss of ability to relate to others: preoccupation with trauma-related
constructs and affect means that other people are at best largely irrelevant
to the child thus affected. At worst, other people are misinterpreted as
threatening and treated accordingly. Since trauma victims are uncomfortable to be with, this social exclusion is likely to be two way. Group
learning activities are difficult for children in this situation, and social
interactions in and out of school are likely to be impaired.

Loss of social intentionality: a key element in the development of social
accountability, which Shotter (1984) suggests is crucial in human
development, is the recognition that intentions and not just actions are
central to human interaction. The victim of PTSD is 'trying to survive.
This supersedes all other intentionality' (Cairns, 1999, p 61). Motivation
to interact with others is severely limited when the child cannot generate
social intentions.

Loss of ability to perceive or construct meaning: traumatic stress destroys
central constructs of meaning (Janoff-Bulman, 1992), leaving the victim
of PTSD unable to discern connections or make sense of their universe.
Since connectedness is at the heart of sound education, this functional
impairment critically damages the ability to learn either extensively or
intensively.

The basis of effective treatment programmes

PTSD affects body, mind and society. It is a bio-psycho-social condition,
and effective treatment must address all three dimensions of the disorder
simultaneously. The victim needs to learn to manage their own physiological and biological stress reactions, to bring the autonomic hyperarousal and kindling of the limbic system to a level of tolerability and to

recover or create some conscious control over autonomic processes. They also need to process and come to terms with the horrifying traumatic memory fragments, and to restore or create personal constructs of meaning and intention. At the same time they need to recover or discover social connectedness and the possibility of joy.

They also need the disorder to be recognised, of course. This hardly happens at all at present. In a recent study of the mental health needs of looked after children in Oxfordshire, Jacinta McCann (BMJ, 1996; Davies, 1999) discovered that 67 per cent of these children were suffering major psychiatric disorder, as compared with 15 per cent in a reasonably matched comparison group. PTSD, a disorder recognised by DSM-IV (APA, 1994) and the World Health Organisation, is not mentioned and was not apparently part of the detailed screening process, despite the fact that it is often co-morbid with (or misdiagnosed as) several of the disorders which were identified.

This lack of recognition is widespread. One possible reason for the profound silence around PTSD is that it is very difficult for any one discipline to address itself to a disorder which requires connections across several professional disciplines even to recognise its existence. Yet once it is recognised, there is an increasing body of knowledge about how to treat it effectively (e.g. Chu, 1998), provided that the various disciplines can get their heads, and their budgets, together.

The need for treatment to be three-dimensional has led to the recognition that every practitioner involved with the child needs to be part of the treatment programme if it is to be effective. The disorder is global, and treatment must therefore address every aspect of the disordered functioning. Trauma experts generally agree that this is most elegantly and effectively achieved by 'phase-oriented' treatment which 'divides the overall trauma treatment into discrete phases or stages of treatment' (Brown, Scheflin and Hammond, 1998, p 437). Three stages or phases are recognised: stabilisation, integration, and post-integrative self and relational development. Each of these phases in turn needs to be addressing the three dimensions of the disorder: biological and physiological functioning; emotional and cognitive functioning; and social, cultural and spiritual functioning

Children who are victims of PTSD need safety, stabilisation, therapy, secure social attachments and the possibility of joy (Tedeschi and Calhoun, 1995). Many children in the public care are receiving none of these, as the Utting Report made clear (Utting, 1997), and very few receive all of them. Yet this is not a list from which options may be selected. For the child to recover, all of these elements – stability, appropriate therapy, lasting social connectedness and restitutive emotional experience – must be present, and the whole healing process must be based on effective treatment of post traumatic disorders.

In conclusion

Consider Article 39 of the UN Declaration on the Rights of the Child:

> *States Parties shall take all appropriate measures to promote physical and psychological recovery and social reintegration of a child victim of: any form of neglect, exploitation, or abuse . . . Such recovery and reintegration shall take place in an environment which fosters the health, self-respect and dignity of the child.*

We now know what such child victims need in order to recover and reintegrate. They need a safe, stable, loving home; they need access as and when required to therapists who understand the root problems; and they need a social milieu in which schools and doctors and police officers and the criminal justice system all recognise the effects of childhood trauma and work together to provide appropriate treatment and prevent further deterioration into disorder. Only when these needs have been met will we be coming close to honouring our commitment to uphold the rights of the child.

References

APA (1994) *Diagnostic and Statistical Manual of Mental Disorders*, Washington DC: American Psychiatric Association.

Barn, R, Sinclair, R and Ferdinand, D (1997) *Acting on Principle: An examination of race and ethnicity in social services provision for children and families*, London: BAAF.

Brown, D, Scheflin, A W and Hammond, D C (1998) *Memory, Trauma Treatment and the Law*, New York: Norton.

Cairns, K (1999) *Surviving Paedophilia*, Stoke-on-Trent: Trentham Books.

Carter, R (1998) *Mapping the Mind*, London: Weidenfeld & Nicholson.

Chu, J A (1998) *Rebuilding Shattered Lives: The responsible treatment of post traumatic and dissociative disorders*, New York: Wiley.

Davies, G (1999) 'Fragile Minds: supporting young people with mental health problems', *Foster Care*, 97, pp 12–14.

Fahlberg, V (1994) *A Child's Journey through Placement*, London: BAAF.

Farmer, E (1998) *Sexually Abused and Abusing children in Substitute Care*, Chichester: Wiley.

Goleman, D (1996) *Emotional Intelligence*, London: Bloomsbury.

Ivaldi, G (1998) *Children Adopted from Care: An examination of agency adoptions in England – 1996*, London: BAAF.

Janoff-Bulman, R (1992) *Shattered Assumptions: Towards a new psychology of trauma*, New York: Free Press.

Joseph, S, Williams, R and Yule, W (1997) *Understanding Post traumatic Stress: A psychosocial perspective on PTSD and treatment*, Chichester: Wiley.

Kinchin, D (1998) *Post Traumatic Stress Disorder: The invisible injury*, Didcot: Success Unlimited.

McCann, J (1996) 'Prevalence of psychiatric disorders in young people in the care system', in *British Medical Journal*, 313: 1529–1530.

Shotter, J (1984) *Social Accountability and Selfhood*, Oxford: Basil Blackwell.

Tedeschi, R G and Calhoun, G C (1995) *Trauma and Transformation: Growing in the aftermath of suffering*, Thousand Oaks: Sage.

Performance and Innovation Unit (2000) *The Prime Minister's Review of Adoption*: London: PIU.

Utting, Sir W (1997) *People Like Us: The Report of the Review of the Safeguards for Children Living Away From Home*, London: The Department of Health.

van der Kolk, B A, McFarlane, A C and Weisaeth, L (eds) (1996) *Traumatic Stress: The effects of overwhelming experience on mind, body and society*, New York: The Guilford Press.

12 Maintaining looked after young people in mainstream education

Eric Blyth

Introduction

As other contributions to this volume testify, care leavers are 'ill-prepared to compete in an increasingly competitive and shrinking youth labour market' (Stein, 1994, p 354). Being out of school is 'undoubtedly a significant risk factor in terms of undesirable outcomes for young people' (Vernon and Sinclair, 1998, p 4). As a corollary, for young people in local authority care, 'school can provide one element of stability, continuity and belonging in an otherwise disrupted life' (Bullock *et al*, 1994, p 307).

Yet, a decade after Jackson (1987) had drawn attention to the educational disadvantage experienced by young people in public care, the authors of the Children's Safeguards Review commented:

> The importance of health and education services for looked after children has been emphasised in a sequence of reports. The Review received vigorous representations about the inadequacies of both . . . Whatever the cause, it produces **a scandalous situation in which the life prospects of these young people may be irretrievably damaged and their immediate safety put at greater risk**. (Utting *et al*, 1997, s2 para 16 – my emphasis)

In response, in 1998, the Government indicated its view that 'the quality of the public care system in which children are looked after by local authorities is unacceptably low' (Government's Response to the Children's Safeguards Review [1998], cited in DfEE/DH, 2000, p 5).

Two years later, government data indicated that many children looked after by English local authorities were still leaving care without GCSE or GNVQ qualifications (DfEE/DH, 2000).

Self-evidently, contemporary aspirations to improve the educational achievement levels of looked after young people are crucially dependent on their active engagement with the education system (DH, 1998a; Social Exclusion Unit, 1998; DfEE/DH, 2000).

Why maintaining looked after young people in mainstream education is an issue

A number of different studies have shown that school-age children and young people in public care ("looked after" young people) are disproportionately represented among those who are neither attending school (for a variety of reasons) nor receiving any kind of education. Further, looked after children are more likely than their peers to be educated in educational units provided by social services departments (SSDs) or social work departments or in special schools.

Stirling's (1992) study of a single local authority showed that, of 60 residents of the authority's children's homes, two young people were permanently excluded while another 30 were either excluded indefinitely or unoffically. A "snapshot" single-day survey of children in residential care provided by Lothian Regional Council Social Work Department revealed that 16 of the 115 school-age residents were permanently excluded from school, and nine more children were receiving no education while an alternative school placement was sought (Maginnis, 1993). Maginnis states that children in residential care represented approximately 0.3 per cent of the total secondary school population in the region, but 23 per cent of the annual total of permanently excluded pupils. Comparing the two groups, Maginnis calculates that 'the residential care population was eighty times more likely to be excluded than the average'. Based on a one-day census, the Audit Commission (1994) noted that ten per cent of looked after children were being educated in social services units and just over a third were not attending school. Of these, over 40 per cent were permanently, indefinitely or temporarily excluded; 39 per cent were "refusing to attend" and seven per cent had no school place. In one local authority, 40 per cent of 5–16-year-olds in children's homes were receiving no education at all. Berridge and Brodie (1998) concluded from their study of children's residential care experiences that non-attendance had become a much greater problem between 1985 and 1995. A study of four English local authorities conducted jointly by the Social Services Inspectorate (SSI) and the Office for Standards in Education (OFSTED) (1995) showed that overall 12 per cent of looked after children were either excluded from school or did not attend on a regular basis, although this rose to over 25 per cent among 14–16-year-olds. Smith (1998) and Sandiford (1999) cite unpublished Department for Education and Employment data indicating that looked after children account for 33 per cent of all secondary school exclusions and 66 per cent of all primary school exclusions in England and Wales, although they comprise less than half of one per cent of the total school population (Fletcher-Campbell, 1997). Such data are consistent with the findings of Hayden's (1997) study that over three-quarters of children excluded from primary schools were already receiving help from social services.

The outcome of exclusion in particular may also be more severe for looked after young people. While there is little evidence of parents generally putting to effective use their rights to challenge the exclusion of their children from school (Department for Education, 1993), Fletcher-Campbell and Hall observe that SSDs were unlikely to take on education as 'real parents' because 'we're all fellow employees' (Fletcher-Campbell and Hall, 1990, p 40). Similarly, SSI and OFSTED identify a general reservation in social services to press for appeal in respect of exclusion from school:

> *because of the likelihood of the harmful effects on relationships with schools. Appeals were viewed as a criticism rather than an opportunity to coolly discuss the events leading up to exclusion, to enable the child to understand the reasons for exclusion more clearly and for the school to reconsider the decisions in the light of any additional information.* (SSI and OFSTED, 1995, p 39)

Smith's (1998) survey of exclusions conducted in January–February 1998 reveals a different concern – the level of accurate knowledge within local authorities about the educational experiences of looked after young people. Of the 104 English and Welsh local education authorities (LEAs) surveyed, 66 responded, of which only 38 per cent replied to the question about the number of looked after children excluded from school. Fewer than half of these LEAs had any idea how many excluded students were in local authority care.

In addition to the impact of high levels of both exclusion and absenteeism militating against the engagement of these young people in the education system, two other major factors have been shown to exert a disproportionate impact on the physical presence in school of young people in public care: the disruptive effect on schooling of care placement changes and the failure by local authorities to make adequate educational arrangements. There is considerable evidence about the adverse educational effect of care placement changes, especially multiple placement moves (e.g. Fletcher-Campbell and Hall, 1990). Further, Stein (1994) warns that statistics alone might fail to convey the nature and impact of repeated placement disruptions. Since a high proportion of young people enter care as teenagers, placement moves are compressed into a relatively short time period and 'education as a developmental process is therefore likely to have little meaning given the disruption to syllabuses, course work and examination preparation' (Stein, 1994, p 353). Several studies have also highlighted the relatively high numbers of looked after young people who are not receiving any education or are not registered on any school roll (Maginnis, 1993; Audit Commission, 1994).

The educational prospects for those looked after young people who are educated within facilities provided by SSDs themselves or who are provided with "special education" because they are considered to have "special education needs" appear little brighter. Reviews of social services' education provision, despite occasional accolades, have been almost uniformly negative (Department of Education and Science, 1978, 1992; Department of Health and Social Security, 1981; Fletcher-Campbell and Hall, 1990; SSI and OFSTED, 1995), while all too often, "special education" has in effect been second rate education (Barnes, 1994).

Corporate parenting and "joined up" government

Given the impact of their legislative programme on the fragmentation of public services during the 1980s and early 1990s, Conservative Government exhortations to improve inter-agency co-ordination, including provision for the care and education of young people (Department for Education and Department of Health, 1994), were rather like a burglar promoting "Neighbourhood Watch" (for a fuller discussion, see Blyth and Milner, 1997). Unsurprisingly therefore, despite Department of Health support for the development of the *Looking After Children: Good parenting good outcomes* scheme (1995) materials for recording information, reviewing progress and ensuring that young people's needs are met while they are looked after (Parker *et al*, 1991) and adapted for use in Scotland (Wheelaghan *et al*, 1999), there is little evidence of effective inter-agency effort regarding the education of young people in public care (Utting *et al*, 1997). In similar vein, the OFSTED (1996) report on exclusions concluded that support strategies for looked after young people in school remained inadequate because of the failure of effective liaison between social services, schools and LEAs. Research conducted by Parsons *et al* (1994) demonstrated that problems were not simply the result of insufficient resources, since a considerable amount of professional workers' time appeared to be spent, unproductively, on what they describe as 'débris management'. For example, residential care staff may need to be employed for additional hours to care for young people without a school place, whether as the result of exclusion or for other reasons, and frequently doing little more than "containing" the young person, while the time and effort of teachers, carers, social workers and others may be spent in dealing with the consequences of individual youngsters' disaffection and alienation, which may include the breakdown of a care placement. Where resources are limited, there is even less excuse for wasting them.

Meanwhile both Jackson (1994, 1998) and Ward (1995) – two of the authors of the *Looking After Children* scheme – acknowledged that some social workers were reluctant to set standards for children for fear that this would 'set them up to fail' or considered it 'unfair to give looked-after children educational advantages that poor parents looking after their own children are not able to give' (Jackson, 1994, p 277). There was certainly little evidence that the Department of Health mandate for care authorities 'to remedy the educational disadvantage of children in their care, and do all that a good parent would do to ensure that children's needs are met' (DH, 1991, p 10) was being seriously addressed by many of them.

In 1997, Felicity Fletcher-Campbell published the findings of a study developing her earlier research with Chris Hall (Fletcher-Campbell and

Hall, 1990). Just over half of the 114 English and Welsh local authorities surveyed responded to the written questionnaire and fewer than half of the respondents appeared to have made what could be described as real progress in promoting the educational experiences of looked after young people. As Campbell (1998) notes, while Fletcher-Campbell identifies the 'real and dynamic progress made in a small number of local authorities . . . this only serves to highlight the patchiness of the response in the majority of authorities' (Campbell, 1998, p 153), a finding replicated by the Government's own analysis of the educational qualifications of looked after children in English local authorities (DfEE/DH, 2000).

Nevertheless, some local authorities have taken up the challenge to develop a "corporate approach", a concept emphasising that the care of looked after young people is the responsibility of the local authority as a whole and not simply that of its social services department (Utting *et al*, 1997).

Murray and Godfrey (1997) outline an interdepartmental policy statement between education and social services to promote joint commitment and ownership in Bradford. At the local authority level, two project officers, one each from social services and from education, are responsible for awareness-raising, dissemination of information, staff training, and for providing advice and support in individual cases. Operational units of the social services and education departments, local colleges and careers services each have identified "link officers", while each school has a designated teacher with responsibility for looked after young people and each school is required to have a policy to identify what a looked after young person can expect from the school.

Vernon and Sinclair (1998) report on a survey of English and Welsh SSDs undertaken in 1997 by the National Children's Bureau and the Association of Directors of Social Services to identify the involvement of SSDs in preventing the exclusion of children from school. Almost a quarter of responding departments reported current projects targeting looked after young people, although the number of existing initiatives was more than matched by those planned for the relatively near future: 'The encouraging findings of this survey are that increasingly SSDs and LEAs appear to be tackling this issue in partnership – in line with local government responsibilities as corporate parent' (Vernon and Sinclair, 1998, p 12).

The *Guidance on the Education of Children and Young People in Public Care* (DfEE/DH, 2000) cites a number of collaborative initiatives in different parts of the country designed to improve the educational experiences and outcomes for looked after children and young people. However, none of the case studies highlighted were among the top performing local authorities according to the 1999–2000 Social Services Performance report (DH, 2000). Indeed, one of the featured local authorities was among the worst performing local authorities, prompting the Government to indicate a 'very urgent need for council to investigate the practices that have led to this performance . . .', while the perform-ance of another was judged to demonstrate a 'serious need for council to investigate . . .'. This tends to reinforce the contemporary perception that, while '[t]here are noteworthy examples of effective local practice from which much has been learned . . . there is little evidence of the spread of sustained good practice' (DfEE/DH, 2000, p 7).

Promoting a culture of achievement for looked after young people

In the longer term, one of the most significant contributions that national government, social services and education authorities, individual carers and professionals can make to the lives of young people in public care is to ensure their acquisition of marketable skills, in particular literacy and numeracy, with the Government suggesting that specific educational attainment may be the 'most significant measure' of the effectiveness of local authority parenting (DH, 1998a).

The evidence from research and formal inspections of services by government bodies has prompted concrete recommendations for policy frameworks and improved professional practice at national, local author-ity, institutional and individual levels (Fletcher-Campbell, 1997) and further elaborated by Borland *et al* (1998). The cornerstone of such initiatives is an explicit acceptance of the need to prioritise the education of looked after young people, replacing the 'non-achieving welfare culture' (Stein, 1994, p 358) with a culture of achievement.

Many of the measures advocated by Borland and her colleagues have been incorporated in the Government's *Guidance on the Education of Children and Young People in Public Care* (DfEE/DH, 2000).

The Government's contribution to the improvement of service provision has been directed at services for all young people in school as well as those specifically for looked after young people. It has issued guidance on social inclusion and pupil support (DfEE, 1999a, 1999b) based on earlier work undertaken by the Social Exclusion Unit (1998). Additionally, the Government's targets for reducing fixed-term and permanent exclusions and unauthorised absence for all school children by one-third by 2002 (DfEE, 1998; Social Exclusion Unit, 1998) should be expected to impact on the school attendance of looked after young people. More specifically, through the Quality Protects programme announced in November 1998, the Government has set up a three-year programme (recently extended by a further two years) designed to improve social services provision for children. One of the programme's eight main targets is 'to ensure that children looked after gain maximum life chance benefits from educational opportunities, health care and social care' (DH, 1998a, objective 4.0). The targets set for local authorities regarding the educational attainment of looked after young people are designed to bring their overall educational performance more closely into line with that of other young people in the same locality. By 2001, at least 50 per cent of care leavers (at 16 or older) should have a GCSE or GNVQ qualification. By 2003, the Government has set a target of 75 per cent (DH, 1998b). Although no targets for attainment have been set for earlier than 2001, the fact that only 15 English local authorities met or exceeded the 50 per cent threshold for GCSE or GNVQ qualifications in 1999–2000 indicates the scale of the task facing local authorities (DH, 2000).

In addition, OFSTED inspections of LEA services now include provisions for the education of looked after children and young people as part of the monitoring of LEAs' social inclusion activities.

Two new initiatives, specifically focusing on the educational experiences and attainments of looked after young people, both supported by the Department for Education and Employment (as well as other sponsoring organisations) have been developed by the Who Cares?

Trust and the National Children's Bureau. Both are designed to complement the Government's legislative and policy framework and the Looking After Children scheme. The Equal Chances Programme (the Who Cares? Trust, 1999), more fully discussed in Chapter 9, is intended to help local authorities improve their corporate parenting in relation to the educational opportunities and outcomes for looked after children and young people. Materials developed by the programme and piloted in Bradford and Brighton and Hove will help local authorities to improve practice and begin to meet the targets and objectives set out by the Government, especially in relation to the Quality Protects Programme.

The National Children's Bureau has produced documentation to assist in the drawing up of a Personal Education Plan for each looked after young person in public care (Sandiford, 1999). The purpose of the Plan is to provide those working with young people in public care with a tool that will enable them to create strategic plans which meet the young person's educational needs. The Personal Education Plan will ensure that:

- all the necessary people have the information they require in order to design an action plan to meet the young person's educational needs;
- the educational needs of each looked after young person are identified and agreed and a process put in place in order to meet them;
- relevant information is submitted to the statutory Child Care Review and is included in the resulting Care Plan;
- each young person may choose whether they want their teacher to be at their statutory review; and
- a record of each looked after young person's education is maintained while being looked after.

Conclusion

Concerns about the educational experiences and achievements of looked after young people have generated a flurry of activity at both national and local levels in the UK, although, because many of the initiatives now under way are of fairly recent origin, it will be some time before their impact can be evaluated. Given that all-too-few local authorities have taken seriously their responsibilities towards the young people in their care, evidence of a heavier hand of government in terms of setting and meeting targets is at least partially welcomed, although as Vernon and Sinclair (1998) warn, the creation of an ever-increasing bureaucracy consisting of plans, meetings and form-completion should not be allowed to distract attention from the central task of ensuring that the needs of looked after young people are recognised and appropriately addressed.

Maintaining looked after young people in school and promoting a culture of achievement among looked after young people requires positive action at all stages of the young person's educational career. It means recognising that many young people entering public care will already have been educationally disadvantaged by their previous experiences (DH, 1991, para. 3.23; Sinclair *et al*, 1993) and explicit commitment to remedy such disadvantage. It means making appropriate efforts to encourage and ensure regular school attendance, whatever the young person's level of attendance prior to him or her becoming looked after. The practicalities of reversing a history of chronic absenteeism have, not infrequently, thwarted the best intentions of care staff, while some have not even bothered to try. However, there is evidence that entrenched patterns of absence can be effectively challenged if staff are sufficiently motivated and supported (Fletcher-Campbell, 1997). It means having appropriate expectations, setting achievable attainment targets and ensuring they are regularly monitored, and providing appropriate support to carers, professionals and young people. There is a self-evident case for developing close working relationships between parents, carers, social services staff, schools and education welfare/social work services.

The minority of local authorities which appear to be taking seriously their responsibilities towards the educational needs of young people in their care provide models of good working practices for others to emulate. For the most part, however, it is a clear case that the majority of corporate parents can, and must, "do better".

References

Audit Commission (1994) *Seen But Not Heard: Co-ordinating community child health and social services for children in need*, London: HMSO.

Barnes, C (1994) *Disabled People in Britain and Discrimination: A case for anti-discrimination legislation*, London: Hurst & Company.

Berridge, D and Brodie, I (1998) *Children's Homes Revisited*, Oxford: Basil Blackwell.

Blyth, E and Milner, J (1997) *Social Work with Children: The educational perspective*, Harlow: Addison Wesley Longman, Chapter 3: 'Education reform in Britain'.

Borland, M, Pearson, C, Hill, M, Tisdall, K and Bloomfield, I (1998) *Education and Care Away from Home: A review of research, policy and practice*, Edinburgh: Scottish Council for Research in Education.

Bullock, R, Little, M and Millham, S (1994) 'Children's return from state care to school', *Oxford Review of Education*, 20:3, pp 307–16.

Campbell, K (1998) review of Fletcher-Campbell, F (1997) 'The education of children who are looked after', *British Journal of Social Work*, 28:1, pp 153–4.

Department for Education (1993) *A New Deal for 'Out of School' Pupils*, Press Release: 126/93, London: Department for Education.

Department for Education and Department of Health (1994) *The Education of Children Looked After by Local Authorities*, Circular 13/94. DH LAC (94) 11, London: Department for Education and Department of Health.

Department for Education and Employment (DfEE) (1998) *Morris Reveals Ambitious New Plan to Cut Truancy and Exclusion from School*, Circular 386/98, London: DfEE.

Department for Education and Employment (DfEE) (1999a) *Social Inclusion: Pupil support* (Circular 10/99). London: DfEE.

Department for Education and Employment (DfEE) (1999b) *Social Inclusion: The LEA role in pupil support* (Circular 11/99). London: DfEE.

Department for Education and Employment (DfEE) and Department of Health (DH) (2000) *Guidance on the Education of Children and Young People in Public Care*, London: DfEE/DH.

Department of Education and Science (1978) *Community Homes with Education*, HMI Series: Matters for Discussion 10, London: HMSO.

Department of Education and Science (1992) *Education in Social Services Establishments: A Report by HMI*, 4/92/NS, London: Department of Education and Science.

Department of Health and Social Security (1981) *Observation and Assessment: Report of a Working Party*, London: HMSO.

Department of Health (1991) *Children in the Public Care* (The Utting Report), Social Services Inspectorate, London: HMSO.

Department of Health (1995) *Looking After Children: Good parenting, good outcomes*, London: HMSO.

Department of Health (1998a) *Quality Protects Programme – Transforming Children's Services*, LAC (98) 28, London: Department of Health.

Department of Health (1998b) *Modernising Health and Social Services: National Priorities Guidance1990/00–2001/02*, London: Department of Health.

Department of Health (2000) *Social Services Performance in 1999–2000*, www.gov.uk/pal

Fletcher-Campbell, F (1997) *The Education of Children who are Looked After*, Slough: National Foundation for Educational Research (NFER).

Fletcher-Campbell, F and Hall, C (1990) *Changing Schools? Changing People? The education of children in care*, Slough: NFER.

The Government's Response to the Children's Safeguards Review (1998) Cm 4105, London: The Stationery Office.

Hayden, C (1997) *Children Excluded from Primary School: Debates, evidence responses*, Buckingham: Open University Press.

Jackson, S (1987) *The Education of Children in Care*, Bristol Papers in Applied Social Studies, Bristol: University of Bristol.

Jackson, S (1994) 'Educating children in residential and foster care', *Oxford Review of Education*, 20:3, pp 267–79.

Jackson, S (1998) 'Looking after children: a new approach or just an exercise in formfilling? A response to Knight and Caveney', *British Journal of Social Work*, 28:1, pp 45–56.

Maginnis, E (1993) *An Inter-Agency Response to Children with Special Needs – The Lothian experience – A Scottish perspective*, paper presented at Conference: Exclusions from School: Bridging the Gap Between Policy and Practice organised by the National Children's Bureau, 13 July, London: National Children's Bureau.

Murray, V and Godfrey, E (1997) *The Education of Looked After Children and Equal Chances Projects*, Bradford: Bradford Metropolitan District Council.

OFSTED (1996) *Exclusions from Secondary Schools 1995/6*, a report from the Office of Her Majesty's Chief Inspector of Schools, London: The Stationery Office.

Parker, R A, Ward, H, Jackson, S, Aldgate, J and Wedge, P (1991) *Looking After Children: Assessing outcomes in child care*, London: HMSO.

Parsons, C, Benns, L, Hailes, J and Howlett, K (1994) *Excluding Primary School Children*, London: Family Policy Studies Centre.

Sandiford, P (1999) *Personal Educational Plan for Children and Young People in Public Care*, London: National Children's Bureau.

Sinclair, R, Garnett, L, Beecham, J and Berridge, D (1993) *Social Work and Assessment with Adolescents*, London: National Children's Bureau.

Smith, R (1998) *No Lessons Learnt: A survey of school exclusions*, London: The Children's Society.

Social Exclusion Unit (1998) *Truancy and School Exclusion*, London: The Stationery Office.

Social Services Inspectorate and OFSTED (1995) *The Education of Children who are Looked After by Local Authorities*, London: Department of Health and OFSTED.

Stein, M (1994) 'Leaving care, education and career trajectories', *Oxford Review of Education*, 20:3, pp 349–60.

Stirling, M (1992) 'How many pupils are excluded?' *British Journal of Special Education*, 19:4, pp 14–18.

The Who Cares? Trust (1999) *Equal Chances: Project summary*, London: The Who Cares? Trust.

The Who Cares? Trust (undated) *Equal Chances: The framework*, London: The Who Cares? Trust.

Utting, W Sir, Baines, C, Stuart, M, Rowlands, J and Vialva, R (1997) *People Like Us: The Report of the Review of the Safeguards for Children Living Away from Home*, London: The Stationery Office.

Vernon, J and Sinclair, R (1998) *Maintaining Children in School: The contribution of social services departments*, London: National Children's Bureau.

Ward, H (ed.) (1995) *Looking After Children: Research into practice*, London: HMSO.

Wheelaghan, S, Hill, M, Borland, M, Lambert, L and Triseliotis, J (1999) *The Looking After Children Materials: An evaluation of the Scottish pilot*, Edinburgh: The Stationery Office.

13 The place of education in a mixed economy of child care

Tim Walker

The education of children in public care is almost certainly at the highest point on the political agenda it will ever reach. The extent to which levels of educational attainment for looked after children and young people are likely to influence their future life chances has been fully recognised and understood and provides a new context within which specific central government policy and guidance is now based. The DfEE/DH guidance on the education of looked after children provides powerful evidence that central government has been prepared to act and promote the interests of children in public care through a degree of prescription that seemed inconceivable only a few years ago.

While there is little doubt that significant progress has been made, there is no room for complacency. A significant minority of looked after children continue to be disproportionately represented among pupils who are excluded from, or do not attend school, and may feature among those who present teachers and schools with significant challenges. The majority of looked after children attend mainstream schools without apparent difficulty and yet continue to underachieve at an alarming rate and become significantly over-represented in national statistics on homelessness, unemployment, poverty and within the adult prison population.

With these clear links in mind Frank Dobson, then Secretary of State for Health, publicly stated in 1998 that he considered education outcomes for looked after children as possibly the single most important indicator of the overall effectiveness of the public care system. As a consequence, local authority structures and professional practices which comprise the public care system have been provided with a unique opportunity to adapt and change against the background of a sympathetic and supportive political climate. That many of the most disadvantaged of all children continue to be systematically denied educational entitlements that others take for granted is particularly scandalous as we have reached this point with no shortage of hard evidence and remarkably few inconsistencies within research findings on both causes and effects. In meeting this challenge, local authorities would be wise to take into full account the reasons for our collective past failures.

In 1987, the "structural marginalisation" of children in public care, where their educational interests fall rather than are shared between local education and social services departments, was identified by the editor of this book as providing the conditions under which so many so disastrously and disproportionately underachieve in comparison with almost all other groups of children. Those who left public care in the subsequent 12 years may be forgiven for being reminded of George Bernard Shaw's 'The speed with which absolutely nothing happened was breathtaking'. The evidence provides a strong indication that in the past we have either resisted change or simply have not known in what direction we should move. We have usually agreed on the ends, but not the means.

The problem of organisational boundaries

All children, including those in public care, have a fundamental entitlement to access the highest quality educational opportunities and the means to sustain them. For the overwhelming majority of pupils within the general school population, the distinct and separate roles and functions of local education and social services authorities are largely irrelevant and lead, therefore, to very little adverse effect. The opposite is more frequently the case for children who are looked after, whose only uniform characteristic is that their interests legitimately cut across departmental boundaries.

Social workers commonly identify education disadvantages which significantly impede their own planned objectives for children in and on the margins of public care. They then instinctively look to their local education authority which, they understand, has the responsibility to respond to what it is that they have identified, only to discover that the nature of local education department administration, its statutory framework and organisation of services is such that it is frequently unable to deliver within social work time-scales, and in a manner which takes into account what may be termed the "looked after" context.

Field social workers regularly report too that a small investment of support at critical points in children's educational lives would have prevented much higher costs to their own departments even in the shorter term. That their managers were unable or unwilling to make the investment, and then incurred the greater cost directly themselves, provides a clear enough indication of the extent to which they consider the delivery of direct education services to children who are looked after as outside their own terms of reference and a matter exclusively for their counterpart education departments. Within any complex bureaucracy it is a great deal easier to overspend a budget that exists than to commit smaller sums from those which do not.

Furthermore, the prevailing education climate creates additional difficulties for many looked after children with its culture of open competition between schools, performance league tables and a renewed emphasis on raising educational standards for all children. These factors are, however, frequently the subject of exaggerated claims that they are somehow incompatible with the educational interests of disadvantaged children and lead to disproportionate levels of school exclusions and other difficulties faced by children in public care. They are often used to explain the educational underachievement of children who are looked after as if previously these children somehow thrived and succeeded alongside their peers in the general school population.

The schools' perspective

The challenge for the public care system is to develop new ways to meet the needs of children who face significant difficulties and simultaneously to meet the requirements of our mainstream schools. The pressures on classroom teachers and schools in general are immense and need to be taken into full account in circumstances where they are expected to provide high quality education to children who may, at times, present serious challenges to teachers and to other pupils. The vast majority of schools are invariably prepared, willing and able to provide high quality education for all pupils where they feel adequately supported, practically and psychologically. They also widely perceive the present levels of support available to them as at best well-intended but wholly inadequate in their nature and extent. This perception frequently leads to entrenchment, defensiveness and reluctance on the part of many schools to provide opportunities to those children they perceive as having the potential to drain their own resources and to have a negative impact on the smooth operation of a school, including its public reputation and standing.

Additionally, school teachers may suffer from considerable stress and low morale, made more acute by the extent of social deprivation in some regions, the fragmentation of information systems and a lack of cohesion within external support services. There may be concentrations of pupils with entrenched difficulties within individual schools and locations, with disproportionate numbers of exclusions particularly affecting black children and those who are looked after. These factors may be further exacerbated where schools are facing falling rolls and deficit budgets leading to a downward spiral of despair and falling morale within staff teams. It is becoming increasingly clear that the looked after system is not only failing to meet the needs of its children but is also becoming increasingly detached from the expectations and requirements of mainstream schools.

A further impediment to change lies in the instinct of most local authorities and most of the independent child care sector to interpret the extent and nature of the education "problem" within public care in terms of the numbers of children who are not in school or in some other kind of day provision. One local authority reported recently that it did not see any major difficulty with the education of their own looked after children as there were only 16 per cent of them out of school. The local authority's "problem", as they viewed it, was this 16 per cent cohort. The strong likelihood that many of the other 84 per cent were failing disastrously within their mainstream schools and within other education provisions, according to almost all the research, was either not recognised, understood or considered a particular priority for action. The difficulties faced by looked after children were of concern to the local authority for the inconvenience they created for professionals and carers, rather than for children's collective educational underachievement.

Whose failure?

Almost all research and analysis on the educational difficulties faced by looked after children points strongly to the inherent weaknesses within the public care system which then inexorably lead children towards failure. Collectively we have always behaved as if the opposite is true, as if the real difficulty with foster care and group care is the degree of disturbance children carry with them into these provisions. The assessments of education, social work and health professionals and our responses to them still largely reflect the powerful professional instinct to pathologise individual children, with the child constituting the "problem" rather than how he or she may respond to external factors such as our institutions, professional structures and services, including the looked after system itself.

We continue to place too much emphasis on what we assume looked after children are incapable of, or unwilling to do, and as a consequence pay insufficient attention to their capabilities, strengths and potential. In this way, aspects of the current organisation of education and social work practice facilitate a traditional drift of children through processes which may unwittingly take them out of their families, schools and communities, by drawing them into a cycle of identification, assessment, treatment and deepening dependence on the very systems they should be helped to escape.

If we are serious about the need to have a real and positive impact on the lives of children and young people who are looked after, we must comprehensively re-examine the detail of the public care system and consider what it should consist of, and how it should be organised, staffed, trained and supported. One of the more obvious and yet most difficult starting points for this process has to be an understanding and recognition that the status quo has persistently failed to deliver. The present looked after system is in significant parts of it at least, an anachronism, which not only does a great disservice to those children who rely on it but also to the many thousands of dedicated professional carers and staff who commit much of their lives to working within it. The Children Act 1989, and in more recent times an even greater emphasis on the role of the whole authority as corporate parent, have not led to the kind of sea-change in professional attitudes and patterns of service delivery that children and young people in public care might have expected and certainly deserved.

Foster care and education

Within the looked after system itself, the general trend away from residential or group settings has re-emphasised the role of foster care as being the main placement provider for children within all local authorities. Foster carers are now routinely expected to meet the needs of children and young people who formerly would have been looked after within institutional settings. However, local authorities have not in strategic terms reviewed the extent to which children and their carers are supported as a direct consequence of this shift in emphasis and the greater demands placed on individual placements. The picture which emerges is one of foster carers under considerable pressure to care for children who are experiencing increasing levels and degrees of difficulty. At the same time local authorities frequently testify to the deficits in the overall number of available foster carers, many of whom leave the fostering service because of what they perceive as inadequate professional support. These factors are further exacerbated by overt competition for experienced carers from a significant number of independent fostering agencies.

Within local authority and independent sector foster care, placements frequently become vulnerable and break down as a direct and indirect consequence of what may present as the intractable educational difficulties faced by individual children. Similarly, any instability within such placements, and in many cases their complete collapse, further impedes successful educational outcomes for individual children. It is clear that, in establishing and maintaining high quality foster care, social work and educational objectives are completely interdependent. However, there are at present no local authorities within the United Kingdom whose fostering services are specifically staffed and structured to take this fully into account.

The extent to which the absence of effective educational arrangements within the public care system leads to inefficient and ineffective local authority social work practice is still largely unclear. It is highly likely, however, that children are not the only casualties of inadequate education arrangements within foster care as local authorities routinely invest huge sums of money in residential provisions for children whose foster placements continually break down in circumstances where successful attendance at school might have led to stability within the foster home. In these circumstances, residential care admissions are invariably attributed to the changing needs of the child, rather than being seen as the result of any inadequacies in the nature of professional services to children and their foster carers.

The role of the independent fostering sector

Within the mixed economy of child care provision, the independent fostering sector in particular has been much maligned and in part deservedly so. The general acceptance of the validity of the role of the independent residential sector, in contrast to the independent fostering sector, is partly borne out of the misplaced view that residential provision is an end-of-the-line service which must cater for children whose difficulties are so severe that they will have previously exhausted all local authority resources. In this regard, the independent residential sector is considered to complement local authority resources by providing specialist services which local authorities do not see themselves as being able to develop.

In contrast foster care represents the first, most widely preferred and least restrictive local authority placement option for looked after children. The independent fostering sector is not, therefore, regarded as complementary by many local authorities but as being in direct conflict with the strategic and operational concerns of their own service managers and providers. Furthermore, the absence of an effective regulatory framework and of inspection arrangements for this sector, long overdue and now planned by central government, has undoubtedly led to dubious professional and financial practices through the scandalously high levels of remuneration paid to a few agency directors, as well as the deliberate poaching of existing foster carers with cash inducements, at levels local authorities are unable to match. Many local authorities are concerned, too, about what they perceive as being held to ransom by some agencies as significant numbers of foster carers transfer their allegiance to the independent sector with children remaining in placement, with the local authority then subjected to substantially increased costs.

These factors, both singly and in combination, have provoked a widespread political and professional hostility to the independent foster care sector in general rather than seeing individual agencies as specifically culpable. There is little doubt that this has served to deny what might otherwise constitute a dispassionate and informed exploration of the professional contribution of independent foster care to services for looked after children as part of a vibrant mixed economy of child care provision. The sector is, in truth, as varied and diverse in nature and quality as its residential equivalent, with many local authorities developing successful partnership arrangements with individual agencies to provide a wider choice of accommodation placements for children who may have a range of complex needs.

The majority of independent agencies have reacted to the adverse educational circumstances faced by many of their children by developing direct education provisions. These range from small teaching units and home tuition services, to teachers employed in advocacy roles who focus on access to schools and untangling administrative impediments and bureaucratic delays within and between local education authorities.

Almost all of these initiatives, however, constitute a largely pragmatic response to the understandable difficulties presented to their foster carers by children being out of school rather than being motivated by the need to raise substantially children's levels of educational attainment or to relieve the pressures on mainstream schools. In this respect, much of the independent sector continues to mirror the prevailing attitudes and concerns of their professional colleagues within local authorities.

Placing education at the centre of care

In contrast, a number of Independent Fostering Agencies (IFAs) have undertaken a reappraisal of professional services to looked after children and their foster carers which has led to new approaches and patterns of service delivery being established. These agencies include Premier Foster

Care (Manchester), Foster Care Services (North West), Safehouses (North & Essex) and SWIIS Foster Care (Birmingham, Newcastle and Manchester). As a consequence, these independent agencies are demonstrating a capacity for developing services for children and their carers which appear to be highly innovative and from which the public care system may have a great deal to learn as educational and other outcomes for children within these agencies become clearer.

Within these IFAs there has been an explicit rejection of the current and traditional organisation of foster care provision as an exclusively social work led and delivered professional activity. The agencies are seeking to leave behind the inherent weaknesses and the established failures of the public care system and move towards a new internal structure of inter-disciplinary professional services which take full account of the difficulties faced by children, their foster carers and, significantly, of mainstream schools.

Education is no longer seen as an area of peripheral concern on occasions where foster carers themselves may be put under pressure through children's difficult educational circumstances. The education of children is now placed at the heart of professional activity and understood as almost certainly the only means through which corporate aims and objectives for children may be effectively realised. It is considered, too, an area of practice with a crucial role to play in the recruitment, assessment, support and professional development of foster carers themselves.

High expectations are placed on children to attend and succeed in mainstream schools. No alternative education facilities such as separate units or classrooms are provided within these agencies as experience has demonstrated that they may prolong rather than reduce the exclusion of many children from mainstream schools. Furthermore, schools are valued not only as centres of learning but equally for providing important opportunities for the personal and social development of children outside the classroom itself. As one social work manager stated, 'We don't think that educating children on the premises is the right thing to do. Normalisation is the idea, encouraging children to do what other children do, and most don't go out each morning into a classroom in the garden.'

Mainstream schools are too often caricatured as hugely resistant to providing education to children who may present significant challenges to teachers and other pupils. Experience demonstrates that the majority of schools are genuinely sympathetic to providing mainstream opportunities for all children where they feel adequately supported by professional teachers who understand not only the social work system but, critically, the context in which schools themselves operate.

A key professional objective of these agencies, therefore, is to develop a practical response which acknowledges the potential dichotomy of interests of the mainstream school and the child facing serious difficulties and then provides ways in which this may be prevented and resolved. Furthermore, for those children who do attend mainstream schools without any overt difficulty, there is an important focus on raising levels of educational attainment rather than being satisfied with their regular attendance and general compliance with the school's code of conduct and routines.

The social work service provided by each of these agencies is now equally matched and complemented by a team of teachers directly employed by the National Teaching & Advisory Service (NT&AS) who provide each child with an individual education casework service. Teachers are deployed to work within and across each respective agency to provide children and mainstream schools with the quantity and quality of professional support they require to secure access to schools and successful learning within them. This may include up to full-time teacher support within each school for those individual children facing the most serious and challenging difficulties.

Schools equally value the intensive preparation and research of each school placement prior to the pupil's admission, which is undertaken by NT&AS teaching staff. School teachers, young people, their parents, foster carers, social workers and other professionals are all active participants in the planning of school induction programmes. NT&AS teachers administer baseline curriculum assessments, prepare differentiated and extension materials in support of each curriculum area where required, and plan with the school to determine the nature and style of support appropriate to each teacher and pupil setting, in advance of pupil admission.

After two or three weeks of full-time support, the programme is formally reviewed and evaluated and used to determine the specific requirements for the next phase of establishing successful attendance and learning. This takes into account the experience of the first phase as to how the individual child has responded to each element of school life. Through this process it is possible to gradually reduce and effectively focus professional support on any continuing weak spots within the school placement, including those within individual subject areas. The review also takes account of other aspects of the child's personal life and routines that may support or impede their educational progress. The process of planning, support and review continues until the child is successfully included in school. Continued monitoring also ensures informed and immediate intervention should unexpected difficulties begin to emerge or where new areas of underachievement are identified.

NT&AS teachers also provide education expertise within the agency as a permanent resource for the training and development of foster carers and to promote a range of educational initiatives within each foster home designed to complement the work of teachers within mainstream schools. Teacher assessments of potential foster carers include a perspective on their own educational experiences, attitudes and willingness to prioritise school attendance and successful learning throughout their daily routines. Approved foster carers are visited as regularly by teachers as by social work staff to promote effective home–school communications and to develop their role in supporting children's educational lives. Children themselves are provided with direct assistance with homework, individual literacy and numeracy programmes and, progressively, skills in information technology for which each foster home will eventually be resourced with appropriate computers and software, and the training and support required. Children will have access to NT&AS summer school provision during which they will be able to participate in a range of education-based activities to broaden their educational experiences.

The impact on children placed within these agencies and within those local authorities currently working to the same methodology is being evaluated and measured through monitoring individual and collective outcomes matched against baseline assessments administered during the initial stages of each placement. The participating independent agencies themselves have high expectations on behalf of children in their care.

They are already able to demonstrate significant improvements in levels of school attendance, a higher proportion of children facing significant difficulties being successfully educated within mainstream schools, and substantial reductions in incidences of school exclusion as key indicators of the effectiveness of the service. There should also be a measurable improvement in the efficiency and effectiveness of support as understood by children themselves, their foster carers and by mainstream and special school teaching staff.

In the summer term of 2000, of those young people placed within these IFAs who were eligible to take examinations, all did so, and all exceeded the National Priorities Guidance target. Their results ranged

Table 1

Looked after children placed in IFAs worked with by NT&AS (January 1999 to September 2000)

Total number of school-aged children and young people placed	155
Without school place at point of admission	82%
Without school placement after four weeks following admission	8%
Number attending mainstream schools after two months following admission to IFA	78%
Number attending special schools after two months following admission to IFA	14%

from two to eight GCSE passes, together with other nationally recognised certificates of achievement. Of these, 25 per cent gained eight passes or more, and one achieved the highest possible grade in two subjects. Significantly, 25 per cent of these young people had been out of full-time education for two years or more.

The two case studies that follow illustrate how the service has been able to effect a fundamental change for the better in the lives of individual children while reducing the demand for enormously costly specialist residential placements, thus releasing resources for more constructive purposes.

Table 2

Looked after children placed in IFAs worked with by NT&AS (Information collected after Summer Term, 2000)

Education performance of children and young people in placement	
Key Stage One English Level 2	100%
Key Stage One Maths Level 2	67%
Key Stage Two English Level 4	65%
Key Stage Two Maths Level 4	45%
Key Stage Two Science Level 4	86%
Key Stage Three English Level 5 or above	47%
Key Stage Three Maths Level 5 or above	56%
Key Stage Three Science Level 5 or above	73%

The "acceptable" level of achievement described in *Social Services Performance* in 1999 to 2000 is the National Priorities Guidance target for at least 50 per cent of children leaving care, aged 16 or over, to have one (or more) GCSE pass (Grade A* to G) or one (or more) GNVQ pass(es) by 2000/2001. The average across the looked after population in England was 30 per cent, a figure significantly below the target. In the general school population of 16-year-olds, 94 per cent gained one or more GCSE or GNVQ qualification.

Case study 1

John is aged ten and looked after by the local authority. At the outset of John's four previous foster placements, education was identified as a major area of concern. John had not attended school regularly for two years and was permanently excluded from three primary schools. He had not taken up a place offered to him at the authority's school for pupils with emotional and behavioural difficulties as he was moved by his social worker to new carers outside the borough.

It was recognised that John's education circumstances directly contributed to breakdowns within his previous care placements, leading to moves which further complicated attempts to meet his educational needs. John's new carers expressed frustration that his education difficulties were already creating intolerable pressure on their capacity to care for him effectively. The education department was sympathetic but considered that appropriate education provision had been made available but rendered ineffective due to the number of times John had been moved.

His social worker requested funding for a specialist residential provision with education at a cost of £75,000 per year and suggested there was no alternative. Application was made for joint funding of provision with the LEA which rejected the request as they felt they had met their responsibilities to John through the SEN (Special Educational Needs) Code of Practice, offered a place within their EBD (Emotional and Behavioural Difficulties) school, and should not therefore incur further expense as a consequence of social services moving John out of the borough.

The social services manager referred John for placement within an independent fostering agency which worked alongside the National Teaching & Advisory Service. NT&AS teachers planned and supported John's full induction into a mainstream primary school local to his new foster carers. His carers welcomed the programme as it provided John and his new school with full-time teacher support to maximise the possibility of success within the school and within his foster placement. John's current success in school has greatly contributed to stability in the foster home and prevented significant further costs to his local authority. John is no longer being considered for a specialist residential placement.

Case study 2

Georgina is 15 years old and lived at home with her mother and two brothers until April 1998. Another brother had put himself into voluntary care approximately two years previously. In April 1998, Georgina presented herself at the police station and asked them to find her somewhere to live. There had been allegations of neglect and lack of supervision concerning the family for a period of time prior to this. Between April and September 1998, Georgina had five different foster homes which each ended in crisis as a consequence of what was described as her 'uncontrollable behaviour'. In September she was admitted to a local authority children's home.

Georgina had been on roll at Secondary School 1 since Year 7. Her attendance had always been sporadic, but deteriorated so seriously by the time she reached Year 9 that she attended school on only four occasions during the summer term. At the start of Year 10, in September 1998, Georgina's attendance had become an unusual event and when she did attend she would often leave school after being marked present. Her punctuality was also poor. At one stage during this year, a taxi was provided to support her attendance, but Georgina refused to use it. When Georgina did attend, staff at school felt she had a negative and hostile attitude and regularly distracted other pupils. Academically Georgina had completed little work since December 1997. Her Head of Year felt Georgina was working so far below the level of her peers, given the large gap in her attendance that 'the acquisition of skills was virtually impossible'.

The school showed a high level of commitment to Georgina and was anxious to find a way to help her succeed. However, Georgina seemed to misinterpret their concern and felt allowances were being made because she was in care. Georgina saw herself as needing to be more independent in her life choices. On 28 November 1998, a referral was made to the NT&AS. It became apparent that Georgina needed urgent and intensive help in order to access education within a mainstream school setting.

The NT&AS allocated a teacher who compiled a comprehensive social and educational history and subsequently researched all of the possible education options for Georgina. Following discussion with Georgina, the NT&AS teacher then arranged an education planning meeting. Options were explored and a school about three miles away from the children's home was identified and approached as the option that would be most likely to meet Georgina's needs.

Following a meeting between Georgina, her key worker from the children's home, her social worker, the NT&AS teacher and the school Head of Year, an admission date was agreed. It was also agreed to review formally Georgina's progress after the first two weeks of full-time support, following the date of admission. The NT&AS teacher then arranged to discuss professional support with individual teachers in each relevant subject area within the school and subsequently agreed its detail. The style of support varied considerably across subject areas and took full account of Georgina's level of confidence in different elements of the curriculum and the requirements of individual teachers. The teacher then discussed with Georgina and the residential staff at the home the practicalities of transport, uniform, equipment requirements and the details of her new school timetable.

Georgina started school once more at the beginning of term in January 1999 with the NT&AS teacher supporting her on a full-time basis for the first two weeks. In Mathematics the NT&AS teacher taught the full group on three occasions during the first week and on two further occasions in week two. At the school review it was agreed that there were a number of curriculum areas where Georgina had settled remarkably well and in which there were no concerns. It was agreed that NT&AS support would be withdrawn from each of them on a planned basis. In all other subject areas, in breaks and in lunchtime periods it was felt that intensive support should remain and be further reviewed towards the end of the half-term period.

At the half-term review, further areas of significant progress were identified and support from the NT&AS was reduced significantly. By the end of March, Georgina had become part of an established group of friends and expressed the view that she felt part of the school and no longer an outsider. She continued, however, to experience some difficulties and there were concerns about her attitude to particular teachers within the school. The school acknowledged, too, that Georgina's placement had been far more successful than they had expected, given her previous education history. Of particular note, they felt, was Georgina's excellent attendance which had been around 92 per cent.

On 26 September 1999, the NT&AS was advised that a new foster carer had been identified for Georgina and that her social worker was confident that the prospective placement stood an excellent chance of success in spite of the number of foster placements she had previously had, as Georgina was, 'for the first time in ages, now fully occupied during the day'.

Georgina continues to attend school with enthusiasm and has settled well with her new foster carer. The NT&AS teacher now visits

Georgina at home about once a fortnight and continues to support her in school for around two hours a week.

Conclusion

There has undeniably been significant progress in recent years in addressing the educational needs of looked after children. In this respect we should not underestimate the commitment of central and local government to providing fresh opportunities to those thousands of children in public care who have previously been systematically denied them. At the same time, there is no room for any relaxation in our collective efforts to ensure that the scandalous education underachievement of these most vulnerable of children can confidently be consigned to the past.

The aspiration of central government and of all professionals working on behalf of looked after children is, rightly, that they increasingly and demonstrably achieve in line with other children in the general school population. The extent to which we are able to deliver this without a fundamental re-examination of the nature and extent of those *direct* professional services currently available to looked after children and their carers is an important consideration which requires urgent and rigorous analysis, beyond the rhetoric. As part of this re-appraisal of services, there is emerging evidence that a well-supported fostering service that gives equal weight to care and education can give looked after children their rightful access to mainstream education, substantially improve their levels of achievement and, as a consequence, enhance their longer term potential for full and successful social inclusion within our communities.

14 The education of black and minority ethnic children in care

Randy Lee Comfort

Education commences at the mother's knee, and every word spoken in the hearing of the little children tends toward the formation of character.

Hosea Ballou

We tend to associate the word "education" with the word "school", but small children have been both well educated and well schooled long before they reach the steps of the actual building called school. In the best of circumstances, these well-educated little ones will have learned about love, trust, security, tolerance and inter-dependence. Under less desirable circumstances, children will have learned about survival techniques, about the inconsistency of adults, about fear and shame and brutality and self-protection. Children in care fall into the category of youngsters who have been taught about abuse and neglect, insecurity, mistrust and unpredictability. Black and minority ethnic[1] children may have also learned lessons about discrimination, intolerance, racism and defeat. These are not the tools that help a child to decipher the codes of reading, writing and arithmetic.

James is a ten-year-old boy who lives in kinship care, primarily with his grandparents who were born and brought up in Jamaica. They moved to Britain when James was born in order to care for him as his mother's physical and mental health prevented her from providing an adequate environment for her son. James's father left the city when he found out that James's mother was pregnant.

---

[1] For the purposes of this article, the term, "minority ethnic" is used to refer to all children of non-Caucasian heritage and belonging to a cultural, racial or religious group numerically smaller than the white majority ethnic population. For the most part, the term "black" refers specifically to African-Caribbean, African, Caribbean or British-born black children only.

Throughout the years there have been attempts to reunite James with his mother, but short periods of living together have always resulted in his physical and emotional neglect. His grandparents are able to provide a more stable home for James, except that they are quite elderly and find his energy hard to manage.

After frequent exclusions from numerous schools, a caring Head at James's new school requested an external educational evaluation. She felt that his erratic school performance, his volatile behaviour and his considerable inattention in the classroom did not match his apparent intellectual ability. The independent educational psychologist found that James had significant "visual perceptual difficulties" and some degree of fine motor disorder. Providing James with additional support in these areas and making several educational adjustments to meet his needs resulted in this very bright lad settling down in school and performing above average in most subject areas.

Unfortunately, most children in James's situation have not had the benefit of attentive and persistent heads or teachers who have been able to facilitate their educational career. Looked after children are often neglected by both the social service and the education systems with regard to their school progress (SSI/OFSTED, 1995), while black and minority ethnic children in care suffer from even more severe academic neglect.

The complete dearth of research and literature on the education of minority ethnic children in the care system probably accurately reflects the lack of attention that has been paid to this issue (Jackson, 2000). Increasingly, however, it is becoming obvious that these are children who are at multiple risk for failure in society. Despite the lack of formal research evidence, carers, teachers and the children themselves can produce a wealth of anecdotal evidence documenting the blighted academic careers of black and minority ethnic children looked after by local authorities.

As many chapters in this book testify, looked after children do markedly less well academically and socially in school than any other group of minority children. It is also known, particularly in the United States, that Black and Hispanic children have very poor achievement records in the educational system (Cook, 1997; Parker, Greer and Zuckerman, 1998). In England it is estimated that between 50 and 75 per cent of looked after children leave school with no formal qualifications (Biehal, Clayden and Stein, 1992; Garnett, 1992; Biehal *et al*, 1995), but it has not been reported how many of these children are from black or minority ethnic communities.

It is interesting to note that in Jackson and Martin's study of high achievers from care (1998) minority ethnic girls were over-represented, but these were exceptional cases. Despite the paucity of documenting research, there is no reason to believe that minority ethnic children in care do better educationally than others and much anecdotal evidence to suggest that they may be even more disadvantaged. It is important to look at the factors that contribute to this situation, and to begin to think about how changes can be made.

Black and minority ethnic children in the care system

These children are especially vulnerable on several counts, but it is hard to know how to prioritise the associated aspects of risk. Looking at the care population in general, it is known that a high proportion of the children come from birth families in which poverty, substance abuse, physical and emotional neglect, mental and physical health difficulties, low educational attainment and learning disabilities are prevalent components. Low birth weight is a factor which is often associated with infants born of substance abusing and/or impoverished mothers, and low birth weight is also an at-risk factor for low educational attainment (Brooks and Barth, 1998).

Most children come into care because their home lives have been unstable and because there has been inadequate provision for basic emotional and physical health. As infants, these children have not had opportunities to attain the security or stimulation babies need to grow and develop in healthy ways. Programmes such as Head Start (Advisory Committee on Head Start, 1993) and Early Head Start in the US (Zero to Three, 1997), the inspiration for Sure Start in the UK, have shown that providing toddlers with appropriate stimulation and guided opportunities for play enable them to begin school with better skills and foundations for learning and for socialising.

Children in the care system frequently have not had the chance to develop these vital skills. Moving homes and missing out on routine occasions to play with other young children in groups or in nursery school have impeded their opportunities to learn about growing up in healthy and appropriately stimulating environments, both with stable caretakers and with normally developing peers (Jackson, 1988).

Children in care rarely have stability even after being removed from parents who are unable to provide for their needs. Statistics indicate that young children are moved from home to home, in and out of their birth home, and in and out of a variety of placement settings far too often (Jackson and Thomas, 1999). Twenty per cent of children in care in the UK who are under five years have had more than six placements (Department of Health, 1999; Ivaldi, 1999). The child who experiences this kind of disruption in early life begins to concentrate on survival skills, on techniques of emotional withdrawal, and on adaptability rather than learning about trust, dependency, consistency and pre-academic tasks. Children in care are no less intelligent than their home-reared peers, but they are focusing their cognitive and emotional energies along different tracks (see also Chapter 11).

If we focus on the issues concerning the black and minority ethnic child in care, the difficulties are compounded even further. All of the disadvantages existing for looked after white children apply to black and minority ethnic children except that they are magnified many times over. Let us look at why this happens.

Compared with their numbers in the general population, there are a disproportionate number of black and minority ethnic children in care. Social services departments follow the principle that the placement of choice for children should be with carers of similar ethnic and cultural background. Since there are few of these families coming forward to foster and adopt, black and minority ethnic children tend to be moved even more than white youngsters. Although this practice is now being challenged, it has been common for the former to change families if a family of similar ethnic background becomes available while they are in a white home. This is a controversial issue because there are advantages and disadvantages to be weighed on both sides, but the bottom line is that children get moved, and there is not a single piece of research indicating that multiple moves are beneficial for a child. Stability in even a "good enough" home is always preferable to multiple moves for the developing child (Jackson and Thomas, 1999).

Garry, a nine-year-old of mixed parentage, was four and in his fifth foster home when he began school. His reception class teacher described him as a loner and was annoyed with him because he often threw toys around the room rather than playing with anything constructively. In Year 1 there was a brief note from his teacher referring to her sense that Garry might have a learning disorder but this was never followed up because of a change of schools. In the next two years, Garry moved schools three times. During that time he made no real friends and consistently played by himself in the playground. He was not seen as a troublemaker or a particular behaviour problem but he performed poorly in all of his academic subjects; he was, however, noted for being quite a good artist.

Garry's foster carers received a note from his teacher in Year 4 telling them that Garry would probably never be much of a student, but that guiding him toward a career in an artistic vocation would be beneficial for him.

Since Garry's foster carers, like many other carers, did not experience much success at school either, this note did not seem out of line to them. Most looked after children still leave school at age 16, which is consistent with the educational aspirations of their carers (Aldgate, 1993).

Many of us, however, would feel that an eight or nine-year-old child should be given the chance to learn and to improve his or her academic achievement before suggesting any particular vocation. Ruling out educational possibilities for this young child is typical of the stories that are told repeatedly by carers of black and minority ethnic children. Moreover, no one has addressed Garry's social-emotional needs or the fact that he has difficulty making friends and becoming an integral part of his classmates' activities.

A second strike against educational advancement for the black and minority ethnic child in care concerns poverty (Parker *et al*, 1988). Poverty is one of the factors associated with children in care, and poverty affects more black and minority ethnic families in this society. Many non-white children come into care for reasons of economic insufficiency and its contingent deprivations in the child's birth family. Similarly, substance abuse is prevalent in this population, meaning that many infants enter the world affected by serious drugs or maternal misuse of alcohol, factors which may jeopardise their normal growth and development. Often these are fragile babies, whose birth parents have neither the economic means nor the emotional and physical stability to offer their infants the attention and care they require to overcome early vulnerabilities.

The school scene

In a 1998 study in the US, developmental screening of 52 children under 18 months who were in care indicated that 35 per cent failed the screening test, with the most significant number falling down in the language-communication section (O'Hara, Church and Blatt, 1998). Academic and social success in school are highly dependent upon communication skills, yet children who are developmentally at risk and who are subsequently experiencing inconsistency of family life are not given appropriate opportunities to learn how to communicate. These children often have weak language and communication skills. Those skills that they do learn may have to do with staying safe and with surviving, but they lack the skills that are congruent with what is acceptable in the everyday school or social environment.

Minority ethnic children coming from other countries or from parents for whom English is not the first language are likely to suffer even greater communication disadvantages when they enter the school system. This has both an academic and a social impact on them, with the result that they often fall behind in their studies and that they are bullied in the playground. Children of a different colour or for whom English is a second language are readily picked out as children who can be bullied. Playground life is not an easy part of the day for these youngsters as they usually feel isolated or feel the need to fight to defend themselves. Childline receives more calls about bullying than on any other subject, and research has shown that name-calling and other forms of verbal bullying can cause acute suffering to children (Crozier and Dimmock, 1999). For most children the social aspects of school take precedence over the academic aspects, and the social influences at school have profound effects on their lives. Looked after children and particularly black and minority ethnic looked after children, are prime targets for bullying, ridicule, social exclusion and underachievement at school, leaving their self-esteem lagging way behind that of their peers.

There is much anecdotal information suggesting that the school setting reflects societal assumptions that children in care are "damaged goods", that they are less capable and less academically inclined. Teachers are not immune to these prejudices and some teachers expect less of looked after children, and even less from black children. Lower expectations can turn into self-fulfilling prophecies, so minority ethnic children in care often end up performing at only the minimum level they feel is demanded of them.

A well-meaning teacher says that he has recognised that Shawna is struggling in maths, but he hasn't said anything to her or her carers about this because he knows that she is "looked after" and he doesn't want to make matters even worse for her. He gives her the same work and says he has the same expectations of her as he does of everyone else in his classroom because he is not wanting her to be "different".

As stated above, this is a "well-meaning" teacher, but covering up for Shawna, an 11-year-old African-Caribbean girl living in her sixth foster home and attending her fourth different school, is not going to enable her to acquire the skills she will need to become competent in secondary school. Shawna is also aware that she is struggling in maths, and would very much like for her teacher to help her, but she lacks the confidence to ask for help. Trying to keep up with everyone else when she knows she doesn't understand the work is worse for her than being identified as a student who could use additional support.

While these misguided attempts at non-discrimination are not uncommon, there are, on the other hand, many stories told by minority ethnic students substantiating the low expectations of academic achievement that they have experienced in school and in residential care settings. Many black children will say they had no careers guidance at all, or if they did, they were directed toward sport, jazz or street dance and music, technical and manual jobs, regardless of their academic ability (Ince, 1999). Black boys who move schools are often allocated to remedial classes or low streams without reference to their previous level of performance. In the US, research indicates that, once in a special education class or unit, it is harder for black and Hispanic children to progress and to move back into the mainstream classroom than it is for white children to do this. This is highly likely to be true in Britain as well. There are other problems arising from the prevalent black peer culture. Even those children who are studious and who are encouraged by teachers to study, report being teased, bullied and isolated. Once again this is a problem for boys and looked after children generally, but it particularly affects black boys (Craft and Craft, 1985).

A black psychiatrist in his late 30s reflects back on his school days when he attended school in an inner-city setting:

> My father was a doctor and my mother a scientist. They always had expectations that my sister and I would become professionals as well, but this was totally out of sync with many of my black school friends, who teased me for being a swot. I do remember a lot of black children who were in care because they seemed so "volatile". School wasn't really where they were comfortable. Those are the same kids I see in my office as clients today – scared, defeated, under-educated.

(Personal communication)

Children of mixed parentage often say that teachers seem to favour white students when selecting class leaders, when using examples of outstanding work, or choosing classroom monitors. These children say that they are more likely to be selected for being sports team captains, for leading a game, for beating a drum – if they are selected at all.

Residential care children have the worst record of all in the education system (Jackson, 1989) and a high proportion of these young people are usually black (Robinson, 2000). Students in residential care complain that there has been little or no educational support for them. Frequently there is not even a desk or a quiet area where they can study (see Chapter 16), and there may be little time or investment on the carer's part concerning homework or school achievement. There seems to be virtually no communication between the residential care home and the school unless the child is in deep trouble. The environment is not conducive to studying or to achieving academically, and the care community breeds a rough and tough ambience in which school reputation is based on swagger and power rather than academic attainment.

I learned to fight and fuck at school because that was what was expected of me at the home where I was the biggest, blackest dude.

(Young teenager in residential care)

A poignant scenario is described by a black teenager living in a foster home in a video. She comments on the uniqueness of her situation while studying for GCSEs. Most children in Year 10/11, she says, are able to concentrate entirely on their school work, but her foster family is constantly asking her to think about planning for her life after GCSEs: where she will live, how she will support herself. She states, justifiably, that these considerations get in the way of applying herself to her schoolwork, and that they are not topics with which children in birth families are dealing.

Outcomes for black and minority ethnic young people

Children in care are frequently excluded from school for disruptive behaviour and many of these children are black students. This contributes to the black child's perception of being a trouble-maker and of being a victim. It also serves to interfere with the development of healthy self-esteem. The black looked after child has a hard time developing a positive perception of who he or she is when what that child observes is black children being excluded, isolated from their communities, and viewed as non-achievers. Consequently, black children in care are heavily loaded with baggage which white students in birth families never even think about – which is not to suggest that all white children in birth families have easy lives, but the odds are stacked more in their favour.

Depressingly, the Joseph Rowntree Foundation has recently collected various studies showing that job opportunities for African-Caribbeans and Africans in the UK remain bleaker than for their white counterparts even when they are highly educated. African graduates in their 20s are seven times more likely to be unemployed (Hills, 1995; Great Britain Office for National Statistics, 2000). An additional piece of research from the Work and Opportunity series confirms that 'those leaving school at 16 without work or to join government training programmes have difficulty breaking the cycle of insecure employment, unemployment and training initiatives'. Although these studies were looking at young black people in general, one can only assume that the outcomes for young black people leaving care as well as leaving school are that much worse. Very little seems to have changed since the leaving care studies carried out by Mike Stein and his team over the past 15 years (Stein, 1997 and see Chapter 5)

What can be done?

If the State is an unstable parent and a reluctant educator of black and minority ethnic children in care, how is it possible for these children to become healthy and contributing members of society? At present it is clear that they have a much higher mountain to climb than their white peers who grow up in adequate or better birth families, or even for their black and minority ethnic peers who grow up outside the care system.

Faced with such disadvantages, the educational background of their carers may well be more important than the colour of their skin (Morgan, 1998). Despite the conventional orthodoxy, there is plenty of evidence that black and minority ethnic children can flourish in white foster and adoptive homes (Tizard and Phoenix, 1989, 1993) and that, if this is the best available placement for them, other ways must be found to affirm their racial and ethnic identity. Minority ethnic children must have minority ethnic mentors, teachers, community members, heroes/ heroines, professionals and friends immediately available to them. Parents, carers and teachers must provide evidence that they value and respect the child's heritage by exposing them to a variety of cultural events and holidays, by using shops and restaurants run by minority ethnic entrepreneurs and which people of the child's heritage frequent. Buying and using cards, magazines and literature, pictures and articles that reflect intercultural perspectives, cooking foods from a variety of cultures and nations, attending cross-cultural celebrations, going to parks and shopping areas where people from a variety of cultures go, are but a few of the ways in which foster and adoptive families and schools can help minority ethnic children to know that their heritage is valued.

Positive images in magazines and newpapers, as well as stories and examples of successful black and minority ethnic people in everyday life contribute to enhanced self-esteem and the realisation that alternatives to school drop-out and lives of unemployment and disruption do exist. Contact with peers and with older people who have risen above the faulty system can provide windows of opportunity for minority ethnic looked after children (Rutter, 1998).

Social workers certainly have their work cut out for them, both in the placement of children and in the maintenance of the child's familial and educational stability. Not only is changing families disruptive, but also moving from school to school is disastrous for looked after children (Fletcher-Campbell and Hall, 1990; Jackson and Thomas, 1999). A change of school means loss of friends, the need to make new contacts and friends, constant re-engagement with different teachers and school personnel, interrupted learning and lack of educational support. Children who may have begun the statementing process in one school usually need to start all over again in a new school, losing valuable time and learning opportunities. Inconsistency of family life is mirrored by unpredictable and ever-changing school patterns. The ethnic and racial population of the school is also something to be considered when a minority ethnic child is placed with a new family; it is important for the child to have some neighbourhood and school friends who are of a similar cultural background. Above all, social workers themselves need to work closely with the school and the foster carer or residential home in order to provide more effective acknowledgement that school is an important factor in the child's life.

If social services has much to consider, there is no less for the educational system to take on board. Schools would do well to have a culturally/racially balanced staff – a staff that reflects the population of its pupils. Not only cultural awareness training, but also learning about the situations of looked after children would help to mitigate many of the conflicts arising in schools and would serve to expand the interests of and tolerance of differences in the families attending the school.

Involving parents and extended families of all the children at school in programmes and in classroom support usually creates more understanding and enjoyment among teachers, students and parents/carers. There needs to be much greater knowledge about the care system and about looked after children so that old stereotypes can be put aside and so that children in public care have a chance to be given and to earn the respect awarded to children living with their birth parents. Residential homes and foster carers have many concomitant adjustments to make in their support for students at school and in the home.

The black and minority ethnic child in care today has little chance of attaining the educational and employment opportunities available to others. It is well known that the prison population is disproportionately made up of adults who were in care and/or inmates who have learning dysfunctions that were not attended to while they were at school. There is also a disproportionate number of black people in prison. In addition to the low levels of school attainment and high unemployment among care leavers, other frightening statistics include:

- the high rate of pregnancy among black and minority ethnic teenagers in the care system, almost always young girls who have left school early;
- the numbers of black and minority ethnic children and looked after children who are excluded from school each year;
- the poor physical and mental health which is frequently prevalent in this population;
- the degree of substance abuse among black and minority ethnic looked after children.

All of us – professionals and families, white and minority ethnic – need to learn more from those people who have made it through the care system successfully. What enabled these people to move on from their terrible and debilitating experiences? Repeatedly researchers are told that there was one person who believed in them, who helped them, who became responsible for them (Haggerty *et al*, 1994; Fraser, 1997).

Today's social workers, psychologists and educators must ask similar questions of those who have defied a care and education system that threatened to defeat their achievement. There are examples of black and minority ethnic young adults who are now living independently, holding jobs, maintaining intact families even though they spent all or part of their young lives in foster or residential care (Jackson and Martin, 1998). It would be helpful to hear more from them about the factors that enabled them to succeed.

As is so often the case, the way forward is obviously not to be found in a single or simple solution, but the best resolutions might well lie in the experiences of those who have made it, from those black and minority ethnic teachers, heads, social workers and administrators who work successfully within schools and social services, and from listening to the black and minority ethnic children in care whose daily lives present both the questions and the answers that can help to improve a very faulty social and educational system.

The direction in which education starts a man will determine his future life.
(Plato)

References

Aldgate, J (1993) 'Social work and the education of children in foster care', *Adoption & Fostering*, 17:3, pp 25–34.

Advisory Committee on Head Start Quality and Expansion (1993) *Creating a 21st Century Head Start*, Washington DC: Advisory Committee.

Barn, R, *Black Children in the Public Care System: Child care policy and practice*, London: Batsford/British Agencies for Adoption and Fostering.

Biehal, N, Clayden, J and Stein, M (1992) *Prepared for Living: A survey of young people leaving the care of three local authorities*, London: National Children's Bureau.

Biehal, N and Clayden, J, Stein, M and Wade, J (1995) *Moving On: Young people and leaving care schemes*, London: HMSO.

Brooks, D and Barth, R P (1998) 'Characteristics and outcomes of drug-exposed and non drug-exposed children in kinship and non-relative foster care', *Children & Youth Services Review*, 20:6, pp 475–501.

Cook, R J (1997) 'Are we helping foster care youth prepare for their future?', in Berrick, J D, Barth, R P and Gilbert, N, *Child Welfare Research Review*, 11, pp 201–18, New York: Columbia University Press.

Craft, M and Craft, A (1985) 'The participation of ethnic minority pupils in further and higher education', *Education Research*, 25.

Crozier, W R and Dimmock, P (1999) 'Name calling and nicknames in a sample of primary school children', *British Journal of Educational Psychology*, 69, pp 505–16.

Department of Health (1999) *Children Looked After by Local Authorities: Year ending 31 March 1998*, London: DH.

Fletcher-Campbell, F and Hall, C (1990) *Changing Schools? Changing People?: The education of children in care*, Slough: NFER.

Fraser, M (ed.) (1997) *Risk and Resilience in Childhood: an ecological perspective*, Washington DC: National Association of Social Workers.

Garnett, L (1992) *Leaving Care*, London: National Children's Bureau.

Great Britain Office for National Statistics (2000) *Labour Force Survey Quarterly Bulletin*, London: The Stationery Office.

Haggerty, R, Sharrod, L, Garmezy, N and Rutter, M (1994) *Stress, Risk and Resilience in Children and Adolescents: Processes, mechanisms and interventions*, Cambridge: Cambridge University Press.

Hills, J (1995) *Inquiry into Income and Wealth*, York: Joseph Rowntree Foundation.

Ince, L (1999) 'Preparing young black people for leaving care', in Barn, R, *Working with Black Children and Adolescents in Need*, pp 157–171, London: BAAF.

Ivaldi, G (1999) *BAAF Adoption Survey: 1998/1999: Report on the preparatory phase*, London: BAAF.

Jackson, S (1988) 'Education and children in foster care', *Adoption & Fostering*, 12, pp 6–10.

Jackson, S (1989) Residential Care and Education, *Children & Society*, 2:4.

Jackson, S (2000) 'Promoting the educational achievement of looked after children', in Cox, T (ed.) *Combating Educational Disadvantage: Meeting the needs of vulnerable children*, London: Falmer Press.

Jackson, S and Martin, P Y (1998) 'Surviving the care system: education and resilience', *Journal of Adolescence*, 21.

Jackson, S and Thomas, N (1999) *On the Move Again? What works in creating stability for looked after children*, Ilford: Barnardo's.

Morgan, P (1998) *Adoption and the Care of Children*, London: IEA Health and Welfare Unit.

O'Hara, M T and Church, C C *et al* (1998) 'Home-based developmental screening of children in foster care', *Pediatric Nursing*, 24:2, pp 113–17.

Parker, S, Greer, S and Zuckerman, B (1988) 'Double jeopardy: the impact of poverty on early childhood development', *Pediatric Clinics of North America*, 35, pp 1727–39.

Robinson, L (2000) 'Racial identity attitudes and self-esteem of black adolescents in residential care: an exploratory study', *British Journal of Social Work*, 30, pp 3–24.

Rutter, M (1998) *Psychosocial Adversity: Risk, resilience and recovery*, Social, Genetic and Developmental Psychiatry Research Centre, London: Institute of Psychiatry.

Social Services Inspectorate & Office for Standards in Education (1995) *The Education of Children who are Looked After by Local Authorities*, London: SSI/OFSTED.

Stein, M (1997) *What Works in Leaving Care?* Ilford: Barnardo's.

Tizard, B and Phoenix, A (1989) 'Black identity and transracial adoption', *New Community*, 15:3, pp 427–37.

Tizard B and Phoenix, P (1993) *Black, White or Mixed Race*, London: Routledge.

Zero to Three (1997) *National Center for Infants, Toddlers and Families*, Washington DC.

15 Social support and educational enhancement for students in out-of-home care: An investigation using the school success profile

Jack M. Richman and Lawrence B. Rosenfeld

In the Charlotte/Mecklenberg Communities-In-Schools drop-out prevention program in North Carolina, USA, the decision was made in 1998 to include all children in out-of-home care in the support services designed for academically at-risk students (Cynthia Marshall, personal communication, 18 June, 1999). Regardless of any other risk factors these children in out-of-home care might have, out-of-home placement was recognised as a powerful enough risk factor to warrant the invocation of extra-ordinary educational support.

School failure has severe consequences for both individuals and society – more now than in prior generations (Rumberger, 1987; Hepburn and White, 1990). On an individual level, many students in public schools today experience difficulty adjusting to school and acquiring the skills necessary for pursuing advanced education and training, and succeeding in the workplace. School failure – which seems to affect poor and minority individuals disproportionately more than economically stable and non-minority populations – has been associated with poverty and welfare dependency, higher mortality rates, higher incidence of suicide, and more frequent admissions to state mental hospitals (Rumberger, 1987; Harris, 1991). On the societal level, the impact of school failure includes a waste of human capital, loss of national income, loss of tax revenues, earlier involvement in sexual intercourse, higher risk of sexually transmitted disease, increased use and demand for social services, increased crime, reduced political participation, and higher health care costs (Carnahan, 1994). Keeping students in school and promoting academic success are critical for ensuring greater and more competent adult role performance, which has important implications for the individual, the family system, and the general functioning of society.

Risk factors, protective factors, and school success

In recent years, there has been increasing attention paid to those students who seem to succeed in school even though they are predicted to fail or drop out (Wang, Haertel and Walberg, 1994). In the search for protective factors that buffer the potential effects of risks and promote the positive adaptation of individuals, the concept of *resilience* has been introduced into the literature as a psychological construct (Werner and Smith, 1982; Masten *et al*, 1999). As Apfel and Simon (1996b) defined it, resilience is 'the child's capacity to bounce back from [or not succumb to] traumatic childhood events and develop into a sane, integrated, and socially responsible adult' (p 1). More specific to the concept of educational resilience, Wang *et al* (1994) define resilience as 'the heightened likelihood of success in school and other life accomplishments, despite environmental adversities brought about by early traits, conditions, and experiences' (p 46).

In defining resilience, researchers have considered what character- istics of a child and a child's environment constitute *risk factors* – 'influences that increase the probability of onset, digression to a more serious state, or maintenance of a problem condition' (Kirby and Fraser, 1997, pp 10–11) – and what characteristics constitute *protective factors* – 'internal and external forces that help children resist or ameliorate risk' (Kirby and Fraser, 1997, p 16). Resilience, however, is context dependent: individual factors gain their status as "risk" or "protection" in particular family and community environments in which the individual is embedded (Fraser, Richman and Galinsky, 1999). For example, frequent changes of residence may not be the same high-level risk factor for a child in a family in the armed services as it is for a child in out-of- home care. For both children, change of residence usually means changing schools and adapting to a new community; however, for the child in out-of-home placement, it also means leaving one family and adapting to a new family, often under adverse circumstances.

Although no student is immune to school problems, there are several risk factors that make those students who are exposed to them more vulnerable to academic problems and poor psychosocial adjustment in school. These factors include, for example, poverty, racial discrimination, poor parenting, abuse and neglect, an unstable home environment, few opportunities for education or employment, and racial and ethnic minority group membership (Rumberger, 1987; Carnahan, 1994; Kirby and Fraser, 1997). Children in out-of-home care – who tend to experience many of these risk factors and others – are highly vulnerable to academic problems (Heath, Colton and Aldgate, 1994).

Protective factors counter or buffer the effects of risk factors and, therefore, promote resilience. Internal protective forces include, for example, problem-solving ability, well-developed communication skills, self-understanding, high self-esteem, a belief in one's own personal effectiveness, high intelligence, the ability to attract adult support, resourcefulness, easy-going temperament, and optimism (Apfel and Simon, 1996a, 1996b; Kirby and Fraser, 1997). Regarding external protective forces, children are more likely to respond in positive ways to adversity if their environment provides them with three types of general protective conditions – stabilising and supportive relationships (stability), the balance of environmental demands to the child's capabilities (load balance), and opportunities to participate in meaningful events (participation) (Antonovsky, 1991).

Children in foster and out-of-home care: a vulnerable population

Academic success typically eludes children in out-of-home care – whether in traditional foster care, kinship care, or residential care arrangements. Summarising their cross-sectional analysis of the educational outcomes of UK children placed both in residential and long-term traditional foster care, Heath *et al* (1994) stated: 'Our previous research did not provide much encouragement for the hypothesis that foster care provides "an escape from disadvantage" ' (p 242).

Some of the most basic educational challenges foster children face are those over which they have no control, or are those which they bring into their foster placements. Foster children may change placements frequently, thereby experiencing more school disruptions and changes. Often, these upheavals in the child's life contribute to problems with proper school functioning (Thorpe and Swart, 1992; Ayasse, 1995;

Smucker, Kauffman and Ball, 1996; Tennyson, 1998). For example, Berrick, Courtney and Barth (1993) found that placement in a foster home necessitated changing schools for over 80 per cent of the children in their survey. Blome (1997) found that 36 per cent of foster children changed schools after the fifth grade, while only 20 per cent of the non-foster comparison group changed schools. An earlier Canadian study by Thorpe and Swart (1992) found that 44 per cent of foster children changed schools between grade levels, and 25 per cent experienced school disruption at least once during the school year.

Focusing on school success, Dupper (1997) summarised the dilemma of foster children in this way:

It is easy to understand why challenges at school are not a top priority for these children as they struggle to give meaning to the recent up-heavals in their lives. Often children in foster care must also struggle with the added challenges of low socio-economic status and dis-crimination and the tendency to change schools frequently because of changes in placements. (p 122)

Findings from Blome's (1997) survey revealed that most of the foster youth received 'C' grades, while the comparison group received a mix of 'B' and 'C' grades. In addition, foster children in general were more likely to be retained a grade level, and this likelihood increased when they were diagnosed with emotional-behavioural disorder. Even children who have the seeming benefit of long-term placements tend to perform below the national average for their grade level (Smucker *et al*, 1996), particularly when abuse or neglect has occurred (Colton, Heath and Aldgate, 1995).

The trend of low educational achievement continues into high school, when students are preparing for college or a career. Unfortunately, underachieving foster children are often locked into a "vocational track" by their school administration. For example, Blome (1997) found that children in out-of-home placement were more likely than others to be tracked in vocational education classes and clubs, or to receive on-the-job training, than to participate in college-preparatory classes. Exacer-bating the situation, the involvement of foster carers and caseworkers in the foster child's school career often was limited; for example, foster carers were much less likely to check up on homework assignments (Blome, 1997). Because of time and money pressures, heavy caseloads, and record-keeping requirements, foster children's educational needs can slip past their caseworkers (Ayasse, 1995).

Kinship care

Given the pitfalls (including academic failure) to which children in traditional foster care are vulnerable, kinship care has been studied as an alternative. Kinship care 'includes formal legally sanctioned and informal arrangements for the care and protection of children. It encompasses the private, voluntary, and formal child care arrangements among blood-related, non-related, and fictive kinship network members' (Everett, 1995, p 240). Results of several studies indicate that the hoped-for differences are negligible. For example, a comparison of children in kinship care, traditional foster care, and a non-foster care group found that 33.3 per cent of the kinship group and 39.4 per cent of the foster care group performed below their grade level, as compared with the non-foster group, of which only 11.1 per cent performed below grade level (Iglehart, 1995).

Dubowitz et al's (1994) study of children in kinship care found that these children do not perform significantly better than children in traditional types of foster care; also, like children in traditional foster care, they perform less well in school when compared to children not in out-of-home care. Children in kinship care also demonstrated more behavioural problems at school: their teachers indicated that 47 per cent of them had difficulty paying attention in class, while 53 per cent demonstrated poor study habits. Children in kinship care were also 26 per cent more likely than their classmates to "act out" or engage in aggressive behaviour. These problems are similar to those shown by children in traditional foster care, where even ordinary daily events can significantly impact the child's behaviour (Tennyson, 1998). School attendance, however, was about equal for the kinship group (89 per cent of enrolled days) and the city's public school population (86 per cent of enrolled days) (Dubowitz et al, 1994).

In a survey of teachers of children in kinship care, Sawyer and Dubowitz (1994) found that most of the children performed below average for their age group, although about 66 per cent of them had average or above-average cognitive skills compared to their peers.

The researchers found two factors that influenced how well a child in kinship care did academically: age at the time of placement, and the number of children in the placement home. High school students placed as teenagers did better academically than did children who started off early in kinship care.

Zuravin, Benedict and Stallings (1999) completed a study of 40 adults who were in traditional foster care and 31 who were in a kinship care arrangement. They found that the adults who were in traditional foster care completed fewer years of school, were more likely to be out of work, and to have a lower standard of living. In comparison, the adults who had been in kinship care were simply more likely to have a lower standard of living.

Biological parents' visits to their children in foster care have not been shown to be a significant factor in the children's school performance (Cantos, Gries and Slis, 1997). Regular visits, however, positively affected the children's behaviour, especially 'problems of an internalising nature (i.e. withdrawal, depression, anxiety)' (Cantos, Gries and Slis, 1997, p 324).

Long-term living and life skills

Drawing from the results of a 1988 California Department of Children's Services study, Iglehart (1994) suggested that the amount of education attained determines a foster youth's preparation for future employment and, therefore, his or her future standard of living. Adolescents frequently leave foster care with a 'poor education, poor health and low self-image', which makes finding a job difficult (Aldgate, 1994, p 261). Adolescents and young adults in grades 7 through 12 frequently struggle to stay in school and maintain good academic progress if they enter care during this crucial time (Christmas, 1998).

Some studies indicate that doing well in school can be a protective factor for children 'who have little else to fall back on. Recognition by teachers and/or peers as being good at something becomes very important. It may help them maintain hope for a better future' (Stein, 1997, p 11). Colton *et al* (1995) suggest that perhaps 'early educational intervention may be necessary in order to secure an "escape from disadvantage" ' (p 27). Educational success and support, particularly among female foster children, has been shown to affect their future life choices in a positive way; for example, they are more likely to choose supportive marital partners and carefully plan their work careers, life aspects that relate to overall social functioning (Rutter, Quinton and Hill, 1990).

The Independent Living Programme (ILP), implemented by the Department of Social Services in Maryland's Baltimore County, is being explored as a possible way to prepare foster children (primarily young adults aged 16–21) for living on their own (Scannapieco, Schagrin and Scannapieco, 1995). The ILP focuses on giving foster children the employment, life skills, and education they need to function well. Comparisons of 44 ILP participants with 46 foster children who were non-participants were favourable: the ILP youth 'were more likely to complete high school, have employment history and employment at discharge, and were more likely to be self-supporting at the closing of the case' (p 387). While Scannapieco et al caution on generalising results with a study sample this small, the findings suggest that programmes of this kind are worth further exploration.

Dubowitz et al (1994) suggest that 'services for all children in kinship care should include monitoring of school performance and behaviour, and appropriate interventions should be implemented when needed' (p 102). Zuravin et al (1999) agree that 'educational remediation is paramount . . . it [has] been found to be highly correlated with employment, [and] well-being' (p 220).

In general, foster children leave care less well prepared for independent living than non-foster care peers, although children in kinship care leave moderately more prepared than do children leaving traditional foster care situations (Zuravin et al, 1999). Blome (1997) recommends that local school and social service systems create methods and programmes specifically to help foster children and youth to cope with and overcome their unique problems. For example, financial assistance for independent youth should be offered, on a one-time basis, to make the beginning of their independent lives successful, whether they choose college, the military, or to go immediately into the work force.

Heath et al (1994) argue that, because children in out-of-home placement come to school with above average risk, they require above average educational services. Children in foster care are at heightened risk for school failure; therefore, it is paramount for practitioners – both in the out-of-home system and the education system – to co-operate and attend to the issue of educational success for these children.

The school success profile

One approach to helping students at risk of school failure begins with understanding how they perceive the several ecological environments that form the context in which they live. Developing intervention strategies without this information sets the stage for failure or, short of that, less-than-possible beneficial results. The School Success Profile (SSP) developed at the University of North Carolina at Chapel Hill by Drs Jack Richman and Gary Bowen, is designed to assess middle and high school students' (aged approximately 11–17) perceptions of their family, school, peer and neighbourhood environments, as well as of themselves. These perceptions form the basis for understanding each student's strengths and areas of risk. This information, in turn, can be used to develop knowledgeable interventions based on the particular student's needs.

The SSP is based on three theoretical perspectives: ecological theory, social disorganisation theory, and Maslow's need hierarchy theory (Richman and Bowen, 1997). The primary foundation is ecological theory (Bronfenbrenner, 1979) which argues that the social environment either advances or constrains a child's development. Environmental risk factors, such as living in a dangerous neighborhood, deprive the student of experiences and opportunities that enhance resilience; environmental protective factors, such as social support from teachers, help build resilience. The SSP assesses students' individual adaptation in four areas of their social environment – neighbourhood, school, peers and family – and a fifth area that assesses self-perceptions of their health and well-being. For example, the section devoted to "neighbourhood" contains items related to students' perceptions of neighbourhood safety and satisfaction; the section devoted to "school" contains items related to grades, school self-efficacy and teacher support; the section devoted to "friends" contains items related to how well the student gets along with her or his peers, and the extent to which she or he trusts them; and the section devoted to "family" contains items related to adult caretaker support and family interaction. The "health and well-being" section of the SSP assesses students' feelings of confidence, self-image and self-esteem, and whether they receive various types of social support.

Social disorganisation theory (Sampson and Groves, 1989) argues that community-level characteristics of disorganisation, such as sparse friendship networks and unsupervised peer groups, inhibit the creation of social capital among families and children. Neighbourhood norms and values affect children by serving as their guideposts for behaviour. Vowell and Howell (1998), for example, found that social disorganisation increases perceptions of blocked opportunity, and perceptions of blocked opportunity relate to increases in delinquent behaviour. A well-organised community with positive norms and values, and many educational and recreational resources, provides community members with opportunities to feel supported and enhances the number and quality of their protective factors. In light of this theoretical perspective, the SSP assesses students' perceptions of the extent to which there is drug use and violence in their neighbourhoods, the extent to which their neighbourhoods are stable or transient, and whether there is a sense of cohesion among neighbours.

Psychologist Abraham Maslow (1954) suggests that human needs fall into five categories, each of which must be satisfied before someone can concern herself or himself with the next one. The most basic needs are *physical*, such as sufficient air, water, food and rest. The second category of needs involves *safety*, for example, protection from threats to one's well-being. Beyond physical and safety concerns are *social* needs, such as belonging to groups. Additionally, Maslow suggests that people have the need for *self-esteem*, the desire to believe they are worthwhile and valuable. The final category of needs involves *self-actualisation*, the desire to develop one's potential to the maximum. The SSP incorporates this theoretical perspective by assessing, for example, students' perceptions of their safety, the extent to which they belong to and are accepted by their peer groups, and their self-esteem.

The SSP produces two profiles for each student: (1) the Social Environment Profile, and (2) the Individual Adaptation Profile. The former considers a student's perceptions of his or her neighbourhood (e.g. neighbourhood safety), school (e.g. school satisfaction), peers (e.g. peer acceptance) and family (e.g. family integration). The latter focuses on a student's perceptions of the social support she or he receives (e.g. emotional support), self-confidence (e.g. her or his influence in school), school behaviour (e.g. attendance) and general well-being (e.g. physical health).

The two profiles make up a one-page individual student summary (see Figure 1). Information on the bottom of the page includes the student's identification number, gender, race/ethnicity, age, grade level, and the proportion of valid responses. Practitioners who work with the students – such as advisors, social workers and teachers – are encouraged to meet with each individual student who completes the SSP and review the profile results. The results are presented as one way of looking into the life of the student, and practitioners are encouraged to carefully establish the validity of the findings from the student's perspective. The SSP is designed to augment the observations and dialogue that practitioners have with students on an ongoing basis. It is not a substitute for this process; it is designed to enhance and support this process. An Intervention Planning and Monitoring Form is provided with the Profile to help develop intervention plans together with each student who completes the SSP.

The SSP also provides a group profile. The information on the group profile allows practitioners to become aware of areas that may warrant group interventions and to plan change strategies in these areas.

The SSP has been successfully field tested in middle schools and high schools in the US. Validity and reliability of the over 90 measures on the SSP have been empirically established and supported (Bowen and Chapman, 1996; Richman and Bowen, 1997).

Research investigations using the SSP

Since its development, starting in 1992, and its field tests in North Carolina and Florida in 1995, the SSP has been used to learn about both academically at-risk middle and high school students (i.e. students in Communities in Schools programmes, the largest stay-in-school network in the US), and students not identified as academically at-risk (i.e.

Figure 1

Example of an individual's school success profile

Social Environment Profile

Neighbourhood
Neighbourhood satisfaction
Peer culture
Neighbourhood safety

School
School satisfaction
Teacher support
School safety

Peers
Peer satisfaction
Peer acceptance

Family
Family satisfaction
Family integration
Parent support

Individual Adaptation Profile

Support
Social support
Home academic culture
Parent education monitoring

Self-Confidence
Self-esteem
School coherence
School influence

School Behaviour
Attendance
Trouble avoidance
Grades

General well-being
Physical health
Happiness
Adjustment

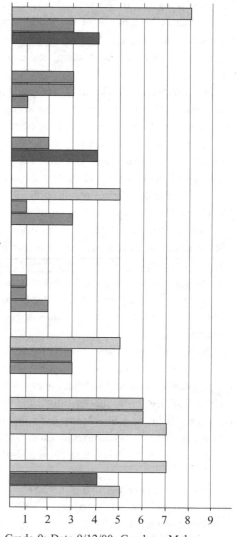

Student JAWS081885; Age 14; Grade 9; Date 9/12/00; Gender – Male; Black/AA

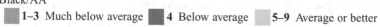 **1–3** Much below average ▮ **4** Below average ▮ **5–9** Average or better

students from a national SSP survey). For example, compared to students not identified as at risk, students identified as at-risk of school failure are more likely to be from an ethnic/racial minority group, to live in single-parent families, and to be from lower socio-economic homes (Bowen *et al*, 1997).

Specific to the focus of this chapter, a series of investigations focusing on social support and school outcomes have helped delineate the relationship between social support and school behaviour, affect, and outcomes (Richman, Rosenfeld and Bowen, 1998; Rosenfeld and Richman, 1999; Rosenfeld, Richman and Bowen, 1998a, 1998b, 2000). In general, results across studies indicate that the receipt of social support is related to some positive school outcome for both academically at-risk students and students not identified as at risk. Also, working with students to access greater amounts of certain types of support from providers in their environment, and helping providers communicate greater amounts of specific support to positively affect particular school behaviours and performance, offer potentially efficient methods of impacting significant school outcomes.

Social support and student outcomes for middle school

Students in out-of-home placement

The literature on risk and protective factors and educational resilience clearly endorses the primacy of the supportive role provided by the family, the peer group, the school, and the community in predicting positive outcomes for students (Wang *et al*, 1994; Bogenschneider, 1996). Findings from a large body of research indicate a positive relationship between social support and outcomes of particular interest to educators (see Rosenfeld *et al*, 2000, for a summary of this body of research), such as student motivation, school adjustment, sense of school coherence, drop-out rate, ability to handle daily school hassles, time studying, academic and behavioural adjustment, attendance and participation. In addition, social support directly or indirectly enhances overall school achievement and academic competence, including performance on examinations and achievement tests and grades.

Social support

Social support is a multidimensional concept that needs to be defined and measured accordingly (Norbeck, Lindsey and Carrieri, 1981; Sarason *et al*, 1983). Each of three broad types of social support – tangible, informational and emotional (Cobb, 1976) – are communicated by support providers when they enact behaviours perceived by recipients as enhancing the recipients' well-being (cf. Shumaker and Brownell, 1984). These perceptions of others' communication behaviours may take eight distinguishable forms (Richman, Rosenfeld and Hardy, 1993):

a) *listening support*: the perception that an other is listening without giving advice or being judgemental;

b) *emotional support*: the perception that an other is providing comfort and caring and indicating that she or he is on the support recipient's side;

c) *emotional challenge*: the perception that an other is challenging the support recipient to evaluate his or her attitudes, values and feelings;

d) *reality confirmation support*: the perception that an other, who is similar to and who sees things the same way the support recipient does, is helping to confirm the support recipient's perspective of the world;

e) *task appreciation support*: the perception that an other is acknow-ledging the support recipient's efforts and is expressing appreciation for the work she or he does;

f) *task challenge support*: the perception that an other is challenging the support recipient's way of thinking about a task or an activity in order to stretch, motivate and lead the support recipient to greater creativity, excitement and involvement;

g) *tangible assistance support*: the perception that an other is providing the support recipient with either financial assistance, products and/or gifts; and

h) *personal assistance support*: the perception that an other is providing services or help, such as running an errand or driving the support recipient somewhere.

The eight forms of social support provide a typology that defines and explains the interaction between individuals and groups as social support is given and received in the environmental context. This typology provides a spectrum of support that practitioners and clients may find useful in assessing social support and in planning appropriate intervention strategies (Richman *et al*, 1993).

Research questions

Three research questions guided this investigation: What are the effects of middle school students' level of academic risk (at risk *vs* not identified as at risk) and out-of-home placement status (in *vs* not in out-of-home placement) on:

a) the proportion of students indicating they receive each of the eight types of social support (RQ_1);

b) the sources of support they identify (RQ_2); and

c) their school behaviour (i.e. attendance and hours studying), school affect (i.e. school engagement) and school outcomes (i.e. grades and years of school repeated/retained) (RQ_3)?

Method

Respondents were 1,209 middle-school students, of which 806 were from a national probability sample of students throughout the US not identified with any formal school programmes designed to provide academic help, and 403 were from a sample of students identified as at risk of school failure and who participated in CIS programmes (CIS services are provided in the UK under the name of "Include"). Eighteen of the 806 students (2.2 per cent) and 21 of the 403 students (5.3 per cent) indicated they were either in foster care or a group home.

Measures used in this investigation to assess perceptions of

(a) receipt of each of the eight types of social support (RQ_1),

(b) the extent to which parent/adult caretakers, teachers, peers and neighbours are sources of social support (RQ_2), and

(c) school outcomes (RQ_3) are embedded in the SSP.

Findings, conclusions and implications for practice

Findings of the investigation support the conclusion that students in out-of-home placement are academically at risk, regardless of whether they are identified as such by school personnel (Blome, 1997; Dupper, 1997).

Also, results suggest a number of directions practitioners may take to respond to the educational needs of children in out-of-home care.

Results of analyses conducted to respond to the first research question indicate that students not identified as academically at risk and who also are in out-of-home placement report receiving fewer types of support than *any* other students. This implies that being in out-of-home care is predictive of lower reported social support unless a special educational support programme, such as CIS, is available. There are three possible explanations for why a school enhancement programme might be successful in the provision of social support:

1) such a programme may create the circumstance for support by mobilising the teacher, peer group, family, and/or neighbours; and/or

2) personnel in the programme may provide the support; and/or

3) work with programme staff may change a student's perceptions of the support available in the environment so that she or he now "sees" and accesses the available support. (Confirming the effectiveness of participating in a school programme that links students and school personnel in positive ways, results of analyses with the variable "school engagement" indicated that at risk students feel more engaged with school than students not identified as at risk.)

These findings suggest that, first, professionals who work with children in foster care and other out-of-home placement should recognise the role and importance of school success programmes for their clients. Second, practitioners should locate and collaborate with the educational support programmes in the schools that their clients attend or the communities in which their clients reside. If these programmes do not exist, practitioners should be among the first to work with community stakeholders to develop them. By working with the educational community, the probability increases of their clients receiving the full range of types of support that positively impact on school outcomes.

Findings from analyses conducted in response to the second research question indicate an interesting phenomenon regarding who is perceived as providing support: out-of-home youth perceive getting more support from their neighbours, and less support from their teachers, peers and adult caretakers than do the other students in this investigation. This may reflect their desire or ability to interact with adults with whom they have less at stake – fewer issues about which to have conflict, less intense emotional ties and reduced mutual obligations – than they have with their teachers, adult caretakers (foster carers, biological parents, and so on), siblings, and the children with whom they share out-of-home residence (cf. Chess, 1989).

Although neighbours may be providing social support to youth in out-of-home placement, social support from a *variety* of sources, as opposed to one or two sources, optimises school outcomes (Rosenfeld *et al*, 2000). The practitioner can enhance support provided by adult caretakers, teachers and peers in a variety of ways. For example, the practitioner can work with community and school resources to develop caretaker and school involvement programmes.

In-service training can be used to help school personnel become aware of the specific support needs of youth in out-of-home placement. This training also can lead to strategies for motivating out-of-home youth to access support as well as to create opportunities for meaningful participation in the school setting. Positive peer interaction and support may be enhanced with extra-curricular programmes, such as "midnight basketball" and after-school curricular activities.

While it is important to enhance support from close members of the students' ecological environments, results of this investigation imply that out-of-home youth perceive much of their support coming from adults with whom they have less at stake. For this reason, programmes that link out-of-home youth with adults capable of caring for them "at a distance" may be the best strategy. For example, mentoring and tutoring programmes that connect the student with community or school volunteers should allow for the provision of social support without many of the usual emotional and interpersonal ties that often accompany support.

Unfortunately, results of analyses conducted to respond to the third research question corroborate the stereotype that students in out-of-home care have poorer attendance and do not perform as well in school (with respect to grades) as other students. However, results also point to the success possible when students in out-of-home care are placed in a school programme designed to provide support and enhance educational outcomes. Specifically, results of this study indicated that students in out-of-home care not identified as academically at risk, and so not participating in a special academic support programme such as CIS, repeated the most years of schooling. The clear implication of this is that children in out-of-home care are at high risk of school failure and can benefit from participation in a school support programme.

Being in out-of-home placement is a significant risk factor – or a proxy variable for a host of complex risk factors – that necessitates the mobilisation of resources to provide services to enhance social as well as academic school functioning. Practitioners working in the out-of-home care system need to recognise the important role that both they and the schools play in the transition from adolescence to adult self-sufficiency, and to work closely with the educational community – regardless that this may require crossing agency boundary lines. The goal, after all, is to create the most promising service delivery for the youth with whom they work.

References

Aldgate, J (1994) 'Graduating from care – a missed opportunity for encouraging successful citisenship', *Children & Youth Services Review*, 16:3/4), pp 255–72.

Antonovsky, A (1991) 'The structural sources of salutogenic strengths', in Cooper, C L and Payne, R (eds), *Personality and Stress: Individual differences in the stress process*, Chichester: John Wiley & Sons, pp 67–104.

Apfel, R J and Simon, B (1996a) Introduction, in Apfel, R J and Simon, B, *Minefields in their Hearts: The mental health of children in war and communal violence*, New Haven, CT: Yale University Press, pp 1–17.

Apfel, R J and Simon, B (1996b) *Psychosocial Interventions for Children of War: The value of a model resiliency* [On-line]. Available: http://www.healthnet.org/MGS/Article3.html

Ayasse, R H (1995) 'Addressing the needs of foster children: The Foster Youth Services Program', *Social Work in Education*, 17:4, pp 207–16.

Berrick, J D, Courtney, M and Barth, R P (1993) 'Specialised foster care and group home care: similarities and differences in the characteristics of children in care', *Children & Youth Services Review*, 15:6, pp 453–73.

Blome, W W (1997) 'What happens to foster kids: educational experiences of a random sample of foster care youth and a matched group of non-foster care youth', *Child & Adolescent Social Work Journal*, 14:1, pp 41–53.

Bogenschneider, K (1996) 'An ecological risk/protective theory for building prevention programmes, policies, and community capacity to support youth', *Family Relations*, 45, pp 127–38.

Bowen, G L and Chapman, M V (1996) 'Poverty, neighbourhood danger, social support, and the individual adaptation among "at risk" youth in urban areas', *Journal of Family Issues*, 17, pp 641–66.

Bowen, G L, Richman, J M, Bowen, N and Chapman, M V (1997) *Contextual Risks, Social Capital, and Internal Assets among Communities in Schools Participants: Comparisons to the National School Success Profile*, Chapel Hill, NC: Jordan Institute for Families, University of North Carolina at Chapel Hill.

Bronfenbrenner, U (1979) *The Ecology of Human Development: Experiments by nature and design*, Cambridge, MA: Harvard University Press.

Cantos, A L, Gries, L T and Slis, V (1997) 'Behavioral correlates of parental visiting during family foster care', *Child Welfare*, 36:2, pp 309–29.

Carnahan, S (1994) 'Preventing school failure and dropout', in Simeonsson, R J (ed.), *Risk, Resilience and Prevention: Promoting the well-being of all children*, pp 102–123, Baltimore, MD: Paul H. Brooks Publishing Company.

Chess, S (1989) 'Defying the voice of doom', in Dugan, T and Coles, R (eds), *The Child in our Times*, pp 179–99. New York: Brunner Mazel.

Christmas, L (1998) 'Looking after learning: making a difference for young people in care', *Educational & Child Psychology*, 15:4, pp 79–90.

Cobb, S (1976) 'Social support as a moderator of life stress', *Psychosomatic Medicine*, 38, pp 300–14.

Colton, M, Heath, A and Aldgate, J (1995) 'Factors which influence the educational attainment of children in foster family care', *Community Alternatives: International Journal of Family Care*, 7:1, pp 15–36.

Dubowitz, H, Feigelman, S, Harrington, D, Starr, R, Zuravin, S and Sawyer, R (1994) 'Children in kinship care: How do they fare?' *Children & Youth Services Review*, 16:1–2, pp 85–106.

Dupper, D (1997) 'A reveille for school social workers: children in foster care need our help!' *Social Work in Education*, 19:2, pp 121–27.

Everett, J E (1995) 'Relative foster care: an emerging trend in foster care placement policy and practice', *Smith College Studies in Social Work*, 65:3, pp 239–54.

Fraser, M W, Richman, J M and Galinsky, M J (1999) 'Risk, protection, and resilience: toward a research-based framework for social work practice', *Social Work Research*, 23:3, pp 131–44.

Harris, K M (1991) 'Teenage mothers and welfare dependency: working off welfare', *Journal of Family Issues*, 12, pp 492–518.

Heath, A F, Colton, M J and Aldgate, J (1994) 'Failure to escape: a longitudinal study of foster children's educational attainment', *British Journal of Social Work*, 24:3, pp 241–60.

Hepburn, L R and White, R A (1990) *School Dropouts: A two-generation problem*, Athens, GA: Carl Vinson Institute of Government, University of Georgia.

Iglehart, A P (1994) 'Adolescents in foster care: predicting readiness for independent living', *Children & Youth Services Review*, 16:3–4, pp 159–69.

Iglehart, A P (1995) 'Readiness for independence: comparison of foster care, kinship care, and non-foster care adolescents', *Children & Youth Services Review*, 17:3, pp 417–32.

Kirby, L D and Fraser, M W (1997) 'Risk and resilience in childhood', in Fraser, M W (ed.), *Risk and Resilience in Childhood: An ecological perspective*, pp 10–33, Washington, DC: National Association of Social Workers Press.

Maslow, A H (1954) *Motivation and Personality*, New York: Harper.

Masten, A S, Hubbard, J J, Gest, S D, Tellegen, A, Garmezy, N and Ramirez, M (1999) 'Competence in the context of adversity: pathways to resilence and maladaptation from childhood to late adolescence', *Development in Psychopathology*, 11, pp 143–169.

Norbeck, J, Lindsey, A and Carrieri, V (1981) 'The development of an instrument to measure social support', *Nursing Research*, 30, pp 264–69.

Richman, J M and Bowen, G L (1997) 'School failure: an eco-interactional-developmental perspective', in Fraser, M W (ed.), *Risk and Resiliency in Childhood: An ecological perspective*, pp 95–116, Washington, DC: National Association of Social Workers.

Richman, J M, Rosenfeld, L B and Hardy, C J (1993) 'The Social Support Survey: an initial validation study of a clinical measure and practice model of the social support process', *Research on Social Work Practice*, 3, pp 288–311.

Richman, J M, Rosenfeld, L B and Bowen, G L (1998) 'Social support for adolescents at-risk of school failure: providers, relationship to school outcomes, and implications for practice', *Social Work*, 43, pp 309–23.

Rosenfeld, L B and Richman, J M (1999) 'Supportive communication and school outcomes, part II: academically "at-risk" low income high school students', *Communication Education*, 48, pp 294–307.

Rosenfeld, L B, Richman, J M and Bowen, G L (2000) 'Social support networks and school outcomes: the centrality of the teacher', *Child & Adolescent Social Work Journal*, 17, pp 205–26.

Rosenfeld, L B, Richman, J M and Bowen, G L (1998a) 'Low social support among at-risk adolescents', *Social Work in Education*, 20, pp 245–60.

Rosenfeld, L B, Richman, J M and Bowen, G L (1998b) 'Supportive communication and school outcomes for academically "at-risk" and other low income middle school students', *Communication Education*, 47, pp 309–25.

Rumberger, R W (1987) 'High school dropouts: a review of issues and evidence', *Review of Educational Research*, 57:2, pp 101–21.

Rutter, M, Quinton, D and Hill, J (1990) 'Adult outcome of institution-reared children: males and females compared', in Robins, L N and Rutter, M (eds), *Straight and Devious Pathways from Childhood to Adulthood*, pp 135–57, Cambridge: Cambridge University Press.

Sampson, R J and Groves, W B (1989) 'Community structure and crime: testing social-disorganisation theory', *American Journal of Sociology*, 94, pp 774–802.

Sarason, I, Levine, H, Basham, R and Sarason, B (1983) 'Concomitants of social support: the social support questionnaire', *Journal of Personality & Social Psychology*, 44, pp 127–39.

271

Sawyer, R J and Dubowitz, H (1994) 'School performance of children in kinship care', *Child Abuse & Neglect*, 18:7, pp 587–97.

Scannapieco, M, Schagrin, J and Scannapieco, T (1995) 'Independent living programs: Do they make a difference?' *Child & Adolescent Social Work Journal*, 12:50, pp 381–89.

Shumaker, S A and Brownell, A (1984) 'Toward a theory of social support: closing conceptual gaps', *Journal of Social Issues*, 40, pp 11–36.

Smucker, K S, Kauffman, J M and Ball, D W (1996) 'School-related problems of special education foster-care students with emotional or behavioural disorders: A comparison to other groups', *Journal of Emotional & Behavioral Disorders*, 4:1, pp 30–9.

Stein, E (1997) 'Teachers' assessments of children in foster care', *Developmental Disabilities Bulletin*, 25:2, pp 1–17.

Tennyson, S (1998) 'Counselling children from foster families: challenges for school', in Palmatier, L D (ed.), *Crisis Counseling for a Quality School Community: Applying William Glasser's choice theory*, pp 337–53, Bristol, PA: Accelerated Development.

Thorpe, M B and Swart, G T (1992) 'Risk and protective factors affecting children in foster care: a pilot study of the role of siblings', *Canadian Journal of Psychiatry*, 37:2, pp 616–22.

Vowell, P R and Howell, F M (1998) 'Modelling delinquent behaviour: social disorganisation, perceived blocked opportunity, and social control', *Deviant Behaviour*, 19, pp 361–95.

Wang, M C, Haertel, G D and Walberg, H J (1994) 'Educational resilience in inner cities', in Wang, M C and Gordon, E W (eds), *Educational Resilience in Inner-city America: Challenges and prospects*, pp 45–72, Hillsdale, NJ: Lawrence Erlbaum.

Werner, E E and Smith, R S (1982) *Vulnerable but Invincible: A longitudinal study of resilient children and youth*, New York: McGraw-Hill.

Zuravin, S J, Benedict, M and Stallings, R (1999) 'The adult functioning of former kinship and nonrelative foster care children', in Hegar, R L and Scannapieco, M (eds), *Kinship Foster Care: Policy, practice, and research*, New York: Oxford University.

16 Making residential care educational care

Joy Rees

This chapter draws on experiences from an action research project, *Residential Care and Education in Wales.*[1] The project was established in response to evidence that attendance and attainment of children in residential care consistently falls below that of those in foster placements. Even within the care population, where all children are severely disadvantaged educationally by comparison with children in their own homes, the minority in residential homes fare worst of all (Utting, 1991). They are significantly more likely than others to be denied their right to schooling altogether, and even if they attend, rarely achieve any success.

As other chapters in this book have illustrated, being looked after by a local authority has in the past done more to reinforce previous educational difficulties than to offer solutions. This chapter focuses on practical measures developed during the project to give better opportunities to children and young people living in residential homes.

Between 1997 and 2000, the project worked with four local authorities to improve the educational environment provided in residential care. One clear lesson from this work is the need for effective multi-agency working at all levels, from front-line staff in residential homes to the most senior levels of management and decision-making. With this aim, a Steering Group was set up to manage the project which included managers from both education and social services departments. During the course of the project, all the participating authorities established joint education/social services groups to improve the education of looked after children and one authority has published a joint strategic plan. Not all problems have been resolved. Funding remains a contentious issue, for example, who pays for transport, which can be a heavy cost in rural

---

[1] The project was funded primarily by the Gatsby Foundation with contributions from the National Assembly and the participating authorities and has been hosted by Children in Wales. The Foundation has also funded a parallel project in England.

areas. Clearly effective dialogue must continue at senior levels in the authority with elected members and senior officers. They need to be kept closely in touch with the educational experiences of young people and with the children themselves. As Firth and Fletcher have outlined in Chapter 9, the whole local authority and its constituent schools need to have a unified, published approach to raising school attainment that makes best use of resources. Many of the necessary steps are spelt out in the joint Guidance issued by the Department for Education and Employment and Department of Health (DfEE/DH, 2000) and the National Assembly for Wales.

Policy initiatives do not diminish the importance of seeking to promote educational opportunities for individual children. Children in public care today cannot wait for the wheels of local authorities to move tomorrow. They need to make the most of their unique chance in education.

Creating conditions for educational success

If we aspire to make residential care educational care, there are powerful cultural factors to be overcome, notably the historical tendency to think of residential homes as "caring" for children, with education assumed to be the exclusive concern of schools and other education services.

The Children Act 1989 (England and Wales) states unequivocally that local authorities have a duty to safeguard and promote the welfare of children in public care, and they have the same rights to education as those in their own homes. All the young people who have participated in the project have given the same clear messages: they want to be in mainstream school, they want to gain qualifications, they want to get good jobs, their hopes are the same as those of any other young people. What they have to overcome are their lack of confidence, the gaps in their learning where their education has been disrupted, and the low aspirations of professionals and carers.

Research by the National Foster Care Association has found that the single biggest cause of foster home breakdown is failure to attend school (see also Chapter 14). This corresponds with the experience of the project that the majority of young people coming into residential homes from

274

foster care had not been attending school regularly. Educational stability and placement stability are closely interrelated. It is therefore in everyone's interest if supporting and promoting education is seen as a central role for residential care. Residential carers should be the education champions for the young people they look after, but they themselves need support and commitment from their managers and access to training and resources.

It is helpful to draw on our experiences as parents to guide our efforts. As parents, we try to provide *the right physical environment* for educational achievement, we are *"interested people"* in our children's school careers and when they run into difficulties we provide *support and assistance* for them. This chapter explores what these three aspects of educational care mean in relation to looked after children in residential homes.

The physical environment

Young people cannot be expected to study if they lack basic facilities. One young man, recently returned to school after being excluded, was keen to keep up with his classmates and do his homework. Finding no desk available he took a drawer from the sideboard and turned it upside down to work on his knees. We might admire his resourcefulness, but what kind of message did that convey to him and other residents about the importance, or lack of it, given to schoolwork?

In contrast, a recently built residential home has equipped each individual bedroom with a desk, study lamp and storage space. Even shared bedrooms can have a writing surface and reading lamps. It should be possible for every home to set aside a quiet room with tables, good lighting, and a supply of reference books. Also needed are basic materials for study: paper, pens, pencils, rulers, rubbers. Children should not be expected to buy, from their own pocket money, essential educational supplies, which most parents would readily provide.

Each resident needs to have his/her own lockable storage space. Among the transient populations of children's homes important papers can easily be lost or taken by others. Proper storage for school project work, especially coming up to GCSE, is absolutely essential. It is not good enough to say that no resources are available for these purposes: this simply reflects the priorities of the past.

Books and reading material

Books and other publications are an important part of the environment. The availability or absence of a good choice of books and reading material gives a strong message about education.

As part of the project I asked about availability of magazines and newspapers. Young people replied that they were expected to buy them out of their pocket money. The only publication regularly available was a tabloid newspaper. The idea that quality newspapers and magazines might be an important educational resource had evidently not occurred to the residential care staff, nor that reading should be encouraged in every possible way among a group of children for whom literacy is known to be a problem. Well-chosen newspapers can provide a catalyst for discussion and provide useful material for school projects. Quality newspapers and magazines should be budgeted for and chosen both for educational purposes and to reflect the interests of young people in the home. All young people over ten should receive *Who Cares?* magazine free.

Encyclopaedias and good, up-to-date reference books are another essential resource which is often lacking at present. We found that sometimes staff would bring in their own reference books for specific requests, but they need to be available all the time and easily accessible. Advice on the selection of books can be given by the library service and by the Education Department's Literacy Advisor. The home needs to allocate a regular sum of money for books and involve young people in choosing and buying them.

A useful addition to the book collection are biographies and auto-biographies of people who have been in care. Their achievements can help young people in dealing with their own lives.[2]

The value of books was demonstrated clearly in the Who Cares? Trust "Book of my Own" project. Young people in care were

---

[2] *Who Cares? My Life in Barnardo's* by Fred Fever; *Cornflake Kid* by Mark Riddell; and *Beastly Beauty* by Andrew Butcher

given the opportunity of choosing and buying books and then reading them with a carer (Bald, Bean and Meegan, 1995). This has now been followed up by "The Right to Read", in partnership with the National Literacy Association and the Paul Hamlyn Foundation, in which five local authorities are participating. This project incorporates Creative Achievement Days, Encouragement Days for carers and Starter libraries in 40 residential homes.

The *Book of My Own* project revealed how few children in residential care routinely have access to books and how unlikely they were to own books themselves, in contrast to children at home, many of whom have dozens before they even go to school. A significant finding from Jackson and Martin's (1998) research on succeeding from care is that most of those who had done well at school were keen readers and had taken the initiative to join a library, but this was rarely encouraged or facilitated by residential care staff. All children in residential care should be enabled to join a library, but in addition, some part of their personal allowances should be specifically allocated for buying fiction and non-fiction of their own choosing.

It is all too easy to assume that children in residential care are not interested in books. I talked with a boy of 15, permanently excluded from school, who told me that his favourite author was Stephen Hawking and that he was keen to own all of Hawking's books. It is sad to think how completely the care and education systems had failed to engage the interest and potential of this young man.

Information technology

Computers can no longer be considered a luxury. Young people need access to them if they are to be on equal terms with others of their age. Also the ability to use IT equipment can greatly improve employability. Young people generally enjoy using a computer more than pen and paper; it can do much to enhance their motivation, especially if they are not confident about their spelling or writing. One teacher, working with young people who had previously often been absent and uninterested in school, said the availability of computers was the single most important aid to involving her group of students.

Many local authorities now provide computers in every residential

277

home, but in some cases these are used mainly by staff and are not freely available to the young residents. Simply having a computer is not enough. Arrangements also need to be made for maintenance, upgrading, expert advice on equipment, internet access, educational software and links to schools educational packages.

Interested people

However good the physical environment, the most important factor is the attitudes of the staff. Genuine and demonstrated interest in the school experience and educational progress of the residents is fundamental. For residential staff who have children, a simple yardstick is: 'Do I care as much about the achievements of the young people for whom I am professionally responsible as I do about my own children?' If not, who *is* going to care about them?

If expectations and interest in education are low, it is likely that outcomes will also be poor but high expectations and hopes can bring positive results, not only for young people but also for residential carers themselves. A young person attending and doing well at school is more likely to be sociable and fulfilled than someone who is hanging about a residential home seven days a week. Moreover, there is a danger that children not attending school will become involved in high-risk activities such as crime and prostitution.

Where the right attitudes prevail in the residential home, it is possible for a placement move to be a change for the better.

Paul came into a residential home, following a foster home break-down. He had been excluded from school before becoming looked after, and had not attended school for some months. His mother was refusing to have him back home. After careful discussions with all in-volved, a Personal Education Plan was agreed in which Paul attended a different school in his home area. With support from residential staff he went to school regularly, did his homework and stopped running away. Contact with his mother increased and he was later able to move back home.

Changing attitudes through training

Training is essential if residential staff are to become more effective in promoting the education of the children in their care. There is now an NVQ accreditation for the education of looked-after children. Not only does this give residential staff an incentive to focus on the issue and read more widely but it gives them an insight into some of the difficulties that children may be facing in returning to study after a gap. *There is a strong case for making it a condition of appointment that residential staff should pursue further professional or personal studies* quite apart from any in-service training that may be provided.

Introductory sessions can look at the rights of children to education and encourage reflection on national and local evidence of education outcomes. It is important to include research findings on care leavers which show their vulnerability to unemployment and insecurity (Stein, 1997; Ince, 1998).

On the other hand, staff also need to be aware of research which shows that looked after children *can* succeed provided someone believes in them and gives them consistent emotional and practical support. There is a large body of American research which shows that young people can be extraordinarily resilient (Haggerty *et al*, 1994). Doing well at school enables them to overcome many of the other problems in their lives and gives them a much better chance of a successful transition to adulthood (Jackson and Martin, 1998; Gilligan, 2001).

All staff need a basic introduction to the *Code of Practice for Special Educational Needs* (Department for Education, 1996). A higher than average number of young people in public care are on the Code of Practice register (often as many as 40 per cent in some residential homes). It is important that staff understand that this is not simply a label but can provide resources for children to receive additional help. Some members of staff could be given more intensive training with a view to being designated as Education Liaison Workers. A residential worker with this role needs more detailed knowledge on the relevant legislation, the curriculum, the regulations surrounding exclusions and the powers and responsibilities of headteachers and school governors. An important part of the job is building relationships with education professionals, knowing who to ask for information, becoming familiar with the way schools work, and gaining confidence in negotiating with them on behalf of the young people.

Training materials

A number of organisations publish training materials which can be customised to suit local requirements. Those we have found useful include NVQ Level 3 training packs for residential workers, the Advisory Centre for Education (ACE) Education Guide (1998); an excellent series of checklists prepared by Peter McParlin (1996) and a training guide on the education of looked after children from First Key; National Children's Bureau compact handbooks for residential carers and teachers (Sandiford, 1997a, 1997b), and numerous publications from the Who Cares? Trust (1999a, 1999b, 2001).

Making use of support services

As a social worker by training, I have been impressed to discover the range of educational support services that are available and disappointed at how rarely they are in contact with children's residential homes. These are resources that have great potential for improving looked after young people's educational attainment. Residential workers need to make the best possible use of them, and they in turn need to reach out to their colleagues in residential care who have less specialist knowledge of the education service.

Library services

Staff in libraries have a wealth of knowledge and resources. Many libraries now have internet access. All have staff with expertise. They can advise on books and help young people understand how to look for references.

Literacy and Numeracy Advisers

These are specialists who provide advice and tutoring for schools and further education colleges. Residential carers can benefit from their knowledge to encourage reading and develop literacy skills in the young people in their care. For example, one literacy adviser has prepared *Book*

Bags, a selection of books tailored for individual young people in children's homes in the authority.

Education Welfare Officers

In the past there was little contact between the education welfare service and residential homes. This has changed as a result of the project and education welfare officers now regularly visit the homes. Residential workers sometimes have great difficulty persuading young people who have become alienated from the school system that it is in their interests to start attending again. Education Welfare Officers can be very helpful, both in working with the child and negotiating with the school.

Special needs services

The Code of Practice on Special Educational Need already referred to can be used to help young people make up for gaps in their learning, for example by arranging intensive help with reading or mathematics. Experience from the project has indicated that many residential carers are unaware of the existence of the Code of Practice. Nor do they hold the Statements for young people they are caring for. The result is often that young people in residential care with Statements are on home tuition or in a Pupil Referral Unit (PRU) when they could be receiving support in mainstream schools.

The local special educational needs service can provide training for staff on the Code of Practice and what a Statement of Special Educational Needs means. Residential workers can seek advice for individual young people who may need extra provision; ensure that young people with Statements are receiving the help to which they are entitled, and find out how to help young people to deal with behaviour which may get them into trouble at school (for instance, by learning about anger management). Involving an Educational Psychologist to give advice about the day-to-day running of the home can also bring about big improvements, often at little cost. Two of the authorities in the project are now seeking funding for a full-time Educational Psychologist for children in public care.

Specialist tutors for the arts

Many writers on residential care have commented on the drab and unstimulating atmosphere in too many homes, where kicking a football about, watching television and listening to pop music are the only leisure activities (Berridge, 1985; Berridge and Brodie, 1998; Sinclair and Gibbs, 1998). Many behaviour management problems in residential units arise from boredom. Local colleges can be good contacts for finding specialist tutors for music, poetry, drama, creative writing and a whole range of other pursuits. Young people respond well to these opportunities and I have read a number of excellent poems inspired by an enthusiastic tutor. Not only do such activities fill free time more constructively but they can sometimes inspire young people to go on to further studies.

Local colleges

While it is valuable to bring tutors into the residential home, young people should also visit local colleges on open evenings to find out about courses on offer. These visits can open up possibilities for young people that they may not have the confidence to pursue on their own. Residential staff need to go too so that they know what is available and can offer advice and encouragement.

Careers advisory services

A recent research study in one of the project authorities found that most of the care leavers interviewed had not seen a careers advisor when they were in care (Davies, 2000). Contracts with careers services should specifically include provision for children in public care. Residential carers should establish a good relationship with their local careers adviser, and collect a supply of information leaflets and reference books. The advisers will not necessarily know much about the care system, so they will need briefing on the backgrounds and experiences of the young people. They need help to understand that, compared with home-based teenagers, the residents may be seriously lacking in confidence and self-esteem. They may also lack social and communication skills and have a limited conception of what jobs might be available to them. Advisers need to exercise patience and sensitivity and be prepared not to take apparent lack of interest or unresponsiveness at face value. Careers Advisors can offer personal development training such as the Pacific Institute Program, and so build confidence and motivation.

Youth workers and community education

Many valuable educational and recreational opportunities are provided by these services. Residential workers can access activities for young people, for example, youth clubs, IT, outdoor pursuits, evening classes of all kinds. The City and County of Cardiff is using youth workers to help young people who are looked after to engage in educational activities.

Places of worship

Young people who wish to follow their religion should obviously be supported by residential carers in attending services and social activities. But even those from families with no religious affiliation can benefit from contact with local places of worship. This can be particularly valuable during the transition period between care and independence but can also expand the young person's horizons and may put him or her in touch with useful role models and supportive adults.

Health advisers

Health Promotion Units are part of each health authority. They can be approached to give talks and provide leaflets and information. This is especially important for those young people not in mainstream school who will miss their personal, social and health education and who are at particularly high risk of adopting unhealthy life styles and engaging in health-threatening behaviour (Jackson *et al*, 2000).

Promoting individual interests

Maintaining continuity of interests and building on skills acquired from home or on previous placements is vitally important, and ought to be a natural result of the essential responsibility of residential workers to be "interested people". Too often developing skills, for example, in music or sport, are simply allowed to lapse because carers do not make the effort to sustain them. I met one young woman who had been in the national basketball team before coming into residential care a year before. She had not played basketball since.

Often, leisure activities for residential care will involve groups of young people going in the minibus, for example, to a swimming pool. While this is good to do sometimes, young people should be encouraged to follow their own interests as well, as happens in birth families. Residential carers can play a key part in encouraging individual leisure pursuits and hobbies and by sharing their own personal interests with the young people they look after. Such activities have been shown to contribute significantly to their overall school achievement (Gilligan, 2001)

Links between residential homes and schools

Schools have the potential to help young people achieve academic success – that after all is their raison d'être – but they cannot do this in isolation. Alexander (1997) says, 'they must be part of a learning partnership with parents and all other agencies who work with families and children' (p 19). This is even more true of children in public care, where continuity and communication are especially fragile.

It is important to stress the need for sensitivity to young people's wishes on confidentiality. Many young people do not want schools to know the full details of their circumstances and this should be respected. But the school must know who is the main carer or key worker and how they can be contacted, and any information that may affect a child's safety. Children and young people should be consulted on what information is shared with schools but this does not restrict the opportunity for effective partnerships. Under the Guidance for the Education of Children in Public Care (DfEE/DH, 2000) all schools are required to have a designated teacher with special responsibility for looked after children. Residential workers need to know the name of this teacher in any school where they have a child attending (or who ought to be attending) and should aim to build a close relationship with him or her.

First contact with school

When a child or teenager enters residential care, the key worker or officer-in-charge should make immediate contact with the school to set up a two-way information flow and provide a named contact. We found that schools were often uncertain if they should contact the field worker, residential home or birth parents. A clear agreement from the start avoids these problems.

Keeping in contact

The school calendar generally provides only one or two opportunities a year for speaking to teachers at parents's evenings. While these are valuable, and should be always be attended by residential carers, this is not enough to keep up to date. Much more frequent contact is needed for these vulnerable children, at least once every half-term, so that any problems or learning needs identified in school can be immediately addressed. It should also be an opportunity for the young person's achievements to be acknowledged and to obtain advice on how they can best be helped and encouraged.

National records of achievement

All young people should leave with their Personal Record of Achievement which records extra-curricular activities such as involvement in sports, drama, music, community service or any other interests. These can be a great asset when applying for places in college or for employment and can also provide a useful focus for communication between young people, carers and school. Experience on the project has identified that few children in residential care leave school with these records, which is yet another indication of the absence of an *interested person* in their lives.

Home–school contracts

These are intended to set out responsibilities and agreements between schools and parents/carers. They are at least as important for residential carers as parents. They provide an opportunity for writing down expectations and a focus for communication. Residential carers should discuss them with the designated teacher for looked after children.

Initiatives to reduce exclusion

The Government is giving clear messages that exclusions from school need to be reduced. National research and experience on the project have shown how vulnerable young people in public care are to school exclusion (see Chapter 12). Residential carers need to actively tackle problems with the school before exclusion happens. Are all the education support services needed by the child in place? Does the child need extra tuition for any subjects? Is he or she being bullied? Is he or she able to do the homework? Does he or she have appropriate facilities and help or is the child being blamed by the school for things which are not his or her fault?

Because of the anomaly that local authorities are both "parents" and education authorities, there seems to be an assumption that the "parent" will not challenge the education authority on exclusions in the same way that birth parents do. This can result in young people in public care losing their rights to appeal and makes it even more important for residential carers to be in close contact with schools to try to prevent exclusions from occurring. This means seeking understanding rather than engaging in conflict, trying to see how the problem has arisen and how it can be avoided in future. If this fails, the residential worker should always appeal against the exclusion, *seeking assistance from an independent professional if necessary*, so that both the school's and the child's side of the story can be properly heard. In this situation the residential worker must be an advocate for "their" child just as a parent would be, and not identify with the teachers simply because they are fellow professionals.

The Looking After Children (LAC) system

LAC provides a single set of documents recording key information about a child (see Chapter 11). There is scope for utilising this system more effectively in residential work to safeguard education. Practice in the project indicates there is often a delay in the more detailed second-stage Essential Information and Placement Plan forms reaching residential homes. This results in crucial education information not being available early in the placement. Residential workers need to take the initiative to identify essential information in the first three days following placement, even if the forms have not arrived. All young people in public care should have a Personal Education Plan which should be negotiated and fully involve the young person, to include interests and hobbies as well as academic subjects.

The Assessment and Action Records which form the core of the LAC system are not intended to be used until a child has been looked after for four months. However, the Education section of these forms provides a comprehensive and age-appropriate framework for discussion. It is suggested that residential workers should use these pages straight away as a reference for their work with young people and schools.

The one page Action Plans at the end of the Assessment and Action Records can provide a framework for key workers to use in their on-going work. Young people often want copies of their Assessment and Action Records which they are fully entitled to have but, as mentioned above, it is important to ensure that they have a safe place to keep them which is not accessible to other people – and that should not mean, as in one home I visited, under the mattress.

What difference has the project made?

Raising awareness

At the start only one authority had any plans to try and improve educational provision for children in their care. Neither managers nor residential care workers recognised the existence of a significant problem. Raising awareness was an important achievement of the project.

The first step was to increase understanding of the current situation. This was done by gathering information from young people, carers, teachers and others. Meetings with young people produced many good ideas about what could help. Discussions were held with individual staff and at staff meetings. Flip charts were stuck upon the walls of the office and in the children's space asking: 'What could help with education?' and 'What doesn't help with education?' These were left up for a month and were well used.

Also designed to raise awareness were meetings with other professionals – teachers, social workers and education specialists. An audit of young people was conducted in each authority asking over 40 questions about school and placement experiences and educational needs.

Action plans

All these sources of information were drawn together and presented in a detailed report for each authority. These drew out the key issues and proposed detailed action plans related to government guidance. The authorities have each responded in their own ways. Joint Education and Social Services Working Groups has been set up; reports made to joint Education and Social Services Committees, education welfare officers, educational psychologists and other special needs advisors have been linked to residential homes. Specialised staff training has been arranged.

Dedicated staff

One authority has now established a team of three teachers and an administrator specifically to support the education of children in residential care and the others are planning similar provision. This is already bringing about improvements in the service. It is too soon to know if the developments initiated by the project will result in better school experiences and higher attainment for children living in the homes.

Conclusion

Based on the experience of a three-year project, this chapter has sought to offer a variety of ways in which residential carers, often under-valued and under-used, can positively help young people in their care to achieve their potential. There is no doubt that the crucial factor is for at least one person to take a keen and continuing interest in them as individuals and to act as a caring parent in all aspects of promoting their education. This is the message of all research on resilience, and on the small minority of young people who succeed from care (Jackson and Martin, 1998; Kaplan, 1999). It echoes the finding of numerous researchers over the years that enthusiastic parental involvement in children's education is the key characteristic associated with young people having successful careers, regardless of any other factors.

I will end this chapter with a success story, though one that reminds us how residential care that fails to put education at the centre can critically damage young people's life chances. It illustrates why the Education and Care in Wales project was so badly needed:

Mari's story

I was brought up to believe that education was very important. I lived with my parents until I was about 13; they were both teachers, and the stress they placed on learning has stayed with me. When I came into care I found a completely different culture. School was no longer the focal point of life to everyone around me, it was merely somewhere that kids legally had to go. I was moved around a great deal, and in five years I attended as many senior schools. While I was at my last school, I was placed in a home 35 miles away. In this home there was a "culture" of non-attendance. No staff attended the parents's evening, and no one ever discussed my options with me. The only place I could do my homework was at the kitchen table. These things happened not because anyone tried to make me fail, but because no one ever considered that I might succeed.

But my school believed I *could* succeed. I was transferred to a foster placement, and went on to Sixth Form, which would never have been thought of 18 months earlier. When I got my 'A' Level results, several of my social workers, and ex-social workers, set aside half an hour to come and congratulate me, which was wonderful.

I expect to have a career when I leave university. I am considering whether I eventually want to do a Masters or a Doctorate. That is not to say all is plain sailing. As I now start university in Leeds, I am still struggling to get the help I need from social services. I have nowhere permanent to return in my holidays.

I was incredibly lucky to get the support I did when I really needed it and that people around me had hopes and aspirations for me. Looking back now, I realise how different my life would have been if I hadn't had that encouragement and support, because I see so many ex-care young people who didn't get it. I was lucky that someone valued my education but should a teenager's future chance depend on luck?

References

Advisory Centre for Education (1998) *A Guide to Duties and Responsibilities and Education Welfare*, London: ACE.

Alexander, T and Klyne, P (1995) *Riches Beyond Price: Making the most of family learning*, Loughborough: National Organisation for Adult Learning.

Bald, J, Bean, J and Meegan, F (1995) *A Book of My Own*, London: Who Cares? Trust.

Berridge, D (1985) *Children's Homes*, Oxford: Blackwell.

Berridge, D and Brodie, I (1998) *Children's Homes Revisited*, London: Jessica Kingsley.

Davies, G (2000) *The Experience of Looked After Children in Accessing Careers Services*, unpublished M.Phil thesis, University of Glamorgan.

Department for Education (1996) *The Code of Practice on the Identification and Assessment of Special Education Needs*, London: HMSO.

Department for Education and Employment (DfEE) and Department of Health (DH) (2000) *Guidance for the Education of Children and Young People in Public Care"* London: DfEE/DH.

Gilligan, R (2001) *Promoting Resilience*, London: BAAF.

Haggerty, R, Sharrod, L, Garnezy, N and Rutter, M (1994) *Stress, Risk and Resilience in Children and Adolescence: Processes, mechanisms and interventions*, Cambridge: Cambridge University Press.

Ince, L (1998) *Making it Alone: A study of the care experiences of young black people*, London: BAAF.

Jackson, S and Martin, P Y (1998) 'Surviving the care system: education and resilience', *Journal of Adolescence*, 21, pp 569–83.

Jackson, S, Williams, J, Maddocks, A, Love, A, Cheung, W and Hutchings, H (2000) *The Health Needs and Health Care of School-age Children Looked After by Local Authorities*, Swansea: University of Wales, Swansea and Swansea NHS Trust.

Kaplan, H B (1999) 'Towards an understanding of resilience', in Glantz, M and Johnson, J (eds), *Resilience and Development: Positive life adaptations*, New York: Kluwer.

McParlin, P (1996) *Education of Children Looked After: Checklists for teachers, residential social workers, foster parents [sic], field social workers, independent visitors, employers*, Leeds: First Key.

National Foster Care Association (1997) *Foster Care in Crisis: A call to professionalise the forgotten service*, London: NFCA.

Sandiford, P (1997a) *The Education of Looked After Children: Guide for teachers*, London: National Children's Bureau.

Sandiford, P (1997b) *The Education of Looked After Children: Guide for residential social workers*, London: National Children's Bureau.

Sinclair, I and Gibbs, I (1998) *Children's Homes: A study in diversity*, Chichester: Wiley.

Stein, M (1997) *What Works in Leaving Care?* Ilford: Barnardo's.

Utting, Sir W (1991) *Children in the Public Care: A review of residential child care*, London: Department of Health, HMSO.

Who Cares? Trust (1999a) *Equal Chances Information Pack: Finding the facts*, London: WCT.

Who Cares? Trust (1999b) *Equal Chances Stage II: Acting on the facts*, London: WCT.

Who Cares? Trust and National Literacy Association (2001) *Right to Read*, London: WCT.

Resources

ACE, 1b Aberdeen Studies, 22 Highbury Grove, London N5 2DQ. Tel: 020 7354 8321.

First Key, Oxford Chambers, Oxford Place, Leeds LS1 3AX. Tel: 0113 244 2898.

The Pacific Institute runs a training course for people and professionals supporting the education of looked after children. 145 Kensington Church Street, London W8 7LP. Tel: 020 7727 9837.

Who Cares? Trust, Kemp House, 152–160 City Road, London EC1V 2NP. Tel: 020 7251 317.

About the contributors

Jane Aldgate is Professor and Head of Child Care Studies at the Open University. She was previously Professor and Head of Social Work at the University of Leicester and earlier Lecturer at the University of Oxford and a Fellow of St Hilda's College.

Eric Blyth is a Professor at the University of Huddersfield and the co-author of two books on school exclusion and social work in education.

Professor Roger Bullock is a researcher and sociologist and a Director of the Dartington Social Research Unit, undertaking scientific research applied to policy and practice with vulnerable children and their families. He is the author of numerous books, articles and publications and regularly contributes to national and international conferences and courses.

Kate Cairns is a psychologist and social worker who has also been a foster mother for 20 years. She is the author of *Surviving Paedophilia,* about the effects of trauma on children and professionals. She now works for BAAF as a Trainer/Consultant.

Matthew Colton is Professor and Head of Applied Social Studies, University of Wales, Swansea and is a Professor in the Department of Child and Adolescent Psychiatry, University of Science and Technology, Trondheim, Norway.

Dr Randy Lee Comfort is a psychologist and Director of "Our Place", an independent community resource centre for adoptive and foster families.

Dr Ray Evans is an educational psychologist who runs the Education Access Service for Coventry Social Services.

Howard Firth is Commissioning Officer, Children and Families, Hampshire County Council, seconded to the Department for Education and Employment as Implementation Adviser.

293

Barbara Fletcher is Manager of the DfEE Implementation Programme, Education of Children in Public Care.

Felicity Fletcher-Campbell is Research Director of the National Foundation for Educational Research and the author of two books and many articles on the education of looked after children.

Anthony Heath is an Official Fellow of Nuffield College, Oxford and a Fellow of the British Academy. His specialist interests include the sociology of education and political sociology.

Sonia Jackson is a Research Professor at the University of Wales, Swansea and Professorial Fellow at the University of London Institute of Education. She helped to develop the Looking After Children materials and has been researching and writing about children in care for many years.

Professor Michael Little is a Co-Director of the Dartington Social Research Unit and a Senior Research Fellow at the University of Bristol with visiting appointments at the University of Exeter and the Chapin Center for Children at the University of Chicago. He has written or contributed to over 100 publications, including books and articles in refereed and professional journals.

Peter McParlin is a consultant research child and educational psychologist working in North Yorkshire. He was in care from the ages of two weeks to 19 years.

Professor Spencer Millham was the founder Director of the Dartington Social Research Unit and is a distinguished academic and commentator on delinquency and the lives of children in need.

Dr Albert Osborn (deceased) was the Senior Research Officer in the Department of Child Health, working on the Child Health and Education Study, and subsequently at the School of Education at the University of Bristol.

Dr Jack M. Richman is Professor at the School of Social Work at the University of North Carolina at Chapel Hill. His research is focused on the areas of at-risk students, social support, and violence and trauma in childhood. He developed and researches the School Success Profile, an evaluation and practice monitoring instrument for practitioners, youth at risk of school failure and their families.

Joy Rees is a social worker with extensive experience of children's services. She has the lead role in action research for the Gatsby-funded Education and Care in Wales project based at Children in Wales – Plant yng Nghymru.

Dr Lawrence B. Rosenfeld is Professor of Communication Studies at the University of North Carolina at Chapel Hill. He is the author or co-author of 14 books and over 70 articles and chapters. His primary research areas focus on the effects of disasters on children and families, the role of social support in education, and marital and family communication.

Dr Tricia Skuse works for the Dartington Social Research Unit on a project to transform data from the Looking After Children materials into management information.

Mike Stein is Professor and joint Director of the Social Work Research and Development Unit in the Department of Social Policy and Social Work at the University of York. For the last 20 years he has been researching the problems faced by young people leaving care and more recently the experiences of young people living on the streets and running away from care.

Dr Lindsey St.Claire is a part-time Lecturer in social psychology and health in the Department of Psychology, University of Bristol. She previously worked on the Child Health and Education study.

Tim Walker is a teacher by profession, a former Principal of a Community Home with Education and latterly, Head of the Manchester Teaching Service. He became the Chief Executive of the first national education organisation for looked after children in need, in July 1988. The National Teaching & Advisory Service is a campaigning organisation which provides direct educational services to local authorities and the independent sector.